Chinese Export Porcelain

A. Plate with powder-blue ground and polychrome decoration.
First quarter eighteenth century

Chinese Export Porcelain
Chine de Commande

D. F. LUNSINGH SCHEURLEER

PITMAN PUBLISHING CORPORATION

New York / Toronto / London

Pitman Publishing Corporation
Library of Congress Catalog Card No. 74–82704
© this translation Faber and Faber Limited 1974

ISBN 0-273-07083-5

Text and color plates printed in Great Britain by
R. MacLehose and Company Limited
The University Press Glasgow
and Fine Art Engravers Limited
Godalming, Surrey
Monochrome plates printed in the Netherlands by
H. Veeneman & Zonen, B.V., Wageningen

This book is dedicated to
MISS MINKE DE VISSER
in gratitude for the many valuable contributions
with which she has enriched our knowledge of
Far-Eastern ceramics

Contents

Contents

Colour Plates

Acknowledgements

When Miss Minke de Visser, Keeper of the Groninger Museum, asked me to write a book about Chinese porcelain exported to the Netherlands, I consented to do so after some hesitation on condition that she would render assistance by word and deed. I am very grateful for the corrections she has made in the text and for her useful hints.

Miss Louise Spruit, who for many years has made a study of Chinese porcelain with the decoration often described by the term *encre de chine*, was, much to my satisfaction, prepared to write the chapter on this subject for my book.

I am particularly grateful to Her Majesty Queen Juliana for allowing me to reproduce some of the pieces in the Noordeinde Palace at the Hague as illustrations.

In the preparation of this book, I met with much help and assistance in museum circles, and to all those who gave me their unstinted aid, directors and staff alike, I here express my deep gratitude.

I have also to thank Miss J. Harkema and Mr. H. Flinterman who were so helpful in correcting and amending my text; Mr. O. Verhagen for the drawings in the text; Mr. F. Berkhout who helped me by providing data, particularly concerning the Bal collection at Middleburg; and the photographers Messrs. A. Karreman and R. A. van der Zwan who among other things took the photographs of the Bal collection.

The Hague
March 1966

Introduction

The expression *chine de commande* is well known in the Netherlands to everybody who is in any way interested in Chinese porcelain. Commonly, Chinese eighteenth-century porcelain is given that name when decorated to the order of Europeans with representations provided by them, in blue and white as well as in polychrome. In this book, however, the name is also given to the Chinese porcelain ordered by the Dutch East India Company and by private individuals from the beginning of the seventeenth century onwards. There are two distinct groups: one which is Chinese in shape and decoration and was only incidentally made for export, and the other which was painted with some western decoration. Names given to this porcelain in England and in the United States include East India Company China, East India China, China ware and Canton China. It also used to be called Oriental Lowestoft in these countries, although this is a misleading term.[1] The French refer to it as *porcelaine de la compagnie des Indes*.

With the aid of paintings showing porcelain,[2] old estate inventories and sales catalogues, I have tried to build up a picture of the different kinds of porcelain shipped to Europe, and especially to the Netherlands, from China. Sometimes, too, European ceramic wares made in imitation of Chinese porcelain have given helpful indications.

The so-called 'coarse porcelain', which probably did not reach the Netherlands until the nineteenth century, is also briefly discussed.

In several cases it was not possible to ascertain whether a given kind of porcelain was first ordered in China by the Dutch or by the trading company of some other country. During the second half of the eighteenth century, much porcelain was imported into the Netherlands for which, judging from the similarity between English objects in daily

---

[1] This name was used by J. A. Lloyd Hyde in his book *Oriental Lowestoft*, published in 1954. For details of how it first came to be used, see page 151.

[2] See also Dr. A. I. Spriggs, 'Oriental Porcelain in Western Painting', *Transactions of the Oriental Ceramic Society*, 1964–65, 1965–66, pp. 73ff.

use and this Chinese porcelain, England must have provided the models. Much of the porcelain decorated with scenes and scenery, apart from that with typically Dutch representations, was perhaps made to the order of other nationalities.

I have given special attention to the dinner, tea and coffee services made to order for Europeans, since they form an important part of Chinese export porcelain. The same goes to a lesser extent for the *garnitures de cheminées,* sets of vases and beakers for cupboards, cabinets, bookcases and so forth.

I have tried to find as many examples as possible of porcelain made in China to European demand. It should be added that, for the most part, I have discussed pieces which can be seen in museums in the Netherlands. It is regrettable, but unavoidable, that only a few pieces from each museum can be shown in the illustrations.

COLLECTIONS AND EXHIBITIONS

The interest in China, which had flourished during the eighteenth century and culminated in the *chinoiserie* of the rococo period, declined towards the end of the century and during the first half of the nineteenth, but from books published in Europe after 1850 it is clear that the West had again become interested in the arts of the Far East.

During the nineteenth and to a lesser extent the twentieth century until after the First World War, the 'china cabinet' was for many people evidence of prestige, a status symbol, and there are certain indications of a revival in this field. Many of these collections have ultimately found a place in a museum by gift or by bequest.[1] In this connection, the partial translation of the *Ching-tê Chên T'ao-lu* by Stanislas Julien, published in Paris in 1856, was significant.

As a result of the looting of Peking's Summer Palace by French and British troops in 1861 and the troubles that followed, many Chinese works of art came onto the market and found their way to Europe, America and Japan.

The first original European book on porcelain was written by two collectors, A. Jacquemart and E. Le Blant, and it was Jacquemart who coined the terms *famille verte, famille rose,* etc., still in general use. At that time, knowledge about Chinese and Japanese porcelain (the difference between them was hardly recognized at all) was minimal, but growing. Several collections of Chinese porcelain came into being, like those of Franks, now in the British Museum[2] and Grandidier, now in the Musée Guimet.[3] They were followed by many others of varied importance for the study of Chinese porcelain.

The Victoria and Albert Museum has a number of excavated pieces acquired from Dr. Stephen Bushell of Peking, whose books are of great interest to the collector of Chinese porcelain. The same museum, together with the British Museum, now possess

[1] Raymond Dawson, *The Legacy of China* (Oxford, 1964) p. 170.
[2] A. W. Franks, *Catalogue of a Collection of Oriental Porcelain* (London, 1879).
[3] E. Grandidier, *La Céramique chinoise,* Paris, 1894.

parts of the big collection formed by George Eumorfopoulos, and the collection of Sir Percival David is housed in the Foundation of that name in London.

One of the first people in Holland to bring together a collection of Chinese ceramics in the first half of this century was Nanne Ottema of Leeuwarden. Through systematic buying, he built up a collection giving a good overall picture of the development of Chinese porcelain from the earliest times to the present day. This is now in the Princessehof Museum, of which Ottema was the creator and first director. His *Chineesch Ceramiek*, published in 1943, is a handbook describing the museum's collection.

Of the exhibitions of porcelain so instructive for students and collectors, probably the most important were those held in Berlin in 1929,[1] in London in 1935–36[2] and in New York in 1941.[3] Other exhibitions of interest, though they included very few pieces of *chine de commande*, were those organised by the Oriental Ceramic Society in London, for instance *Enamelled Polychrome Porcelain of the Manchu Dynasty* (1951), *Chinese Blue-and-White porcelain 14th to 19th centuries* (1953–54), *The Arts of the Ming Dynasty* (1957), *The Arts of the Ch'ing Dynasty* (1964) and *The Animal in Chinese Art* (1968).

Chinese Art under the Mongols, the Yüan Dynasty (1279–1368) was an important exhibition held in the United States in 1968, and *Ming Blue-and-White* organised by the Philadelphia Museum of Art in 1949 was also of importance for the study of blue-and-white porcelain. A fine exhibition, *Kostbare Chinesche Keramik*, was shown in Germany at the Museum für Ostasiatische Kunst in Cologne in 1965.

An exhibition consisting entirely of *chine de commande*, called *De Chinese porseleinkast*, was organised by the Dutch museum authorities in 1968. From Holland, the exhibition travelled to Germany, Sweden, Denmark and France.

PUBLICATIONS

The early European writers about Chinese porcelain already distinguished between porcelain made to order for the West and that made for native use. This appears from *Histoire artistique, industrielle et commerciale de la porcelaine*, the work by Jacquemart and Le Blant already referred to and published in 1862. In a chapter headed '*Commandes et dessins d'Europe*', they deal with *chine de commande*. In books on Chinese porcelain after this date, our subject is usually discussed in one or more chapters. In 1887 W. Griggs published *Illustrations of Armorial China* which is devoted exclusively to coats-of-arms on Chinese porcelain. In 1907 it was followed by *Armorial China* by F. A. Crisp. Stephen

---

[1] O. Kümmel, *Chinesische Kunst, Ausstellung Chinesischer Kunst*, Berlin, 1929.

[2] *Exhibition of Chinese Art—A commemorative Catalogue* (London, 1936).

[3] Joseph Downs, 'The China Trade and its Influences', *Bulletin of the Metropolitan Museum of Art* (New York, 1941) pp. 84ff.

Introduction

W. Bushell's *Oriental Ceramic Art* of 1899 and *Chinese Art* of 1904, Vol. I and 1910, Vol. II, are landmarks of their period, and R. L. Hobson's magnum opus *Chinese Pottery and Porcelain* of 1915 is still indispensable today. Many other English authorities have written books contributing greatly to the knowledge of our subject; notably W. B. Honey, E. E. Bluett, A. D. Brankston and Soame Jenyns. Another work that retains its value is Ernst Zimmermann's *Chinesisches Porzellan,* the second edition of which was published in 1923.

In 1925, Sir Algernon Tudor Craig published *Armorial porcelain of the Eighteenth Century,* but before the Second World War not a single book was published devoted exclusively to export porcelain. The real interest in Chinese export wares began during that war. This became apparent from the exhibition *The China Trade and its Influence* already mentioned, and the books which appeared after the war also show that a real interest in export porcelain had only just begun. The first books published on the subject were by J. A. Lloyd Hyde: in 1954 it was his *Oriental Lowestoft, Chinese Export Porcelain,* and in 1956 *Chinese Porcelain for the European Market,* which dealt particularly with Chinese porcelain in Portugal. Meanwhile T. Volker had published *Porcelain and the Dutch East India Company* in 1954, and in 1959 *The Japanese Porcelain Trade after 1683.* Both books are illustrated and contain much data about the porcelain subjects of the books. Of particular interest and value for research into this Company's seventeenth-century trade is Dr. H. E. van Gelder's *Gegevens omtrent Den Porseleinhandel der Oost-Indische Compagnie* (Data relevant to the porcelain trade of the Dutch East India Company) published in 1924. It is a pity that the archives of the Company dealing with the eighteenth century have not yet been published, and as it would take many years to go through them for the relevant material, data concerning the porcelain trade of the Company with Canton have been taken from the interesting articles published by J. de Hullu in 1915 and 1917[1] and from a little book by J. G. A. N. de Vries, published in 1923 and entitled *Porselein.*

In *China Trade Porcelain* by J. G. Phillips, 1956, the author discusses the Helena Woolworth McCann collection among others in the Metropolitan Museum, New York, and the Museum of Fine Arts in Boston, and the history of the porcelain trade. Michel Beurdeley's *Porcelaine de la Compagnie des Indes,* 1962, gives a survey of export porcelain with shapes taken from Europe and of the histories of the several East India Companies established after the arrival of the Europeans in the Far East. *Chinese Export Porcelain for the American Trade, 1785–1835,* written by Jean McClure Mudge and published in 1962, should also be mentioned in this connection. The book deals with the trade between America and China and discusses decorations which are also present on porcelain exported to the Netherlands at the end of the eighteenth century, thus proving that export of decorated ware was not confined to one country.

Among scholarly publications on Chinese ceramics that have appeared since then are

[1] See the first section of the Bibliography, page 232.

Introduction

'Chinese ceramic' by J. Fontein in *Sprekend Verleden* (1959) and Maria Penkala's *Far Eastern Ceramics,* which was published in 1963.

Finally among books and articles, the publications may be mentioned here of Stig Roth, *Chinese Porcelain imported by the Swedish East India Company in the Gothenburg Historical Museum,* Gothenburg, 1965, and Bredo L. Grandjean, *Dansk Ostindisk Porcelain importen fra Kanton ca. 1700–1822,* Copenhagen, 1965, because these books give an idea of the porcelain exported from China by the Swedish and Danish Companies and not much has been published as yet about this porcelain.

The knowledge of Chinese ceramics has also been advanced by many articles in learned periodicals, many of them bulletins of museums or of societies. Notable among these are the *Transactions of the Oriental Ceramic Society,* published in London, the bulletins published in Stockholm by the Museum of Far Eastern Antiquities and the *Archives of the Chinese Art Society of America* (New York, 1945).

For other publications, the reader is referred to the Bibliography (pages 232–42).

1 · Trade relations between the West and China

There is ample evidence of trade between China and the West from ancient times and it is clear that porcelain was one of the articles of that trade: very early pieces of the ware dispersed over several European countries provide evidence of this. The inventories of the Dukes of Normandy (1363) and Jean de Berry (1416), refer to Chinese ceramic wares. The Doge of Venice, Pasquale Malipiero (1461) and Lorenzo de' Medici (1487), were presented with large porcelain vases by the Sultan of Egypt. One of the oldest pieces in Europe is the so-called 'Gaignières ewer' (Plate 1) which was fitted to the order of Louis the Great of Hungary (1348–82) with silver-gilt enamelled mounts and presented by him to Charles III of Durazzo. A water-colour of this ewer, by Gaignières, *circa* 1713, is preserved in the Bibliothèque Nationale, Paris. The ewer itself, denuded of its mounts, is now in the National Museum of Ireland, Dublin.

THE PORTUGUESE IN THE FAR EAST

The Portuguese rounded the Cape in 1497 and arrived at Calicut in the following year. They founded establishments in several countries of the Far East after this, and came to control the sea-routes to and from China. In 1517 the first Portuguese ship arrived at Canton. After they had been ousted by the Chinese from the ports of Ningpo and Chuan-chou in 1545 and 1549, they were allowed to establish themselves at Macao in 1557. From there they were permitted to sail for Canton twice annually to trade there. Among other merchandise they purchased porcelain which they shipped all over Asia and to a lesser extent home to Lisbon where other Europeans came to buy it. Spain, which colonized the Philippines in 1565, is of minor importance in this respect.

After the Dutch East India Company had been founded in 1602, the Dutch gradually took over the sea routes from the Portuguese and with them the rôle as chief pur-

veyor of porcelain for the Asian and European markets during the seventeenth
century.

THE DUTCH EAST INDIA COMPANY

The first contact between the Netherlands and the Indies occurred in 1596 when
Cornelis de Houtman sailed round the Cape and reached Bantam on Java. Soon after
this the Dutch began the long and difficult negotiations which were eventually to lead
to the uniting of the various companies then trading into the Dutch East India Company.[1] Extensive trading already took place between China and Malacca, the Philippines
and the Indian archipelago. From Fukien in South China coarse porcelain was sent to
India, Malaysia, Ceylon, Persia and Egypt. Later The East India Company was to take
over a great part of this trade from the Portuguese. After the Dutch had set up posts on
the most important islands in the Archipelago, the trade of the Spaniards and Portuguese
was even more curtailed (they were driven out in 1600). Just like the Portuguese, the
Dutch wanted to have a factory in China. Efforts were first made in the beginning of
the seventeenth century. Without permission from the Chinese, the Company set up an
establishment in 1623 on the island of Pehoe (one of the Pescadores). Under pressure
from the Chinese, the Dutch left this island, and Amoy which they had possession of for
a short time, setting themselves up in Formosa in 1624.

ENGLAND IN THE FAR EAST

The fourth country to pursue trade with the Far East, by means of the East India Company set up in 1599, was England. Englishmen reached Indian waters about twenty-five
years before the Dutch. In 1620 this company established itself at Bantam, where they
had a trading post, with intervals, until 1694. From 1612 they traded porcelain with
Thailand, where there were also Chinese traders. In the course of the seventeenth century

[1] The Dutch East India Company was established on 20th March 1602, and consisted then of six
chambers: Amsterdam, Hoorn, Enkhuizen, Delft, Rotterdam and Middelburg. Each chamber had a
large measure of independence and controlled its own ships. Initially the company was directed by the
shareholders, directors of the seventy-six companies who were members, a number later reduced to sixty.
Amsterdam chose 20 of the directors, Zeeland 12 and the four other cities 7 each. Above the general
body of directors was the college of the Seventeen Gentlemen; these were elected for every meeting by
and from the shareholders. The Amsterdam chamber chose 8, Middelburg 4, Delft, Rotterdam, Enkhuizen, Hoorn each 1, and the 17th member was chosen by Zeeland or one of the small chambers. The
Seventeen Gentlemen met for a few days two or three times a year. The Company had a trade monopoly
and a sovereign position. In the course of the eighteenth century its prosperity declined, until in 1798 it
was taken over by the Batavian Republic, and thus ended the 200-year-old Company.

Immediately after the Company had set up a post in the Indies, the Gentlemen named a governor-
general (the first was G. C. Both) and a council to support him.

the Company established various settlements in the continent of India, including Gombron.[1] An attempt in 1637 by four English ships to start direct trade with Canton was thwarted by the Portuguese.

[1] From Gombron, then called Bandar Abbas (lying across from Ormusz in the Persian Gulf), the English East India Company shipped the first Chinese porcelain to England. Thus Persian earthenware as well as Gombron was known. Horace Walpole in his Catalogue (1770) called Chinese porcelain 'most ancient Gombron China'. Later this Company imported Chinese porcelain as 'India-China' from Calcutta and Bombay for England, Europe and America.

2 · Ching-tê Chên

Ching-tê Chên, which was originally called Ch'ang-nan, owes its name to the Emperor Ching Tê (1004–08). Although throughout China porcelain was made at large and small factories, the emperors of the Ming dynasty (1368–1644) concentrated its production at Ching-tê Chên. The *T'ao-lu*[1] informs us that Emperor Hung Wu (1368–98) had a kiln built at the Jewel Hill and that inspectors were commissioned to supervise the manufacture of the porcelain and its transport to the capital. According to other sources, it was only under the Emperor Yung Lo (1403–24) at the earliest that porcelain of good quality was made. It was this porcelain especially that was to become known in Europe from after the time of the coming of the Portuguese at the beginning of the sixteenth century. Apart from the royal factory, other factories were also built, such as that of Ts'ui-kung yao (second half of the fifteenth century).[2]

Ching-tê Chên is situated about thirty miles up river from Po-yang, formerly Jao Chou in the province of Kiangsi in a valley basin surrounded by mountains (fig. 1). The town itself is favourably placed, connected by waterways with the great city of Nanking. Fortunately, there are several early accounts of the manufacture of porcelain, among the first being that in the journals of Marco Polo (1254–1324). Since the few Europeans who reached China before the sixteenth century all mention porcelain in their descriptions, it appears to have been regarded by them as something remarkable. In his book

---

[1] *Ching-tê Chên T'ao-lu or The Potteries of China,* being a translation and an introduction by Geoffrey R. Sayer (London, 1951) p. 1. The *T'ao-lu* was written by Lan P'u (Lan Pin Wan). After his death it was published in 1815 by his pupil Cheng-Ting Kuei under the rule of Emperor Chia Ching (1795–1820). Stanislas Julien translated some parts of this into French: *Histoire et Fabrication de la Porcelaine Chinoise.* This translation contained a few misinterpretations, because of which various passages were not understood for years. See p. 15, R. Soame Jenyns, *Later Chinese Porcelain* (London, 1951), 2nd impression.

[2] R. L. Hobson, *The Wares of the Ming Dynasty* (London, 1923) pp. 59, 123.

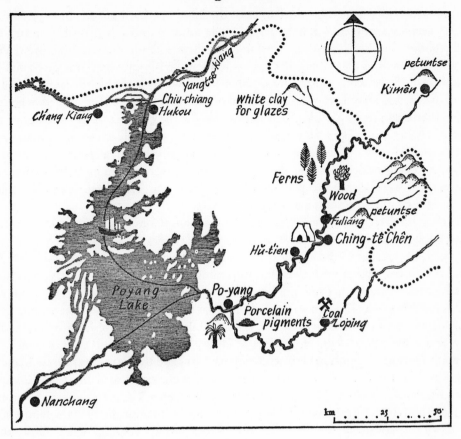

Map labels: petuntse / Kimên / Yangtsê-kiang / Chiu-chiang / Hukou / Ch'ang Kiaug / White clay for glazes / Ferns / Wood / petuntse / Fuliang / Ching-tê Chên / Hŭ-t'ien / Po-yang / Poyang Lake / Porcelain pigments / Coal / Loping / Nanchang / km . . . 25 . . . 50

1. Pottery-centre of Ching-tê Chên and surrounding country

published in 1569, Caspar du Cruz[1] describes how the clay was purified and the blue applied. Jan Huygen van Linschoten also mentions porcelain in his *Itinerarie*; and Jan Nieuhof describes in his book his visit to Ching-tê Chên (see Bibliography).

The fullest and most valuable information about the manufacture come from the pen of Père d'Entrecolles.[2] In two letters to Père Orry at Paris in 1712 and 1722 he writes that at Ching-tê Chên there were three thousand porcelain kilns and that at night it was

[1] After he reached Indies in 1548, he went in 1556 to China, to return thirteen years later to Portugal, where he died in 1570. His discoveries were made known in his *Treatise in Which are Sketched Chinese Things,* re-published at Barcelona in 1937.

[2] Père d'Entrecolles was born at Limoges or Lyon in 1663. He went to China in 1689. After having lived for some time at Jaochow or Jao Chou (now Po-yang), he died in Peking in 1741.

as if the town, illuminated by the flames of the kilns, was itself aflame. In 1735 Père du Halde[1] mentions only five hundred kilns. The latter number is probably nearer the truth; about five hundred kilns working for three to four thousand factories. Père d'Entrecolles tells us that Ching-tê Chên was no walled-in city and was governed by an imperial officer who, assisted by a police force, was responsible for law and order. Every street was served according to its length by one or two police officers who had under them again ten constables, each responsible for the conduct of the inmates of ten houses. The total number of the inhabitants was about one million, all of them in some way connected with the porcelain industry. The majority by far were artisans, most of the others being traders. During the night the streets were closed by barrier gates and no strangers were allowed to pass the night in the town. They were allotted a place in one of the numerous ships anchored in the river.

Apart from descriptions by foreigners, there are also Chinese sources of information about Ching-tê Chên, such as the *T'ao Ch'êng Shih Yu Kao* (instructions for the making of porcelain) inserted in the annals of the district of Fou-liang for 1735 and *T'ao Yeh T'ou Shuo,* a description with twenty illustrations[2] of the porcelain industry, published shortly after 1743. Both these publications were written by T'ang Ying[3] who was director of Ching-tê Chên from 1736 to 1749 or 1753. Well known too are the *T'ao Shuo* which, written by Chu Yen and published in 1774, was translated by Bushell in 1910 under the title *Description of Chinese Pottery and Porcelain* and the *Ching-tê Chên T'ao-lu.*[4] During the fighting between Ming partisans and the forces of the new Manchu dynasty, which continued even after the Ch'ing were established in 1644, Ching-tê Chên was largely destroyed by fire in 1675.[5] The Emperor K'ang Hsi had the town and the factories rebuilt in 1683 with Chang Ch'i-chung as director. In 1677 the land-tax of the district of Fou-liang was placed at his disposal, which enabled him to buy much needed materials and to pay the labourers. In 1683 Ts'ang Ying-hsüan was appointed director. He reorganized the imperial factories and under him they began to flourish again; he also invented several new glazes. In this year the revival of the Chinese porcelain industry became an accomplished fact.

Another great director was Nien Hsi-yao, appointed by the Emperor Yung Chêng in 1726. The fine white porcelain, covered with clear white glaze, came into being through

---

[1] Père du Halde, *Description géographique, historique, chronologique et physique de l'Empire de la Chine et de la Tartarie Chinoise* (Paris, 1735, 4 vols.). In the 2nd volume parts of Père d'Entrecolles' letters are inserted. See also R. Soame Jenyns, *Later Chinese Porcelain,* p. 16.

[2] Translated by S. W. Bushell in *Oriental Ceramic Art, Illustrated by Examples from the Collection of W. T. Walters* (New York, 1899). See R. Soame Jenyns, *Later Chinese Porcelain,* pp. 7, 61, 70. The illustrations have probably been lost.

[3] R. Soame Jenyns, op. cit., p. 62.

[4] Translated with notes and an introduction by G. R. Sayer.

[5] In 1853 during the Tai Ping rebellion it was once more destroyed by fire and many labourers were killed. The factories were rebuilt in 1864. See R. Soame Jenyns, op. cit., pp. 24–25.

the efforts of Nien. There was hardly ever a flaw to be found in the glaze. Nien became famous in connection with fine copies of Sung monochromes.

A third director of note was T'ang Ying, mentioned already as an author. He was appointed by the Emperor Ch'ien Lung as director of the Imperial factories in 1736. By mixing with the artisans he learned all the details of their craft and became an expert himself. He had a great knowledge of different kinds of clay and was well acquainted with the effect of fire on clay. Under his direction a very fine, thin, translucent porcelain was successfully made and, according to the *T'ao-lu*, Ching-tê Chên reached its zenith under this director.

METHODS OF WORK

Improved working conditions for the porcelain workers and other personnel were introduced by Chang Ch'i-chung. He changed the system of recruiting workers from the various districts of Fou-Liang and Po-yang for statute labour at Ching-tê Chên. A few thousand workers could now have the pleasure of working in the porcelain factories; and these were probably contented with their lot. Père d'Entrecolles on the contrary found them poorly paid. This judgement held also for the porcelain-painters, who painted so admirably the porcelain flowers, animals and landscapes. Unfortunately, the *T'ao-lu* does not give details of amounts of salaries,[1] but rather with the manner of paying them. The workers, for example, who made the objects from the raw clay, received their wages in the fourth and the tenth months, with a further small payment at the end of the year. The artists and foremen were paid on the day of the Dragon boat festival and also in the middle of the seventh and tenth months and on the last day of the year. In the first and third months money was paid out to buy provisions on the market; this was contrived by the head of the customs at Kiukiang.

A sort of conveyor-belt system was further developed under Emperor K'ang Hsi. According to Père d'Entrecolles, the factories were departmentalized to the utmost. There were different studios for the decoration in relief or in openwork for gilding, for the drawing of the marks, the painting, and so forth. Specialists appeared: one man would paint water or mountains, another birds and animals. On the whole, wrote Père d'Entrecolles, the human figures were the least good. This system meant that the painting had less personal character.

According to the *T'ao-lu*, living things, such as flowers, birds, insects and fish, had to be painted, and here nature had to be faithfully portrayed. Tradition has it that the first Ming Emperors had had great fish-bowls made that took up a whole oven and took nineteen days to bake. The story goes that when the baking of one bowl (diameter 90 cm.) repeatedly went amiss, one of the bakers, Tung by name, threw himself into the kiln as a sacrifice, after which the fish-bowl came out perfectly. Over and over again,

[1] *T'ao-lu*, op. cit., p. 35.

the Emperors gave commissions that were impossible or almost impossible to execute. For instance, they did not manage to make a 30 cm. high organ with 14 pipes; though they did succeed with ducks and turtles that could float in the water. Père d'Entrecolles tells us that the mandarins yearned for many other articles from Europe that could be imitated in porcelain, for they wished to flatter the Emperor with them. 'The Christians' (converted Chinese), writes Père d'Entrecolles, 'begged me not to give such things to the mandarins, because they would be beaten with sticks if they could not copy them.'

TRANSPORT

The transport of the finished product of the porcelain to Peking, about 1200 miles away, was by boat down the Ch'ang river to Jao Chou, from there via the Poyang lake down the Yangtse to Nanking and from there by the Grand Canal to Peking. The transport to Canton, about 600 miles, was also via Jao Chou; from there southwards on the Poyang lake to Nanchang, the capital of Kiangsi and from there upriver again to the border of that province; it was then carried by bearers over the Meiling pass (Plate 55) and shipped down the Pekiang to Canton. When transport to Amoy or Canton by sea was wanted, the porcelain was shipped via Nanking to the sea-port of Hang Chou where it was trans-shipped and carried by sea-going junks to these southern ports. In 1736 T'ang Ying wrote about the transport of porcelain destined for the royal court at Peking; this was carried out in flat-bottomed boats in the autumn of each year. A quantity of between 16,000 and 17,000 pieces of first quality was shipped yearly, and further 6,000 to 7,000 pieces of the best quality of the second class. The first quality porcelain made in private factories was reserved for the Emperor and the court.

3 · The manufacture of Chinese porcelain

As it still frequently happens that stoneware and porcelain are taken for earthenware and conversely, the difference, which arises from the clay used—more or less refractory— and the temperature at which it is fired, may be very concisely outlined in this short survey of the manufacture of porcelain. Earthenware, fired at a temperature of about 800–1900 degrees C., is comparatively soft, porous, easily scratched, not translucent and not resonant. Stoneware, fired at a temperature of 1250–1300 degrees C., is hard, not porous, not easily scratched, not translucent and, when thinly potted, may be resonant. Stoneware potted from a special white clay is called porcelain. It is resonant and, when thinly potted, translucent. Chinese porcelain was fired at a temperature of 1200 degrees C. and perhaps even 1300 degrees.

The white clay used in Chinese porcelain was a combination of two kinds, *kaolin*,[1] so called after a hilly forest district east of Ching-tê Chên where it occurred abundantly, and *pai-tun-tzu* (petuntse[2]), so called from the small white blocks into which it was pressed for transport. The Chinese called the kaolin and the petuntse, the bones and the flesh of the porcelain. The origin of both materials had great influence on the quality of the porcelain.

Kaolin came as a very fine white clay out of the river bed. In contrast to petuntse, it did not need to be broken, ground or purified, though it did require some refining which was done by stamping. The petuntse and the kaolin were mixed in correct

[1] W. B. Honey, *The Ceramic Art of China and other Countries of the Far East* (London, 1945) pp. 11–22. Kaolin consists of approximately 50 per cent silica, 30 per cent alumina, 2.5 per cent potassium, iron and other elements. When in the reign of Wan Li (1573–1619) the good porcelain clay of the Ma Ts'ang mountains was used up, the royal factory got it from Mu-men.

[2] The name petuntse, *pai-tun-tzu*, 'little white blocks', was given in the eighteenth century to the clay containing feldspar. Père d'Entrecolles writes that both the Dutch and English used small pieces of petuntse but forgot the kaolin so their attempts to make porcelain were doomed.

proportion with the required amount of water, and kneaded and stamped until a homogeneous mass without air-bubbles was formed. According to Père d'Entrecolles this process was the most important and the trickiest of the whole operation. The tiniest impurity in the clay, such as a grain of sand, could make the porcelain crack in the oven.

Here must be mentioned Carletti's[1] explanation about the best clay: he says, 'The kind of clay called "the flower of the clay-bed" may not be sent out of the Kingdom and may only be put at the disposal of the King and the governors of the land.' This law must have been broken a number of times, for in the collection of Augustus the Strong, for instance, there are pieces that were not intended for export.

The *T'ao-lu*[2] indicates that there were two sorts of 'foreign' porcelain meant for export. The best pieces were made of *hua-shih* (slippery stone). The cheap and the coarse porcelain was made of *tun-ni* (brick mud).

The Chinese knew two methods of manufacture: by the wheel and by the mould. Père d'Entrecolles describes how a cup was made on the potter's wheel. The procedure, rather like that of a modern assembly line, was as follows. The first labourer threw the cup on the wheel, a second one finished the shape by means of a mould (Plate 4) into which it was pressed, a third one smoothed and thinned it with a spatula till it became very thin and translucent and a fourth put on the prefabricated handle. All this happened very quickly and according to our informant a piece of porcelain was handled by seventy workers before it was completely finished. Large pieces were thrown in two or more parts which were then luted together with porcelain clay. In the same way handles were fixed to bodies. Pieces which because of the shape wanted could not be thrown on the wheel, manysided ones or those of irregular shape, were moulded.[3] The same procedure was followed in the making of statuettes and human or animal figures and small objects such as arms, heads or ornaments.

After being shaped on the wheel or in the mould the body was set out to dry.

EGGSHELL PORCELAIN

In Chinese this porcelain is called *t'o-t'ai* which might be translated as 'without a body'.[4] The cup, dish or vase was put on the wheel and pared down till it became as thin as possible—more than half the clay was removed. After the porcelain treated in this way had been glazed and fired it was as if the whole object consisted of glaze only. T'ang Ying was famous for having this kind of porcelain made and used a very special glaze. Sometimes the body is so thin that the outside and inside glazes seem to touch.

[1] Francesco Carletti, *My Voyage around the world, 1594–1606* (London, 1965).

[2] *Ching-tê Chên, T'ao-lu*, translated by G. F. Sayer, p. 32.

[3] The moulds were made of stone or fired clay.

[4] Eggshell porcelain was spoken of for the first time in the reign of the Emperor Yung Lo (1403–24). The Yung-chêng list (see p. 35) mentions, under No. 24, copies of Yung Lo porcelain.

The manufacture of Chinese porcelain

DECORATION

Besides painted decoration, which will be dealt with presently, porcelain was also decorated with incised design or in relief. The name lacework is given when the decoration, deeply incised into the body, is covered with a greenish-white glaze. Sometimes a vessel was covered with a slip of a colour different from that of the body clay and the decoration was carved or modelled therein. Because of this the decoration stands out clearly. This technique known as *pâte-sur-pâte* or *bianco-sopra-bianco*. At times a decoration occurs where the representations, for instance a dragon or leaf scrolls, are engraved on the body itself. This decoration is called *an hua*, secret design, and is visible only when the piece is held against the light or in a slanting light.

OPENWORK DECORATION

Quite different from the above is the openwork decoration, in Chinese called *ling lung*. It demands very good craftmanship since openings are cut through the as yet unglazed dry body and the whole piece then covered with glaze. After firing the openings become quite transparent. It is also called *kuei lung,* devil's work. During the eighteenth century and after, openings about the size of a grain of rice were cut through the body and filled in with glaze and this decoration is therefore sometimes called rice-grain decoration. Porcelain so treated was also called Gombroon ware.[1]

GLAZE

Feldspathic glaze is made from petuntse. After the clay had been cleaned with water it was pounded with a hammer into small pieces which were then pulverized in a mortar. After being diluted with water and mixed with vegetable ashes, for instance fern-ashes, and with a small quantity of lime, the glaze was ready for use. The *T'ao-lu* states that small objects were dipped in a vessel filled with glaze. Larger objects were squirted with glaze by means of a piece of bamboo covered with gauze. In the heat of the kiln kaolin and petuntse are fused at a temperature of 1200–1300 degrees C. into a homogeneous whole, the glaze now forming a hard glassy surface. In the case of Têhua porcelain (see Chapter 18) the fusing is so complete that it is impossible to discern where the glaze stops and the body begins. In general, the glazes of the Ming period are thicker than those of the Ch'ing. Sometimes a glaze shows crackle, originally the result of a different reaction of body and glaze in the heat of the kiln. Later, when this mishap had caught the public fancy, the porcelain makers started to produce crackle intentionally. The glaze of the fifteenth-century porcelain is frequently as it were pockmarked. This

---

[1] The term 'Gombroon' is derived from the port Gombron (the modern Bandar Abbas) on the Persian Gulf, from which both Chinese and Persian wares in this technique were exported.

so-called 'orange peel' effect was purposely imitated in the eighteenth century. In 1722 Père d'Entrecolles writes that in order to prevent scaling of the glaze at the rim of a piece (a rather frequent occurrence in 'carrack' porcelain) a special glaze was added which had the same colour as the body glaze. In the seventeenth and the beginning of the eighteenth centuries, rims of dishes and plates were sometimes covered with a brown glaze.[1]

PAINTING

As soon as a potted piece of porcelain was dry enough, the decoration was painted on. Every stroke of the brush was at once soaked in by the still porous body, which considerably limited the freedom of the porcelain painter. Because of the high temperature at which the porcelain was baked, the number of colours which could stand the heat was restricted to blue from cobalt and red from oxide of copper.

Blue

Two kinds of cobalt were used, the native kind which contains an amount of manganese and the cobalt imported from Persia which contains arsenic. The latter, which results in a magnificent blue, is called Persian or Mohammedan blue,[2] *su-ma-ni, su-ni-po* or *hui hui ch'ing*. It was imported rather irregularly. Native cobalt, perhaps mixed with the imported material, was probably used during the sixteenth and seventeenth centuries. It was found according to the *T'ao-lu*,[3] in the provinces of Chêkiang, Kiangsi, Kuang-tung and Yunnan. During the eighteenth century large quantities of cobalt were imported from Europe.[4] Finely ground cobalt, which in the raw state is black, was mixed with water after being cleaned. The pigment thus created was painted on the object it was to decorate and resulted, after glazing and firing, in a splendid silvery blue gloss which reminds one of the feathers of a kingfisher. It occurs of course in various tints depending for instance on the purity of the cobalt and the thickness of the liquid paint. The potters were able to eliminate the iron so well from the raw cobalt that a prime quality blue was obtained. A blackish tone resulted when the cobalt was insufficiently covered by the glaze. When the concentration of the cobalt was too weak, the result was a pale blue. When refined and impure cobalt were mixed different tints of blue were obtained.

[1] W. B. Honey, *Guide to the Later Chinese Porcelain*, London (Victoria and Albert Museum, 1927) p. 32.

[2] The Ming annals tell us that the cobalt was brought from Sumatra as tribute in 1426, 1433, 1434 and 1486. So far as we know, cobalt was first used towards the end of the T'ang dynasty (618–906). Sir Harry Garner, *Oriental Blue and White* (London, 1954) p. 15.

[3] Op. cit., p. 6.

[4] B. Watney, *English Blue and White Porcelain of the 18th Century*, p. 6.

B. Washing set of water jar with lid and wall-basin all with polychrome
decoration on Y-diaper gold ground. Second quarter eighteenth century

The manufacture of Chinese porcelain

Red

In the fourteenth century, the Chinese began to paint decorations in red from copper oxide on porcelain. This method was common especially during the reigns of emperors Hsüan Tê (1426–35), Ch'êng Hua (1465–87) and later of Wan Li (1573–1619). Underglaze red was used alone or together with underglaze blue. Because this red was found to be difficult to use, especially by the later porcelain painters, iron-red enamel was employed in place of copper-red, and this was put on top of the glaze.

Powder blue

To get the effect of powder blue, before the body was quite dry cobalt in powdered form was blown on to the porcelain by means of a bamboo pipe covered with a piece of gauze. In this way thousands of small cloudy specks of colour appeared. If any part of the body was to remain white, it was covered with a piece of paper of the desired shape and size. After being glazed the piece was fired as usual. Gold was occasionally painted on the blue background after firing.

Enamel colours on glazed porcelain or biscuit fired in the muffle kiln

In addition to the colours that were baked at high temperature in the main kilns (*grand feu*) there were many that could only withstand the low temperature of the muffle kiln (*petit feu*). These enamels, which included iron-red (Chinese *fan-hung*), could be painted over the glaze or on the baked unglazed porcelain, generally known as 'biscuit'. Colours painted on the biscuit are more matt, softer and less sparkling than those painted over the glaze.

SAN-TS'AI OR 'THREE COLOURS'

The decoration known in China as *san-ts'ai* is produced by applying coloured lead glazes, generally but not always limited to three in number, to the biscuit. This type of decoration was first applied to pottery in the T'ang dynasty and afterwards to the Tz'ŭ-chou stonewares of the Sung dynasty and to Ming porcelains. The outlines of the designs were first engraved on the body or applied in thin lines of slip (cloisonné style) to contain the colours. The colours were turquoise and green (derived from copper), aubergine (manganese), blue (cobalt) and yellow (iron). A colourless flux derived from arsenic was also used. The porcelain was fired in a muffle kiln. Biscuit figures such as Buddhist deities, Taoist immortals, children, animals, birds and ornaments in relief were decorated in *san-ts'ai*, as well as vessels.

c   33

The manufacture of Chinese porcelain

WU-TS'AI OR 'FIVE COLOURS'

Decoration in 'five colours' (*wu-ts'ai* in Chinese), applied over the glaze, came into being during the early years of the Ming dynasty. The number 'five' is only intended to imply a number of colours which in fact may range from two to five. Underglaze blue, applied in the first stage of firing, may be used in addition to the enamels. The colours are red, green, turquoise, yellow and aubergine, and outlines in black and red are generally used. Sometimes gold decoration is applied in a third firing.

FAMILLE VERTE

Although a green transparent enamel was in use in Chinese pottery from the T'ang dynasty onwards and was included both in the *san-ts'ai* and *wu-ts'ai* enamels, the term *famille verte* is only strictly applicable to the enamel decoration of the early part of the Ch'ing dynasty. The enamels may be applied over the glaze or on the biscuit.[1] The former may be combined with underglaze blue or an overglaze blue enamel peculiar to the K'ang Hsi period may be added. The enamel colours are similar to those of the Ming dynasty but a number of gradations of the green enamel are a new feature. Gold decoration, in a separate firing, was often added.

FAMILLE NOIRE

This is a variation of *famille verte* on the biscuit in which a green enamel is applied over areas of brownish-black pigment, which is identical in composition with that used for the black outlines. The result is a glossy black enamel, generally used to provide an effective background for the *famille verte* decoration.

FAMILLE JAUNE

This is also a variation of *famille verte* on the biscuit, in which yellow provides the ground for the rest of the decoration.

FAMILLE ROSE

In China *famille rose* is known under different names such as 'foreign colours' (*yang-ts'ai*), 'pale colours' (*fên-ts'ai*) or 'soft colours' (*yüan-ts'ai*).

The decoration, in which the principal colour is a rose-red enamel, was painted over the glaze. This colour, derived from gold, was used in Europe in enamels on copper in

[1] Père d'Entrecolles writes that enamel colours were mixed with gum and water.

34

in the seventeenth century and was introduced to China before 1720.[1] It was not fully developed until the third decade of the eighteenth century. Shading was achieved by mixing a white enamel derived from arsenic with the pink and because of this a more naturalistic style of painting was achieved than had been possible in the *famille verte*. The other enamels were green, blue, yellow and aubergine. Gold was added in a further firing. T'ang Ying pointed out that the same colours were used for enamelling on metal.

THE YUNG CHÊNG LIST

This list gives a selection of the types of porcelain made in the kilns at Ching-tê Chên for the court. It was compiled between 1729 and 1732 by Hsieh Min, the governor of the province of Kiangsi.[2] It is possible that the list records the porcelain made annually or biennially for the court. There is evidence of western influence in the document, where such terms as 'foreign colours' (*yang-ts'ai* in Chinese), are found. The words 'foreign' or 'Europe' are frequently mentioned. For example, numbers 37, 38, 53 and 54, referring to porcelain covered with yellow, purplish brown, green and black all mention 'European style'. Copies of European wares are mentioned in No. 29. According to the *T'ao-lu*[3] the decoration of porcelain with silver, No. 39 in the Yung Cheng list, was an invention of T'ang Ying. This, however, is contrary to the information given by Père d'Entrecolles in his second letter, published in 1724, which mentions decoration with silver. As T'ang Ying became assistant to Nien Hsi-yao only in 1728, he cannot have invented this decoration; at the best he can only have improved it. Silver decoration after a time becomes black through oxidation and is not generally satisfactory.

STEATITE OR CHINESE SOFT-PASTE PORCELAIN

In 1712 Père d'Entrecolles writes that recently the porcelain bakers had replaced kaolin by *hua-shih* (slippery stone)[4] which, he says, is more expensive than kaolin. Ceramic objects made with it stand in relation to porcelain proper as paper to vellum. It is lighter in weight, and more brittle than genuine porcelain. It is difficult to get the right temperature for firing it. Sometimes porcelain proper was covered with a slip of this clay which

[1] The invention of rose-red enamel has been attributed incorrectly to Andreas Cassius of Leyden in 1650, but it was in fact known to Benvenuto Cellini in the mid-sixteenth century. Cassius applied the principle to the manufacture of ruby glass.

[2] This list was published for the first time in 1732, in the *Chiang-hsi T'ung Chih* or general description of the province Kiangsi. In the *T'ao-lu* (op. cit., p. 22) there is also a list, which differs to some extent from the Yung Chêng list. The first is published in R. L. Hobson, *The Later Ceramic Wares of China* (London, 1925) and also in Warren Cox, *The Book of Pottery and Porcelain* (New York, 11th Edition 1963) p. 582ff.

[3] Op. cit., p. 49.

[4] *Hua-shih*, steatite or soapstone, is a silicate of aluminium and magnesium.

gives a more creamy-white, oily tint to the glaze. As *hua shih* was costlier than porcelain proper, it was used mostly for small objects only. The ware made from or with it is opaque and shows a fine crackle. When fractured the planes are less sharp than in the case of true porcelain (though not so granular as European soft-paste porcelain with which it should not be confused). The blue decoration, which is in general finely executed, was carried out by able porcelain painters.

THE KILNS

Various kinds of kilns (Plate 4) were used for the firing of large and of small objects, for muffling, for the making of seggars of refractory clay, and for the firing of glazes and colours. Kilns stoked with faggots of pine wood were used for the finer porcelain, while for the firing of coarse pieces undergrowth was good enough. Père d'Entrecolles informs us in his letter of 1712 that at Ching-tê Chên coal was also used,[1] which may well be true as it was present in the soil about thirty miles to the south of the kiln-sites. Various shapes of kilns appear on Chinese prints from the end of the eighteenth century, for example those shown on Plate 3: hive-shaped kilns with only one compartment under a shed, and tunnel-like kilns built on the slope of a hill and having several compartments. The former had a round opening in the conical roof for the smoke to escape, but there were also kilns with a chimney about twenty feet high. Du Halde wrote in 1735 that one kiln was 16 metres high and 4 metres wide. Kilns were built by members of the Wei family, who specialized in this work.

To protect the porcelain in the kiln from whirling ashes and dust, it was frequently placed in seggars made from refractory clay. In the seggars the pieces were placed on some sand sprinkled with pulverized kaolin to prevent the footring from sticking to the bottom of the seggar. Various stands were also used, the spur marks[2] of which are sometimes visible on the bottom of a piece. The seggars were filled and then stacked in rows to enable the flames to play around them. The less expensive kinds of porcelain, and probably also the lesser export ware, were placed near the entrance or near the chimney. To protect them as much as possible against the greatest heat, the seggars with the best pieces were placed in the middle.

With the aid of pieces of raw clay[3] which were put in the kiln which had vents and peepholes, it was possible to ensure that porcelain got the right heat and see when it had had enough. Very able potters could also see from the colour of the flames whether everything was going well. The duration of the firing depended among other things

[1] Coal was used in Northern China in Sung times. The Chinese kilns, incidentally, were copied in Korea, Japan and Tongking.

[2] These may be seen for example on Japanese plates and dishes, though seldom on Chinese porcelain of the Ming and Ch'ing dynasties.

[3] What follows is partly taken from the *T'ao-lu,* op. cit., p. 19.

upon the size of the pieces. Large pieces were fired for ten days at a high and for seven at a lower temperature, after which the kiln was left to cool for ten days. For smaller pieces a firing of from three to five days was sufficient with a cooling period of five to three days. If the kiln was opened before the porcelain was sufficiently cooled, the latter would break without fail; the kiln was therefore opened when still moderately warm. This was done by labourers wearing moistened gloves and their heads wrapped in damp cloths. As soon as it was empty the still warm kiln was instantly filled again with porcelain.

Père d'Entrecolles writes that after firing the contents of the kiln were but rarely entirely perfect. When the kiln was opened it was frequently found that porcelain and seggars had fused into one hard mass and all was lost. About fifty per cent, he says, of all the porcelain baked was wasted.

In the stoking of the kilns two methods were used, just as in Europe, that which had a reducing and the other which had an oxidizing effect. The first effect was obtained by severely restricting the supply of air, as a result of which the kiln became full of carbon monoxide which gave a clear tint to the blue, and to celadon its green splendour. The second effect was obtained by letting in air more freely, with the result that the glaze took an ivory tint, the cobalt became blackish and iron oxide yellow or brown or even black instead of green.

EUROPEAN PORCELAIN

When Chinese porcelain became known and fashionable in Europe, potters, glass-blowers and alchemists all tried to imitate it. An early and partly successful result was achieved around 1575 at Florence in the factory of Francesco I de Medici, where a porcelain was made based on Chinese blue-and-white of the sixteenth century. In the seventeenth century Europeans succeeded in making, from materials such as rock crystal and sand, a kind of soft-paste porcelain that could be fired at a high temperature. The first porcelain with kaolin as a base—hard-paste—was made by Böttger at Meissen in 1709, after he had made red stoneware. In 1710 the royal factory was established at Meissen. The second factory making kaolin porcelain was at Vienna. The discovery of kaolin in 1768, at Saint Yrieix near Limoges, led Count de Milly to write his book *Art de la porcelaine* which appeared in 1771. Before porcelain clay was found in France, the so-called *pâte tendre* (soft paste) porcelain was made. This was composed of clay, chalk, sand, plaster of Paris, soda and sometimes soft soap. Towards the end of the seventeenth century there was *pâte tendre* porcelain at Rouen and St. Cloud (1679 or 1722) and in the eighteenth century at Chantilly (established 1725), Mennecy and Vincennes. In England, burnt bonemeal and steatite were used in place of feldspar at the factories of Chelsea, Derby, Bow, Worcester and others. William Cookworthy, who had studied the letters of Père d'Entrecolles, discovered in 1768 at Plymouth how to make porcelains differing in composition. In the first, less than fifty per cent kaolin is used; this percentage is considerably higher in Meissen and Berlin porcelain. In contrast with European porcelain which was first fired at a temperature of 800 to 1000 degrees C. and then glazed, in China the unfired porcelain was first glazed and then fired in the kiln at a temperature of about 1300 degrees C.

4 · Martabani, Swatow and celadon wares

There has been a growing interest during the last fifty years in the above-named ceramic wares,[1] made especially for export. In particular many pieces have been brought to the Netherlands by repatriates from Indonesia. The largest and most important collection is in the Princessehof at Leeuwarden. Interest in other European countries has also increased.

Europe has been acquainted with the first of these groups, the so-called Martabani wares, since the early seventeenth century. One piece in the Ashmolean Museum, similar to that illustrated in Plate 6, is known to have belonged to Sir John Tradescant before 1627.[2] Other pieces are illustrated in a painting dated 1655,[3] which shows three small jars of Martabani ware, of a type known as 'Martavan', on a rack placed against the back wall of a shop-interior. Other jars of this type, about 37 cm. high, are in the Princessehof (Plate 7). These would have been brought from Indonesia by ships' captains as storage-pots.

It is not certain whether the so-called 'Swatow wares' were known in the West before the present century. The celadon wares, of which the dish in Plate 2 is a typical example, were exported over a large area, stretching from South East Asia to the Near East.

MARTABANI WARES

The name 'Martavan'[4] is given to storage pots made from stoneware covered with a black, brown or golden-brown lead glaze. The name comes from the harbour Martaban, corrupted to Martavan, where the pots were seen by Arabian travellers. These storage

[1] Nanne Ottema, *Chineesche Ceramiek* (Amsterdam, 1946) pp. 115, 121, 134.
[2] W. B. Honey, *The ceramic art of China and other countries of the Far East* (London, 1945) Plate 81.
[3] A. Staring, *The Dutch at Home* (The Hague, 1956) pl. VIII.
[4] H. Miedema, *Martavanen*, Princessehof Museum, Leeuwarden.

pots were taken from China overland to Bhamo (Boven-Birma), to be shipped from there to Martaban at the mouth of the Salween and the Gulf of Martaban or Pegu. (They are also called Pegu pots.)

In all probability, these pots were not only made in the Chinese provinces of Kuantung and Fukien and at Soo-Chou (near Shanghai), but also in Annam and Thailand.[1] The Malayans, Siamese, Mohammedans and Chinese shipped them to the Philippines, India, Egypt and the Indonesian Archipelago. Most of the pots in the Princessehof are originally from Borneo, Celebes, Sumatra and Malacca.

It is not known when the Martabani wares were first made. It has been suggested that they were in use towards the end of the T'ang dynasty (618–906). The big pots, which are shown on reliefs of the Borobudur and Prambanan Temples in Java, bear such a striking resemblance to martavans that they can be said to be identical.

Most martavans, having a slightly hollow bottom and usually without a foot-rim have the shape of an upturned pear ending in a narrowed flared rim. On the shoulder are loop-holes for ropes or straps which held tight leather or vellum coverings (Plates 6, 7). They are decorated with engraved or relief motifs of plants (Plate 6), flowers and animals, especially dragons: these last are also known as dragon jars. The decoration may also include horizontal bands with a zigzag motif, as on the brown earthenware vats of Soo-Chou (Plate 5) which have a round or a square base; and decoration is carried out in yellow slip with lead glaze. The colour of the glaze is mostly brown, sometimes yellow and green.

The well-known Arabian traveller Ibn-Batuta (1304–74) tells how in 1365 the daughter of the Indian king Kaylikan presented him with four jars, filled with ginger, pepper, lemons and mangoes. Other travellers too, such as the Portuguese Durante Barbose and sea captains mention these jars. Pieter van Dam, in his descriptions of the E.I.C. around 1700 writes thus: 'Martavans are large pots for storing fresh water; of which there are three sorts—whole, $\frac{3}{4}$ and $\frac{1}{2}$; nowadays the warehouse only stocks one kind.' So it appears that they were handled by the East India Company. In the second half of the seventeenth century—many of the Princessehof ones are eighteenth century—they were difficult to obtain; in the Day Registers[2] not more than 1300 are listed, which were shipped among other places to Batavia and Borneo by the E.I.C. The captains took them on board for storing water (including holy water from the Ganges), oil, wine, opium and also rice and other foodstuffs. Some of these pots measured 1 m. The large number of pots found in the Indonesian Archipelago show that the people found these

[1] Thus martavans are still manufactured at Chienmai (Thailand) ill. 48 in Nelson Spinks, Ph.D., *The Ceramic Wares of Siam* (Bangkok, 1965).

[2] T. Volker, *Porcelain and the Dutch East India Company, 1602–1682* (Leiden, 1954) pp. 4, 20, 221. In this book are published the registers for 1602 to 1682 of the Dutch East India Company's factories in Batavia, Hirado and Deshima. These, which contain a few gaps, list the porcelain that was shipped from the Indonesian Archipelago by the East India Company to Holland.

almost unbreakable pots extremely useful. In particular the Dajaks on Borneo attached great significance to the jars; they used them for preserving the mortal remains of their ancestors and also for the presentation of dowries. They were frequently used on ceremonial occasions, and it seems that the Dajaks attributed to them magic properties.

SWATOW WARES[1]

The name 'Swatow' was given by Chinese merchants to a coarse sort of porcelain named after the town of that name on the south east coast of China in the province of Kuangtung. According to the Day Registers of the Dutch East India Company this porcelain was obtained from the river of Chincheuw, by which was meant the coast of Fukien.[2] It was once supposed that this porcelain came from Têhua. Japanese sources on the contrary name Tung-an and Pat-kwoh near Shih-ma.

Swatow ware was probably made from the second half of the sixteenth century to the end of the Ming dynasty (1644). As well as to the Near East it was exported to India, the Indonesian Archipelago, and Japan where it became especially fashionable because of its spontaneous, realistic decoration. The so-called Swatow wares include fairly large dishes (bowls from which to eat rice) sometimes with a wavy rim, baluster pots (Plate 9), cups with lids and oil-pots. These pieces are made of clear, resonant porcelain or stoneware fired to a red-brown biscuit containing all kinds of impurities, covered with a thick, irregularly applied, often crackled, more or less opaque glaze, which may be greenish to milk-white in colour and through which the decoration on the body is often rather indistinct. The underneath is carelessly glazed, so that the colour of the red-brown burnt clay is obvious in places where the glaze is faulty. Ottema held a theory that these dishes were not put on the table at meals, but rather on something soft, because they had rounded rather than flat bases, and this is confirmed by information from a certain John Davies, who in 1598 visited Acheen on the north point of Sumatra. During a dinner given by the ruler, the porcelain vessels were placed on the ground. The fairly coarse, freely drawn decoration on the surface often consists of a landscape with hills, and animals such as deer, rhinoceros, crab, lobster, phoenix (*fêng-huang*, Plate 9), *ch'i-lin*, dragon (Plate 8), crane and duck.

As a result of Western influence, Swatow wares include dishes and plates decorated with European ships and charts (Plate 11), based on Portuguese and Dutch models. For the Eastern market, dishes with sayings from the Koran (Plate 8) were manufactured. The rims are painted with oblong reserve panels on a diaperwork background, or with

[1] H. Miedema, *Swatow*, Princessehof Museum, Leeuwarden. J. A. Pope, 'The Princessehof in Leeuwarden', *Archives of the Chinese Art Society of America*, V, 1951.

[2] Here are situated the harbours of Ch'üan-chou, Chang-chou and along the coast the islands of Amoy and Quemoy.

narrow or broad trapezium-shaped panels. In these plants and flowers and sometimes figures are painted. One also finds rims with a running decoration of floral motifs and animals.

In addition to porcelain with underglaze blue decoration, which is the most common, polychrome was manufactured (Japanese: *gosu akae*; Plates 10, 11). On this opaque red and transparent green and turquoise was applied over the glaze and fired in the muffle kiln.

CELADON WARES

Among the best known and most admired ceramic export wares are the celadons.[1] They have a hard stoneware body approaching true porcelain in the later wares, covered with a thick feldspathic glaze, varying in colour from bluish-green to grey-green and olive-green; sometimes the glaze is brownish, the result of firing taking place in an oxydizing atmosphere. The earliest celadons, the Yüeh wares, which go back to the T'ang dynasty (618–906) and earlier, were exported to the Near East and examples have been found at Fustat and other places. But the celadon wares that provide by far the largest group of export wares were made in the Sung, Yüan and Ming dynasties in the province of Chekiang, mainly in the neighbourhoods of Lung-ch'üan and Hang-chou. Large dishes and plates with plain and foliated edges, stoutly constructed and sufficiently robust to be suitable for transport over long distances make up the bulk of these wares. They were exported over almost the whole of southern Asia, stretching to Egypt, the east coast of Africa and the Mediterranean area as well as Japan and the Philippines. They were decorated with moulded, carved and incised designs of fish, dragons (Plate 2) or flower sprays. People claimed that poisonous spices, if served on a celadon dish, changed their colour or lost their harmfulness. This alleged property, together with other excellent qualities, helped to make the celadons the most popular of all the export wares. Towards the end of the Ming dynasty there was a sharp decline in the quality of the celadon wares and they were replaced by blue and white porcelain.

In Tonkin, Thailand and Annam the Chinese dishes, plates and other vessels were copied in a rather coarse fashion. These and Chinese celadons were handed down as treasures from generation to generation in the Philippines, Borneo, Sumatra and Malacca.

The celadons were probably the first Chinese wares with which the West came into frequent contact. Dishes and bowls of celadon, in the Middle Ages and the Renaissance,

---

[1] According to some authorities the name celadon comes from the leading character, the shepherd Celadon (dressed in a grey-green costume) from the French pastoral novel *d'Astrée*, written by Honoré d'Urfé between 1616 and 1618. It is also possible that celadon is a bastardization of Saladin, the sultan of Egypt of the twelfth century.

were mounted in gilded metal or silver. One of the most famous celadon vessels is the one embellished with a gothic base by Duke Philip von Catzenellebogen some time between 1434 and 1453 (Kassel, Hessisches Landesmuseum). Here too mention might be made of the bowl in a renaissance mounting which it is said Archbishop Warham presented to New College, Oxford, around 1530.

5 · Chinese porcelain made during the Ming dynasty (1368–1644) and exported to Europe

INTRODUCTION

After Chu Yüan-chang, a man of humble origin who later became emperor under the name of Hung Wu (1368–98), overthrew the last member of the Yüan dynasty (1279–1368) he endeavoured to free the land from the Mongols and especially to annex vast territories to his kingdom. Under Emperor Yung Lo (1403–24), who sent expeditions to Mongolia and Annam, the Ming dynasty reached the zenith of its might. Fleets were despatched to the Indian Archipelago, Arabia and Somaliland. In the fifteenth century the Mongols made raids on China and Japanese pirates harassed the coasts. Under the reign of emperor Wan Li (1573–1619) the Japanese general Hideyoshi, in 1592, made a vain attempt to invade China from Korea.

Against such a background of political upheaval, it is not surprising that the Chinese government, who by tradition were antagonistic towards strangers and especially wary of new concerns, did not give the Portuguese permission to set up a trading post at Macao without much hesitation. In the last quarter of the sixteenth century, the Jesuits also set up a post in China. One of the commodities in which these companies wished to trade was porcelain. Fortunately, Ching-tê Chên had been spared the plundering and devastation of the Ming and Japanese pirates, and the Portuguese were able to establish trade in Ming porcelain.

SHAPE

Of Ming porcelain in general it may be said that it has a robust logical shape. The various parts of a vase, for instance the foot, the body, the neck and the rim together form a harmonious whole. While the earliest Ming displays an undoubted sturdiness, the later develops more elegance. The decoration, whether in underglaze blue, carved, or low relief, is closely related to the object itself, though it does not always follow its

44

shape. Not only were various Chinese bronzes imitated in porcelain, but metal and pottery shapes from the Near East were also taken as models. Only those kinds of porcelain which may be taken as having been exported to the West during the Ming dynasty will be dealt with here. This was in the first place the 'blue-and-white' and to a lesser degree the polychrome and various sorts of coarse porcelain.

BLUE-AND-WHITE

The earliest date of blue-and-white porcelain is not yet known. Fairly recent investigations in Kiangsi[1] have unearthed blue-and-white fragments claiming to belong to the Sung (960–1279) and Yüan (1279–1368) periods, but these require confirmation.

It is a moot question whether blue-and-white was an offspring of the ubiquitous Ying Ch'ing wares of the Sung dynasty. However this may be, blue became the fashion at the Ming court and as a result of this patronage it soon reached a high degree of perfection. In the fifteenth century, fine blue-and-white was made under the emperors Hsüan Tê (1426–35) and Ch'êng Hua (1465–87). The wares made during the reign of the first are thought by many to be the finest of all blue-and-white.

The porcelain was painted in the deep blue called Mohammedan blue, showing blackish markings where the cobalt is thicker ('heaped and piled' according to an early description) and then covered with an even glaze. Motifs used in decoration were dragons, fishes, water-plants, peonies, stylized lotus blossom and the cloud motif (fig. 56) together with the Buddhist symbols (fig. 62) and human figures.

After a break of twenty years during which Ching-tê Chên did not function because of political troubles, a new blue period began under Emperor Ch'êng Hua. In his reign paintings from the Imperial collections were sent to Ching-tê Chên to be copied by the porcelain painters. It is believed that the well-known 'chicken motif', which was used as a decoration on cups, was derived from those paintings.

During the reign of Chêng Tê (1506–21), the Portuguese reached China and the first shipload of porcelain sailed to the West. The blue-and-white porcelain made during this reign includes wares with a decoration of playing children, and also Arabian and Persian inscriptions. There were, too, pieces decorated with articles pertaining to writing, made in shapes in the Persian fashion and destined for the Mohammedan eunuchs. After this reign a method of blue painting first used at the end of the fifteenth century became the general usage: the contours were first traced and then filled in with bold and broad washes.

Emperor Chia Ching (1522–66), who was a fervent Taoist, ordered porcelain decorated with Taoist symbols, such as symbols of longevity (*shou*) and the Eight Immortals

---

[1] Fêng Hsien-Ming, 'Important Finds of Ancient Chinese Ceramics since 1949', *Chinese Translations*, issued by the Victoria and Albert Museum, with the Oriental Ceramic Society, No. 1, 1967, p. 29.

and their symbols (fig. 61). At the same time the dragon, lotus-blossom and playing children remained in fashion. In the second half of the sixteenth century, plates with a narrow rim decorated with leaves and flowers were made, the centres decorated with fawns and gazelles in a wood, or a landscape with pagodas (Plate 15).

Towards the end of this reign the painters in the private factories rebelled against the conventional methods of decorating the porcelain for the court which were in force at the time, and began for instance to use illustrations in books as models for their work. This much more free, naturalistic style which is also to be seen from time to time in Wan Li porcelain, is most apparent in work of the so called Transitional period (c. 1620–80).

The *nien hao*, or reign-mark, of the Emperors Hsüan Tê, Chêng Hua and Chia Ching appears on porcelain of the Ch'ing dynasty (1644–1912). It was at one time believed that this porcelain was made during the reigns of the earlier emperors, but this supposition has now been disproved, for most of it was made during the reign of K'ang Hsi (1662–1722). The Japanese too put some of these marks on their porcelain.

PORCELAIN SHIPPED TO EUROPE BY THE PORTUGUESE IN PRE-DUTCH TIMES

At first as trade with the Portuguese was forbidden by the Chinese court, what trade there was must have been on the sly. And so, Vasco da Gama,[1] who had not been in China, must have bought in Molucca the porcelain he took home, perhaps from a Chinese trader. The porcelain which King Manuel of Portugal presented to his queen Dona Maria[2] in 1513 must have been bought either in India or surreptitiously on the China Coast; a similar source must have provided the porcelain which, according to his diary, Albrecht Dürer[3] received from a Portuguese at Antwerp in 1520.

In Portugal the interest in porcelain was so great at that time that in 1522 a third of the cargoes of the ships from India had to consist of porcelain. In Lisbon there were, in 1580, half-a-dozen shops selling porcelain. The Italian Francesco Carletti,[4] who made a world tour from 1594–1604, says that 'white with a blue border' was 'the finest porcelain one usually sees'. Through the agency of the Jesuits he bought the best porcelain to be obtained. In other countries too, Chinese porcelain could be found in the sixteenth century. Henry VIII of England was the owner of a silver-mounted bowl. The emperor Charles V of Germany (1500–58) had a number of plates with his monogram and his son Philip II of Spain (1527–98) had a collection of three thousand pieces. Shortly after the Portuguese had established contact with the Chinese the ewer in oriental shape of figure 2 was made to the order of king Manuel (1469–1521). Together with the

[1] J. A. Lloyd Hyde, *Chinese Porcelain for the European Market* (Lisbon, 1956) p. 48.
[2] J. A. Lloyd Hyde, op. cit., p. 49.
[3] P. T. A. Swillens, *Albrecht Dürer, Zijn dagboek van de zeis door de Nederlanden in 1520-1*, Maastricht.
[4] F. Carletti, op. cit.

Chinese porcelain made during the Ming dynasty

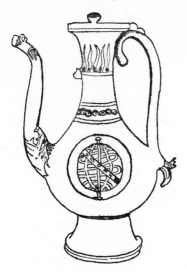

2. Ewer made to order for King Manuel of Portugal (1469–1521), blue-and-white, with decoration of celestial globe. Ht. 26 cm. *Collection José Cortes, Lisbon*

usual Chinese decoration it shows a celestial globe.[1] Prominent Portuguese families also ordered porcelain. Jorge Anrz (short for Anriques or Alvarez) ordered a pear-shaped vase now in the Victoria and Albert Museum. Apart from the Portuguese inscription and the date, 1557, on the shoulder, the decoration is Chinese. This combination of western and eastern motifs is also found on a dish in the Princessehof Museum at Leeuwarden in the Netherlands. Amidst Chinese motifs on the border it shows the coat of arms of King Sebastian I of Portugal (1557–87) repeated four times The centre is decorated with the Buddhist wheel surrounded by four Buddhist lions playing with a ball. The splendid octagonal flagon, in the Victoria and Albert Museum, silver-mounted and marked 1585–6, is amongst the finest pieces of Wan Li porcelain (Plate 13). Similar porcelain was known in the Netherlands as is shown by a still-life painting by W. Kalf (Plate 12).[2]

THE DUTCH MAKE CONTACT WITH CHINA

Towards the end of the sixteenth century, the Dutch discovered the Indies, and came in contact with China. They had seen Chinese porcelain at Bantam in 1596; Cornelis

[1] The mark of Emperor Hsüan Tê (1426–35) was probably put on later: the jug would be made in the reign of Cheng Tê (1506–21). Celestial globes are often to be seen in Portuguese paintings of the time of Manuel I (1469–1521).

[2] Jugs like these (made during Chia Ching's rule) can be seen in the Victoria and Albert Museum in London and in the Museum Für Kunst und Gewerbe, Hamburg (Martin Feddersen, *Chinese Decorative Art*, London, 1961, fig. 54). A similar jug without lid and spout is in the David Foundation of Chinese Art in London (Margaret Medley, *Illustrated Catalogue of Porcelains, Decorated in Underglaze Blue*, etc. nr. 689).

Chinese porcelain made during the Ming dynasty

de Houtman[1] writes about the market stalls where he bought dishes of Chinese porcelain. Although the Dutch by then knew of the existence of porcelain it was not actually seen in Europe until the beginning of the seventeenth century. Undoubtedly, the porcelain brought here in conquered Portuguese ships was the first to appear. In 1602, the first Portuguese galleon (in Spanish *carraca*) was captured near St. Helena. Two years later Jacob van Heemskerk captured the *Catherina* near Patani (Malacca). The porcelain brought in these ships acquired the name of *carrack*[2] porcelain. After some important officials had received gifts, the rest of the porcelain was auctioned in Amsterdam. Great interest was shown in it from beyond the boundaries of the Netherlands, for example by the English King James I (1566–1610) and by Henry IV of France (1533–1610) who on the advice of Louise de Coligny (1555–1620) bought a dinner-service.

On 24th March, 1604, Joris van Spilbergen arrived at Vlissingen from Bantam, bringing among other cargo the first porcelain bought in the Far East. From the very beginning of the seventeenth century, considerable quantities of porcelain were being imported, as can be seen from the Day Registers of the Dutch East India Company, and from the book published in 1614 by Pontanus which describes the trading city of Amsterdam. It appears from this that the porcelain wares were being imported not only as decorative articles but as things for daily use. Although this particular export porcelain from Ching-tê Chên was regarded by the Chinese as second-rate, it is not surprising that the Dutch were delighted by the thin-walled white porcelain, with its delicate blue decoration. The Dutch earthenware of that time was quite different in character—painted in multi-colours and thick walled. Because of their admiration for the Chinese porcelain, the Dutch potters and painters began to attempt to make thin earthenware decorated in Chinese style, and in this they were to succeed admirably.

It was at this time that Chinese porcelain frequently began to appear on paintings, especially still-lifes,[3] and such paintings therefore illustrate the kinds of porcelain which were in use in the Netherlands at the time. Sometimes we come across a porcelain vase with a decoration now seldom seen, like the one on a still-life by Jan Brueghel the Elder (1568–1625), decorated with square panels on a background of meanders. A still-life by the same painter (Plate 34) shows a *kêndi* with the spout turned to the back. Dutch still-lifes often include dishes and plates with fruit, as on a painting by Nic. Gillis of 1611 (Plate 14) one of the oldest paintings showing porcelain. Porcelain appears repeatedly on paintings of the first half of the seventeenth century by, for instance, Fl. van Dyck (1575–1651), Floris van Schooten (c. 1590–1651), B. van Ast (c. 1590–

---

[1] Mentioned in *The First Voyage of the Dutch to the East Indies under Cornelis de Houtman*, Linschoten Society, vol. I, p. 111.

[2] The name carrack is derived from *carraca*, and has nothing to do with breaking; see Volker, *Porcelain and the Dutch East India Company*, p. 23.

[3] Dr. A. I. Spriggs, 'Oriental Porcelain in Western Paintings, 1450–1700', *Transactions of the Oriental Ceramic Society*, 1964–65, 1965–66, p. 73.

C. Oval tureen and stand with *famille verte* decoration. *c.* 1730–1735

1660), W. Cl. Heda (1594–1680), P. Claesz (1597–1661), J. D. de Heem (1606–83), Abr. Bosschaert (1609–45), J. Jansz. van de Velde (1619–62), Willem Kalf (1619–93), Abraham van Beyeren (1620–90) and many others. Foreign painters too have used porcelain as a subject of their still-lifes, such as Sebastien Stoskopf of Strasburg (1597–1657), the French Linard (c. 1600–45), and Louise Moillon (1609–96), the Germans Peter Binoit (worked c. 1611–24) and Georg Flegel (c. 1563–1638) and the Flemings Jan van der Hamen (worked c. 1596–1680) and Fr. Snyders (1597–1657). Such dated still-lifes can of course be a help in fixing the period of a piece of porcelain. This is also the case with the year-letters etc. of silver or silver-gilt mounts which can give an indication of the date of a piece. Old inventories and catalogues of personal estates, on the other hand, give one but little help because frequently the names and terms used are incomprehensible.

According to the T'ao-lu[1] the Wan Li porcelain was of good quality. The body is generally highly vitrified, sometimes brittle, and covered with a greenish-blue glaze without crackle. The blue which at first was like that of the Chia Ching period, later in the reign was frequently a greyish or an indigo blue. The plates, saucers, dishes and bowls were often so thin-walled that they sometimes came from the kiln crooked or even ruptured. This is especially true of the carrack porcelain[2] between 1625 and 1635 when the Transitional wares came into being. The Wan Li dishes, saucers and bowls frequently have scalloped rims. The convex, later flat, bottom rests on a flared footrim. The glazed base often shows radial chatter- and wheel-marks, and sometimes grains of kiln sand are found adhering to the bottom of the footrim.

The shapes most frequently recorded in the Netherlands are the *clapmuts* (Plate 14, right foreground) and the caudle-cup (Plate 24)[3]; the bowl (Plate 26), the bottle (Plate 21), the ewer (fig 2, Plate 23), the *kêndi* or gorgelet (Plates 30, 32, 33, 34) and the wine pot (Plate 18). In this period the shape and the decoration are still wholly Chinese. It is only during the Transitional period that porcelain with a western shape or decoration was made to the order of the Dutch East India Company.

The decoration of Wan Li porcelain is in part that of the Chia Ching period and in addition includes birds and insects in a landscape (Plate 19), playing children (Plate 13), men and women, fabulous animals, and Taoist symbols (Plate 20). Frequently the Eight Buddhist Symbols and several of the 'Hundred Antiquities' are shown. One of the most common shapes is the very deep dish or plate, generally with a broad rim. The division of the rim into panels is characteristic of this period, usually broad panels alternating with narrow ones (Plate 19). A hexagonal or polygonal medallion with contours bracket-shaped or curving inwards, often forms the decoration in the central part

---

[1] G. R. Sayer, *Ching-tê Chên, T'ao-lu*, p. 45.

[2] H. Miedema, *Kraakporselein en overgangsgoed*, Princessehof museum, Leeuwarden, p. 4.

[3] This cup in a silver mount was used for drinking warmed brandy or wine. C. Boschma, 'Brandewijn-kommen uit Friesland', *Antiek*, 1966–67, No. 4, pp. 5–9.

(Plate 20). A more or less naturalistic landscape with birds is painted in it (Plate 19) or the landscape is adorned with insects, tigers, dragons, emblems (Plate 20), a vase with flowers or a 'sage' (Plate 16). This decoration may be separated from that on the rim by a well-border pattern of scales or meanders alternating with the *ju-i* motif (Plates 16, 19). The back of the rim is sometimes decorated with tassels and symbols. On the bottom of the thin-walled *clapmuts,* a shallow bowl with sloping rim, of various dimensions (Plate 17), a landscape with a bird is generally shown. The caudle-cup (Plate 24), which is somewhat deeper and more straight-walled, has a similar decoration on the bottom, of a crow in a tree. Other dishes are decorated with graceful deer (*sika*) near a pine, a prunus and a bamboo—the 'three friends'. These bowls had reached Europe by 1623 (see note describing Plate 29). The pear-shaped bottle, the 'Persian flask', the long neck sometimes crowned by a kind of knob,[1] is quite common in the Netherlands. As in the case of the dishes and the bowls the decoration is divided into alternately wide and narrow vertical panels, the wide panels painted with flowers, birds and insects or (see Plate 21) galloping horses, and the narrow panels with a motif like a jewelled pendant, which may also appear on the neck, linked by a *ju-i* motif. Another type found in the Netherlands is the bottle with the neck nipped in above the shoulders. The bowl is decorated with flowers in panels and the neck with meanders (Plate 22). The plates, saucers and dishes which have a border in relief and bowls with arched walls were probably finished on a mould. This also applies to a wine-pot in the shape of a fruit and perhaps also for the flagon of Plate 23. A similar flagon in the Schlossmuseum at Berlin was silver-gilt mounted by George Berger about 1576–79. From the date it follows that this kind of vessel was already being shipped to Europe by the Portuguese in the second half of the sixteenth century.

A special 'sort of jug is the *kêndi*[2] which was also used in the Near East. This had a round body with a short—later long—neck with a rim. On the shoulder is a hemisphere with a short spout. A *kêndi* appears on the painting, *Het Atelier van Apelles,* by Willem van Haecht (1583–1615) in the Mauritshuis in The Hague. On a painting by W. Kalf (Plate 33) a *kêndi* is shown mounted with a metal handle, cover and spout. From these data it follows that the *kêndi* was already being made at the end of the sixteenth and the beginning of the seventeenth centuries. The fact that towards the end of the seventeenth century, they were being copied in the factory of Samuel of

[1] At Rhages in Persia flasks with a knob-like crown on the neck were made in the twelfth and thirteenth centuries. A. Lane, *Early Islamic Pottery* (London, 1957) ill. 56a, 71b.

[2] The word *kêundi* or *gêndi* is of Malayan origin and is derived from the Sanskrit *kundika.* In Javanese it became *gêndi.* The oldest *kêndis* in South-east Asia were of bronze and earthenware. From the beginning of the fourteenth century or somewhat earlier the Chinese began to make *kêndis* of celadon for export to South-east Asia. When the people of the Mohammedan lands began to smoke, *kêndis* were also used as 'Nargileh Bottles'. T. Volker, op. cit., p. 19, note 5. J. A. Pope, *Chinese Porcelain from the Ardebil Shrine,* p. 116 ff. M. Sullivan, 'Chinese Export Porcelain', *Oriental Art,* 1958.

Eenhorn[1] shows how popular they became. Sometimes the *kêndi* is moulded into the shape of an elephant (Plates 30 and 32).[2] Other vessels are shaped like a phoenix, a fish or a toad.

Many pieces of Wan Li porcelain were mounted in costly metals, which shows how much they were appreciated. In the Metropolitan Museum of New York there are some bowls presented to Queen Elizabeth I (1558–1603) by her treasurer Lord Burghley in 1587 or 1588. It is possible that one or more of these bowls came from the Portuguese cargo-ship *St. Philip* or from the *Madre de Dios,* taken by the English in 1587 and in 1592 near the Azores. Silver mounts like those mentioned above are more frequently found with English than with Dutch or German marks. Recently the Fries Museum at Leeuwarden acquired a caudle-cup with a silver mount (Plate 24) bearing the marks of the silversmith Minne Sikkes of Leeuwarden and the year letters of 1632.

The 'character' bowl generally dates from the first quarter of the seventeenth century. On the outside the character *shou,* longevity, is painted many times round medallions each showing two of the eight Taoist Immortals (Plate 28). The inside shows Shou Lao seated on a flying crane. Related to them are the so-called 'Red Cliff' bowls painted on the outside with the second part of Su Tung-po's poem *Red Cliffs,*[3] and a party drinking wine in a boat. A similar bowl is shown in a painting by J. Linard (1600–45), dated 1627.[4] Bowls with figures in relief on the outside, often in biscuit, generally date from the first quarter of the seventeenth century. The blue-and-white bowl in Plate 27 has pairs of Taoist Immortals in biscuit covered with yellowish-brown and green enamels, separated by openwork swastika diapers. A second bowl with a landscape in underglaze blue and five biscuit plaques with the Eight Taoist Immortals in pairs and Shou Lao belongs to the same group (Plate 25). A similar pot with a Buddhist lion on the cover is shown in a painting by Kalf (Plate 26).

POLYCHROME AND OTHER PORCELAIN EXPORTED TO EUROPE

Porcelain with red and green and underglaze blue decoration also found its way to Europe: for instance a bowl of the Chia Ching period mounted in silver at Augsburg.[5] Within blue contours it is decorated with aigrettes and flowers in blue and red. In the first half of the seventeenth century polychrome porcelain also arrived in Europe as is

---

[1] J. Helbig, *Faïences Hollandaises, XVIIᵉ et XVIIIᵉ–debut XIXᵉ siècle* (Musées Royaux d'Art et d'Histoire, Brussels) Vol. 5, p. 39.

[2] In the collections of the David Foundation in London there is a similar *kêndi* wrongly described as 'goat'. M. Medley, *Porcelain decorated in underglaze blue and copper red,* no. 665.

[3] A. I. Spriggs, 'Red Cliff Bowls of the late Ming Period', *Oriental Art,* VII, 1961, p. 182.

[4] Cf. *Vier Eeuwen Stilleven in Frankrijk,* Boymans van Beuningen Museum (Rotterdam, 1954) cat. 7, ill. 5.

[5] R. L. Hobson, *The Wares of the Ming Dynasty,* pl. 6, fig. 2.

apparent from the Day Registers of Batavia.[1] The round covered box of the late Ming period in the Rijksmuseum at Amsterdam (Plate 36), decorated on the cover with a high official in his chair of state surrounded by courtiers and painted in the *wu ts'ai* manner, is reputed to have belonged to an old estate.

OPENWORK DECORATION

The porcelain decorated with openwork (*à jour* or *ling lung*) mentioned in Chapter 3 was also sent to Europe. Usually the bowls are double-walled, only the outer wall being pierced. They are mentioned under 1642 in the Day Register as '*half doorluchtige*' cups. Sometimes they are decorated in blue.

In the Groninger Museum there is a fine single-walled glazed openwork specimen of the type called a '*doorluchtige*' cup in the Day Register. The decoration includes Chinese characters (Plate 37). Reference has already been made to the bowl in Plate 27, which has openwork panels of a swastika diaper between the pairs of figures in relief.

[1] T. Volker, op. cit., the years 1616, 1623, 1631 and 1644.

6 · Trade between Europe and China during the Transitional period (1620-1680) and the porcelain made during that period

INTRODUCTION

When the Dutch had established themselves in the Indies, the Chinese brought porcelain by junk to Patani, Bantam on Java, from 1619 to Batavia and after that to Formosa. In 1631, 1632, 1634 and 1637 the East India Company sent ships to 'the river of Chincheuw'[1] to buy porcelain—trade that must certainly have been clandestine. The porcelain exported to Europe and Japan was made at private kilns. The death of Emperor Wan Li in 1619 led to serious new disturbances and the war between the followers of the Ming emperors and the Manchus who were trying to conquer China grew desperate. Finally the Manchus captured Peking, in 1644, and the Ching dynasty came to the throne, with Manchu Shun Chih as their first emperor.

In 1644 a small Chinese junk sailed into the harbour of Batavia with the news that owing to internal difficulties in the province of Kiangsi there was probably no further stock of porcelain to ship. Another Chinese captain lamented the fact that many porcelain makers had been killed in the war. A year later the governor of Formosa announced that the porcelain trade had made a loss because of the war. From 1647 the state of affairs grew steadily worse, until by 1657 trade had as good as ceased.[2]

In 1624 the Dutch had built the fortress Zeelandia on the island of Taiowan, about half a mile from the west coast of Formosa (Plate 35) and by 1642 the whole island was in the possession of the East India Company. In the interval it had grown to be a trading post for Chinese goods, among which was porcelain. In 1635, the governor of

[1] T. Volker, *Porcelain and the Dutch East India Company*, pp. 35, 37, 40.

[2] R. Soame Jenyns says in his article 'The Chinese Ko-Sometsuke and Shonsui Wares' (*Transactions of the Oriental Ceramic Society*, 1962–63, p. 15) that during the reign of Emperor T'ien Ch'i (1621–27) the imperial kilns were probably closed. In his *Later Chinese Porcelain*, pp. 21–22, the same author points out the fact that little porcelain exists with the mark of Shun Chih (1644–61).

Trade between Europe and China during the Transitional period

Formosa[1] wrote to Amsterdam that the Chinese had that year delivered more porcelain than he dared to forward. In 1638 the stock stood at 890,328 pieces, intended for the Netherlands, the Indian Archipelago and other parts of the Far East.

Nicolas Verburgh, the governor of Formosa, in an attempt to get trade under way again in 1653 sent the *Bruynvisch* with the merchants Frederik Schedel and Zacharias Wagenaar on board to Canton. The viceroy of that time received the deputation graciously and gave them a gift of 400 plates and 40 bowls of fine porcelain for the governor, but the visit had little effect. In 1655 a delegation was sent to China in the hope of acquiring the right to trade, but again in vain. Then in 1657 a junk with 35 barrels[2] filled with porcelain arrived at Batavia from Amoy,[3] and the captain bore a letter from the ruler Koxinga. This announced that he would not allow his subjects to bring any more Chinese porcelain to Formosa. By this decree he struck at the economy of the Manchus. As a result there was a lack of porcelain from China, which compelled the Company to order it from Japan, and so it was that the first big shipment of Japanese porcelain reached Batavia in 1659.

In 1662, Koxinga conquered the fort of Zeelandia and Formosa itself.[4] The loss of the island was a blow to the Dutch East India Company, but by no means ended the trade with China.

Already in 1608,[5] from the Chinese merchants of Patani on Malacca were ordered: 50,000 butter-dishes, 50,000 'telyeoren' (plates), 1000 mustard-pots, 1000 large plates, 1000 large bowls, 500 wine-flasks, 500 small jugs, 500 large fine cups, 500 small tasting dishes, 2000 fruit dishes and 1000 salt-cellars, etc.

Occasionally prices are given in the Day Registers for the various kinds of articles. So, from one of 1637: 20 calabashes, 1 *reaal* each, 38 large goblets, 1 *reaal* each, small wine jugs with spouts, $\frac{3}{8}$ *reaal*, without spout, $\frac{1}{2}$ *reaal*, *snellekes*, $\frac{3}{8}$ *reaal* each.

Between 1604 and 1657, 3,000,000 pieces of porcelain were exported to Holland. The highest average price, 34 cents, was reached in 1629, and the lowest, $4\frac{1}{2}$ cents, in 1629. That year 2 cents was the price of a tea-cup. In general there was a hundred per cent profit on the sale of a piece.

PORCELAIN

Transitional ware is the name given to porcelain made from the death of the Emperor Wan Li in 1619 to the time when the royal factory at Ching-tê Chên began producing

---

[1] Dr. H. E. van Gelder, 'Data relevant to the Porcelain Trade of the Dutch East India Company', *Economic Historical Yearbook*, 1924, p. 184.

[2] T. Volker, op. cit., pp. 58, 59.   [3] Amoy was the port used for the Dutch trade.

[4] Koxinga was born in 1623, of a Chinese Christian father and a Japanese mother. The son of Koxinga reigned over Formosa until 1681. In 1683 the Emperor K'ang Hsi conquered the island and annexed it to China.

[5] T. Volker, op. cit., p. 23.

again in 1683. It has its own particular character. In general the body is thick and so it is heavy in weight. On the clear white porcelain the decoration is applied in a deep clear blue, of a slightly violet tinge. The finest blue-and-white was not made for the emperor but for private buyers and traders, and because of this Europe became acquainted with the best blue-and-white made up to that time. In addition to Wan Li motifs there were new elements in the decoration, taken from fairy-tales, novels and episodes in the lives of heroes. These scenes, in which beautiful girls also appeared, showed naturalistic landscapes of shrubs and weeping-willows, sometimes with mountains in the background. The landscape is usually peopled by men and women who by their elegant poses look like play-actors. The more spontaneous style undoubtedly sprang from the attempts of the porcelain-painters of Ching-tê Chên to break away from the traditional formality in force before that time; and was influenced by contemporary art as well as by the past.

How highly this decoration was regarded in Holland can be seen from the vases and jugs made in the factory of R. J. Hoppesteyn in Delft at the end of the seventeenth century, on which the same rather hazily painted figures are seen, proving that Transitional ware was exported to Europe. According to Volker, 1657,[1] the year that Koxinga suppressed trade with the Indies was the last year that Ming porcelain was shipped to Europe. Volker also correctly supposes that after this date no more Transitional ware can have been sent, unless clandestinely. It would seem that most of the porcelain in question which was exported to Europe was made before 1657.

Until this time, Europeans had been content with the 'carrack' porcelain, which in form and decoration was Chinese, but there now came a change in taste. The demand was for wares which were European in shape and if possible also in decoration. Here we have the first instances of *chine de commande* proper. Above all, this had to be well made, not like the Wan Li, which was frequently carelessly made. This change in taste is evident in a letter dated 23rd October 1635 from the governor, Hans Putmans, of Formosa, to the Amsterdam Chamber of the East India Company. He said that the Chinese merchants had given him various painted wooden Chinese articles,[2] in order that the potters and painters could copy them.

The merchants told the governor that these models could be made in porcelain and furthermore they promised that the order would be delivered the following year. In 1639 mention is again made of wooden models. That year the captain of the *Castricum* brought to Formosa, from the Dutch East India Company in Amsterdam, an order for 25,000 pieces to be made according to wooden models sent from Holland. In the letter was a short description of the kinds of porcelain wanted, with reference to the numbered

[1] T. Volker, 'Early Chine de Commande', *Bulletin Museum Boymans-van Beuningen*, IX, 1958. T. Volker, *Porcelain and the Dutch East India Company, etc.*, p. 59.

[2] T. Volker, op. cit., pp. 37, 38, suggests that these models were made by Chinese on Formosa. See also Dr. H. E. van Gelder, op. cit., p. 184.

models. It was also stipulated that the porcelain must be fine and clear and painted in clear blue. And the Chinese merchant, Jousit, was required to return the wooden models. The negotiations took place with the help of the interpreter, Cambingh. In this commission were detailed: 300 fruit-plates without rim, with ridges like model 2; 200 small wine-jugs with spouts and without ridges as model 8; 200 jugs as model 9; 300 large deep dishes with flat rims (painted) as model 1. The big plates had to be light with thin bases and well-rounded. Clearly, the Chinese porcelain of that time was influenced by Western shapes. The decoration remained predominately Chinese, but with European elements, for instance Dutch houses and the occasional stylized flower with leaves, which is often a tulip.[1] Considering the Dutch fondness for the tulip, it is highly likely that this flower was copied from the painted models. Or perhaps it was taken from the tiles of the second quarter of the seventeenth century, for it is quite possible that these were known to the Chinese by then. A Chinese encyclopedia of 1686[2] says that Dutch tiles had reached China. This motif on the porcelain can, however, be interpreted in another way: it has been suggested that it might be derived from a similar design on Anatolian wares of the sixteenth century.[3] Miedema[4] thinks that it might go back so far as the so-called grotesque ornament; and it also bears some resemblance to a floral decoration on Italian majolica plate of the sixteenth century.[5] Of these possibilities, it seems most likely that it is this last which influenced the Chinese porcelain painters, though they may well have used a Dutch interpretation of it. In the same way as he had used Chinese figures, towards the end of the seventeenth century R. J. Hoppesteyn adopted this motif using it especially on the necks of pitchers. We also see the tulip on German (Frankfort, Hanau) and French ceramics (Nevers) of the second half of the seventeenth century.

Up to now it has not been possible to trace a connection between much of the porcelain mentioned in the shipping-lists and articles known to us today; this is certainly true of the beakers (fig. 3), pepper and salt dishes, mustard-pots (fig. 4), lamp-holders, 'gorgelets' and various plates and dishes. Apart from these the lists mention other articles: letting- or barber's bowls (after 1637, Plate 48), tasting dishes, cups with high foot, octagonal chalices and cups, flowerpots, pear-shaped wine-flasks with spouts, oil and vinegar sets, wine-coolers, teacups, caudle-cups, chamber-pots and boxes (for keeping medicaments).

As has been said, various of these articles are based on European examples. For

[1] Dingeman Korf, *Tiles* (London, 1963).

[2] Prof. G. Schlegel, 'De betrekkingen tussen Nederland en China volgens Chineesche Bronnen', *Taal, Land en Volkenkunde van Nederlandsch-Indië.* Vol. 42, 1893, p. 26.

[3] Dr. B. Jansen, 'Een Delftse kan uit de fabriek van Rochus Jacobsz. Hoppesteyn', *Mededelingen van de Dienst voor Schone Kunsten der Gemeente 's Gravenhage*, 1952, p. 67.

[4] H. Miedema, *Kraakporselein en overgangsgoed*, p. 31.

[5] B. Rackham, *Italian Maiolica* (London, 1952) plate from Castel Durante, pl. C.

3. Beaker, blue-and-white, with decoration
of Chinese in landscape. Transitional period.
Ht. 17.5 cm. *Princessehof Museum, Leeuwarden*

instance, the beaker is derived from a silver or pewter communion chalice. An example in the Rijksmuseum is painted in blue with Chinese figures in a landscape. Another common drinking vessel is the covered beer-mug or *snelle* (Plate 47).[1] From one Chinese vessel, which bears the date 1642 on its silver lid, we can take it that these were made and imported in the thirties (Hamburg, Museum für Kunst und Gewerbe).[2] Usually there is a hole in the handle for securing the mounting, so it appears they were ordered in China with the intention of having a metal lid put on later in Europe.

The chamber-pot is also known. Plate 38 shows a candlestick of which the foot is an inverted chamber-pot, on which the candleholder and dripcatcher are placed. The lower part is decorated with Chinese figures in a mountain landscape, with a frieze of lambrequins on the rim. The candleholder shows the tulip so characteristic of the period.

We can be fairly certain that the graceful vessel with deep foot and a lipped neck (Plate 39) is a ewer of the kind mentioned in a letter from Putmans in 1635. The body is decorated with a landscape with palaces, banded at top and bottom with a repeating scroll pattern of stylized flowers and leaves and a frieze of lambrequins.

The salt-cellar and the mustard-pot (fig. 4), which has its lid fastened to the handle by means of a metal mount, are taken from silver or pewter examples. The letting or

4. Mustard-pot, blue-and-white, with
decoration of Chinese landscape, silver hinge
and knob. Transitional period. Ht. 14 cm.
Groninger Museum

[1] T. Volker, op. cit., pp. 38, 39, speaks of '*snellekens*'. Here is meant the German *schnelle*. This is an unusually tall drinking beaker, conical and narrowing towards the top. In the sixteenth century, these were made of stoneware, among other places at Siegburg and brought to Holland in quantity.

[2] M. Feddersen, *Chinese Decorative Art*, pl. 58.

barber's bowl, which was also copied in China at this time, is likewise derived from metal or earthenware and the same goes for the porringer. All these pieces are decorated in Chinese style. Another common shape is the jug with handle and pouring lip, which was probably made according to a wooden model sent out by the East India Company (Plate 40). The pear-shaped body, sometimes decorated with a Chinese figure in a landscape, rests on a light curved foot. The shoulder is decorated with a stylized flower with leaves, and on the neck a simplified tulip motif. Round the base of the jug is a frieze of lambrequins. The remarkable thing about this example is the handle, curving slightly outward, with a connecting piece to the body at the lower part: a method of attaching the handle which also occurs on Chinese pieces of this time. Jugs[1] (Plate 42) with an S-shaped spout were made during the reign of Ch'ung Chêng (1628–43). The spout is sometimes reinforced with a porcelain bond (Plate 41).

Porcelain made in Chinese style and exported to Europe included simple or double-gourd flasks (Plate 49), brush pots and also globular bottles (Plate 50) with a long neck. These bottles can be seen in the still-lifes of J. van Streek (c. 1625–84, Plate 53). On the body is a Chinese landscape with figures and on the neck the familiar tulip with leaves. This Dutch influence is also apparent on the large round rice-bowls (Plates 45, 46). The inside and the outside are decorated with a total of twelve panels, alternately broad and narrow. In the broad ones are Chinese figures wearing flat hats (rice-farmers) against a background of Dutch-type houses. In the small panels and some of the big ones are stylized tulips and carnations. The way in which the flowers are drawn is not at all Chinese, and resembles decoration on Dutch tiles.[2] The inside base of these dishes may be decorated with a spinning woman, small houses, etc. (Plate 46).

There are also plates with centre decoration of two Chinese figures and an elephant, and rims like the rice-bowls just mentioned, painted in the Wan Li manner with narrow and wide panels. In the narrow panel is a wide tulip motif, similar to that on a jug with spout, metal handle and hinged lid (Plate 51) and on a round bottle (Plate 50). On the body of this bottle, between the Chinese decoration, is a typical European design, winged angels or heads of *putti*. The same head, with a cap and a radiating collar, is seen on a small Chinese jug in the Boymans-Van Beuningen Museum.[3] We first encounter winged *putti* as majolica decoration (for example, apothecary's bottle, fifteenth century, Caffaggiolo, Milan, Castello Sforzesco). This Italian decoration is also to be found on south and north Netherlands ceramics,[4] silver articles and chests.

Typical Chinese shapes seen in export ware are the double-gourd flask (Plate 49), the cylindrical vase with slightly flaring lips called *rolwagen* in the E.I.C. shipping lists (Plate 60), the flask (Plate 53), the wine-ewer with upright handle (Plate 44) and the

[1] R. Soame Jenyns, 'The Chinese Ko-Sometsuke etc.', op. cit., pl. 15a, p. 25.
[2] Dingeman Korf, op. cit., pl. 252–263.
[3] T. Volker, 'Early Chine de commande', *Bulletin Museum Boymans-van Beuningen*, IX, 1958.
[4] Dingeman Korf, *Nederlandse Majolica* (Bussum, 1962) fig. 94, 111, 112.

teacup. The decoration on these, landscapes, plants and flowers, is also Chinese, of a type that persisted, as can be seen from the square bottle shown in Plate 150, dating from the end of the seventeenth century.

On seventeenth-century still-lifes we see a number of different vase shapes, for instance, the octagonal baluster-shaped vase with lid in the still-life of Corn. Cruys[1] (before 1644–c. 1666). Its body is decorated with a landscape through which a Chinese procession wends its way, and a simple v-shaped border encircles the deep base. A similar vase with flower decoration is to be seen in the Princessehof at Leeuwarden (fig. 5).

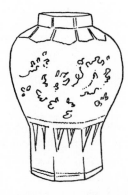

5. Octagonal vase, with decoration of flowers in blue-and-white. Transitional period. Ht. 31.5 cm., D. 23 cm. *Princessehof Museum, Leeuwarden*

[1] Dr. N. R. A. Vroom, *De Schilders van het Monochrome Banketje* (Amsterdam, 1945) p. 142. A. Lane, *French Faience* (London, 1958), Nevers jar dated 1644, pl. 10, Cambridge, Fitzwilliam Museum.

7 · Trade between the West and China at the end of the seventeenth and during the eighteenth centuries

INTRODUCTION

When Emperor Shun Chih died in 1661, he was succeeded by his son K'ang Hsi, who was to reign until his death in 1722. At first there were four regents, but when he was thirteen the young Emperor took the reins of government into his own hands. After years of war, the Emperor in 1681 succeeded in quelling the revolt that had broken out in South China in 1674 under the leadership of Wu San Kuei (a supporter of the Mings). During this war the porcelain factories of Ching-tê Chên were devastated.

The Emperor strove to promote art and scholarship. With this aim in mind, on the advice of Father Ferdinand Verbiest, he had set up near his palace in Peking 27 to 30 work-places for the practice of various crafts. Articles of metal, glass, jade, lacquer, ivory, porcelain and enamel were made here. K'ang Hsi was succeeded in 1722 by his fourth son, Yung Chêng, and he in turn was succeeded in 1736 by Ch'ien Lung, who like his grandfather was to reign for sixty years, giving way at the age of eighty-five to his son Chia Ch'ing (1796–1820).

TRADE BETWEEN EUROPE AND CHINA

At the beginning of the reign of K'ang Hsi, the East India Company once more sent a legation to the Emperor, under the leadership of Pieter van Hoorn. It reached Peking in 1667, and again to little avail. However, three ships sent by the Company to Canton in 1679 did have some success; the captains contrived to get a return cargo of the value of three tons of gold. A second voyage, undertaken three years later, yielded no result; only a small part of the cargo was unloaded at Canton. In order to stimulate trade with China, Governor Rijckloff van Goens in 1680 gave the Chinese citizens of Batavia permission to trade. From 1695, the Chinese went themselves to Batavia, where they sold tea, silk and porcelain. When K'ang Hsi put a ban on all foreign trade, except with Japan, from 1718 to 1722, it was a heavy blow to the Dutch. The Portuguese profited in trading from Macao between China and the Indies. The main Batavian commodity was pepper; and this together with cinnamon, amber, linen, lead and sandalwood, was sold in exchange for porcelain, silk and tea, and also spianter, an alloy of tin, copper and lead, and birds' nests. Tea, which was cultivated in both China and Japan, was shipped in ever greater quantities to Europe, with porcelain as ballast. Attempts to grow tea on Java failed.

TRADE WITH CANTON

An important fact in the history of the trade was that in 1699 the Chinese government decided to open the port of Canton to foreign trade, though in practice the trade was much hampered as only sporadic permission was given. In 1700 the master of the English *Macclesfield* was allowed to put into port at Canton, and he returned home with a rich cargo. Only in the eighteenth century did the the Chinese authorities begin to take a more liberal attitude towards European infiltration, and this led to the English East India Company's becoming the first trading company allowed to open an office at Canton in 1715. One after another, the French (1728), the Dutch (1729), the Danes (1731), the Swedes (1732) and the Austrians, and the Americans (1784),[1] got permission to open trading posts at Canton. Indians and Armenians already had a foothold; and since the end of the seventeenth century Russia had traded with China. From time to time the Ostende Company, established 1721, and the Spanish Manila Company also traded. In 1751, a company was set up at Emden in East Friesland, and this traded with China until its abolition six years later.

In 1727 the Dutch Company decided to order two ships annually to Canton. Direct sailing from Batavia started after 1734 and was kept up until 1756. After this year trade was again directed from Holland. The first ship to arrive from Holland in 1729 was the *Coxhoorn*.[2] This ship, as was customary, sailed round the Cape of Good Hope and on 2nd August 1729, after a fair voyage, reached Macao. She sailed home with a rich cargo, arriving in Holland in July 1730 with 930 cases of tea and 137 of porcelain. Canton, on the Pearl river, lay in an excellent position on the coast, with water connections to the interior. When the trading ships reached West China in October and November, they sailed from the South China Sea about eight miles up-river to Canton, about sixty-six miles from Macao (see fig. 6).

The ships' masters had to touch at Macao first where a pilot was taken on board who guided the ship to the Tiger Gate. After arrival there the customs officers levied two taxes: tonnage or anchorage and a 'present' (really a tribute) for the emperor. From the

---

[1] The dates are only approximate.
[2] Dr. J. de Hullu, 'Over den Chineschen Handel der O.I.C.', *Taal, Land en Volkenkunde*, 73, 1917, p. 59.

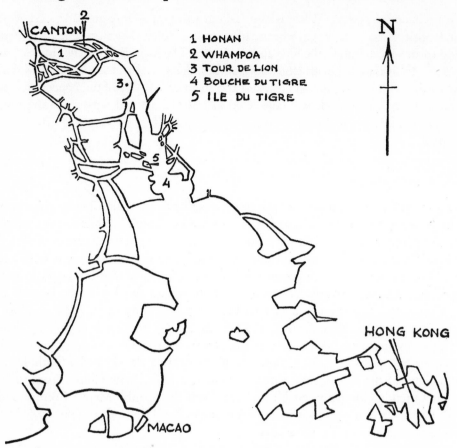

1 HONAN
2 WHAMPOA
3 TOUR DE LION
4 BOUCHE DU TIGRE
5 ILE DU TIGRE

6. The mouth of Pearl river, showing the relative positions of Macao, Canton and Hong Kong

Tiger Gate[1] the ships sailed up the Pearl river to the roads of the isle of Whampoa, about 12 miles from Canton, where they anchored and there were kept till they were due to sail fully laden. From the anchorage the supercargoes—the men in charge of the cargoes—were allowed to sail to their trading posts in Canton in small boats. Their negotiations and transactions had to be concluded before the end of January for the ships to be able to sail home with the favouring north monsoon.

Starting with 1734 large cargoes of porcelain were annually shipped to Holland. But in the second half of the century English pottery increasingly became the fashion in the Netherlands and the interest in Chinese porcelain decreased and so less was imported.[2] During the Napoleonic wars the trade came to a standstill to be resumed by

[1] *Boca Tigre* in Portuguese; *Bouche du Tigre* in French; *Boque* in English.
[2] Even so the Company ordered a total of about 800,000 pieces in 1780.

King William I in 1813. During the nineteenth century Chinese porcelain was once more imported into the Netherlands but, so far as has till now been traced, on a more modest scale.

In the eyes of the Chinese the Europeans were *fan kuei,* queer devils, who should be kept at a distance. Although the Dutch (Holan or red-bearded), because of their common-sense and reliability, were held in fairly high regard, they together with all other foreigners were subject to all sorts of strict regulations: no wives were allowed, nor cannon, guns and powder, and no sedan-chairs. The Europeans were allowed to promenade outside their settlements only three times monthly in groups of ten under the supervision of an interpreter. After the sailing of their ships the Europeans were not allowed to stay in Canton, they were bound to live at Macao during the 'quiet season'. From 1776, however, they were allowed to stay in a Canton suburb. At first the trading posts were set up in any given rented houses, but after 1749 the foreign companies were allowed to hire their own 'comptoir' or lodge.[1] Eight and later thirteen trading posts (each 250 metres in depth) were built in a row on the small island of 'Jongsin-Seeluan' in European style. In 1822 they were destroyed by fire and rebuilt in the same style. In 1855 they were burnt down again, now once for all. Each *hong* (warehouse) consisted of a lower and an upper storey built of bricks and roofed with tiles.[2] The wooden partitions which separated the comfortably furnished apartments were papered with thin white Chinese paper. On either side of the inner yard were the storage buildings. In front of each post there was a terrace giving on to the river and separated by railings from its neighbour. There too were the flag-poles flying the colours of each country.[3] At the back they gave on to 'Thirteen Factory Street'. On the punch-bowl of Plate 54 from left to right, the Danish, English and Dutch flags are visible. Because the American flag is missing the bowl may be dated before 1783.[4] Each trading post had its own name. That of the Dutch was called 'Hong of Justice' and the English one 'Hong which keeps the peace'.

THE CO-HONG

The 'Co-Hong'[5] established by Imperial decree and abolished in 1904, was an association of merchants of which each Cantonese trader who wanted to trade with foreigners

[1] A. M. van Lubberhuizen-van Gelder, 'De Factoryen te Canton in de 18e Eeuw' in *Oud Holland,* 1955, pp. 162 ff.

[2] Dr. J. de Hullu, 'Over den Chineschen Handel der O.I.C.', op. cit., p. 90. 'De Porseleinhandel der Oostindische Compagnie', etc., in *Oud Holland,* 1915, p. 50.

[3] Pictures of the posts may be found in the Kon. Instituut voor de Tropen and in the Nederlands Hist. Scheepvaart Museum, both at Amsterdam.

[4] J. Goldsmith Phillips, *China Trade Porcelain* (London, 1956) p. 14.

[5] Ibid., pp. 32, 33 and 35 and M. Beurdeley, *Porcelaine de la Compagnie des Indes* (Fribourg, 1962) pp. 23 ff.

had to be a member. Their offices were situated near the foreign trading posts. Foreign merchants were only allowed to sell and buy through one of the members of the Co-Hong. For the porcelain trade alone there were no restrictions. According to the Co-Hong decree every one was allowed to buy it because 'Chinese porcelain required technical knowledge'.

The Hong merchants were responsible to the emperor; they had to guarantee the behaviour of the foreign merchants, local staff and ship's company. The number of the Co-Hong merchants varied little: 10 in 1765, 12 in 1817 and 11 in 1838.

ORDERING AND BUYING AT CANTON

Each year the Canton-based staff of the Dutch East India Company received a 'demand of return-cargoes' from home,[1] mentioning how much porcelain of each kind was wanted and how many pieces were to be blue-and-white and how many with enamel colours and how many 'Chinese Imari'—this meant 'a smooth ware, evenly glazed, similar to the coloured Japanese porcelain'. Though it was considered much less fine than the enamelled kind, it was without the defect of cracking and scaling enamel. The 'demand' also listed how many pieces should be painted in the European manner and how many in *encre de chine*. The demand for 1700 was, for instance, for fish-bowls, sets for pickles with their saucers, salt-cellars, pairs of caudle-cups, flasks, toilet-sets consisting of six, eight, ten, even or twenty-nine and more small boxes, ewers, tea-trays, tea-caddies and many other things.

After their arrival at Canton the supercargoes went round the porcelain work shops (Plate 56) of which there were more than a hundred among others on the isle of Honan. The American traveller William Hickey[2] describes a visit to a number of these shops and factories in 1769. In a long hall he saw about two hundred people busy painting designs on porcelain and finishing various ornaments. Some parts were done by old men, others by children 6 or 7 years old. There were only limited supplies of the finest wares most in demand, and here it was a question of first come first served. The more common ware as a rule caused no difficulties because it was plentiful.

Dinner services and other large items had to be contracted for or had to be specially ordered. An agreement was made with a Chinese merchant who was bound to deliver a given quantity of porcelain within a certain time 'everything as to size, shape and painting according to the directions given by the servants of the Company and inserted into the agreement'. To avoid mistakes blank services were sometimes sent down from Ching-tê Chên to Canton to be decorated there.

The Hong-merchants travelled to Ching-tê Chên,[3] there to order the porcelain

[1] Data taken from Dr. J. de Hullu, 'De Porseleinhandel etc.', *Oud Holland*, 1915, pp. 54 ff.
[2] J. G. Phillips, op. cit., p. 37.
[3] *T'ao-lu*, op. cit., p. 36.

D. Tureen and cover with polychrome decoration. *c.* 1750–1760

wanted and to fix a price for a given lot. The order was recorded on a ticket, which the merchant had to produce when taking delivery on an arranged date. Damaged pieces were exchanged for sound ones, but in general the foreign merchant could only hope that the porcelain would be supplied in accordance with the agreement. There was a considerable risk that the transaction would turn out badly as the captain was forced to accept the order, good or bad, otherwise he would be in trouble, for he had to sail with the monsoon, or to stay till the next year.

It was quite often difficult to get all the parts of a service ready at one and the same time, for one manufactory made the cups, a second one the saucers and a third one the dishes. More than once Chinese officials laid an embargo on the junks transporting porcelain from Ching-tê Chên to Canton and sometimes as a result parts of services would arrive at Canton after the rest had already left for Europe. Obviously such incomplete sets did not fetch a good price.

Porcelain bought in the East by the various branches of the East India Company was auctioned, among other places, at Amsterdam, Enkhuizen, Delft, Hoorn, Rotterdam or Middelburg. It was also sold to private persons. When in the course of the seventeenth century the interest in porcelain declined and it could no longer be sold at a reasonable price in the smaller towns, the branch which had ordered the porcelain had it auctioned at Amsterdam.

It is interesting to note that in 1759 the Swedish Company instructed their factor at Canton to 'buy heavy and durable things'. According to this instruction 'all the thin porcelain' should be avoided as much as possible.

The making of porcelain was sometimes impeded by heavy rains or floods so that for months at a stretch there was not enough sunshine for the porcelain to become dry; and occasionally coarse porcelain could not be had because it was impossible to make as labourers or firewood were lacking. Because the tax on porcelain was levied according to weight, the common and ordinary goods were taxed more heavily than the fine ware.

As in the seventeenth century, wooden samples were frequently sent by the Dutch Company with the orders. When they wanted new models earthenware samples were made at Delft and, if this proved impossible, drawings were sent, such as those commissioned by the Dutch East India Company from Cornelis Pronk (see Plates 175, 193, 194, 195, 197). Sometimes samples of porcelain or earthenware were sent back to Canton[1] to show the kind of pieces that were not wanted in Europe. This happened for instance in the case of a decoration consisting of dragons and other monsters, the symbolic meaning of which eluded the Europeans. The samples sent to China had to be returned home in order to control whether the porcelain bought at Canton was made according to sample.

In general, the artisans tried to satisfy their customers to the best of their ability although sometimes the porcelain makers and painters refused to fill an order. In 1775

[1] Dr. J. de Hullu, 'De Porseleinhandel', etc., p. 59.

they refused to make a dinner-set, painted inside with yellow and outside with small bouquets in enamelled colours and golden circles because they were afraid that the colours would not turn out well.[1] Besides miniature plates having motifs painted on the rim, wholly finished pattern-plates were also sent to Europe, their rims decorated with four different decorations to give the customers an opportunity to make their choice.[2]

Complaints about the quality of the porcelain supplied were frequent.[3] Thus in 1767: 'The coloured stuff should be enamelled more exactly because the red flowers, even when dry and without having been touched by moisture, fade away, which proves that they were only painted on and not baked, and evidence of this is that the red paint when it is not baked becomes dull, and to the contrary when it is baked glossy. In future this should be better attended to.' This was probably a case of a decoration put on 'cold', not fired in the muffle kiln, a kind of decoration that soon fades.

Besides the Company many private persons placed orders for porcelain. A large proportion of the armorial services probably originated in this way. In London there were the 'China-men',[4] merchants who placed orders for private persons for the manufacture of porcelain with special decoration. Usually, it took two years before the customers could take delivery.

Merchants and other employees of the Dutch East India Company were forbidden to trade on their own account, but this ban of 1609 was repeatedly broken. In a memorandum of 1675, officials and employees were given permission to take a certain quantity of porcelain to Holland.

PAYMENT

The Western traders paid the Chinese in silver, for instance with Spanish and Mexican coins, or in silver bars. When the merchants paid, the Chinese calculated the worth and weighed the silver on small scales which they always carried in a lacquered box, which hung from their waist.

In gold, the Chinese used the *tael*, of which the worth varied from 2.50 to 3.40 Dutch florins.[5] In the account books the Spanish *real* is sometimes mentioned; its worth was from fl.2.35 to fl.2.60. Although Chinese law forbade the export of gold—which was scarce—it was often traded in secret. Silver also was scarce in China.

[1] J. G. A. N. de Vries, *Porselein* (The Hague, 1923) p. 26.
[2] J. G. Phillips, op. cit., p. 36, fig. 22.
[3] J. G. A. N. de Vries, op. cit., p. 26.
[4] J. G. Phillips, op. cit., p. 34.
[5] In English currency, the *tael* was worth between five and seven shillings. 1 *tael* is worth 10 *maes* which are worth 10 *condorijnen* which are worth 10 *kassis*. Only copper was minted in China, never gold or silver.

8 · The appreciation of Chinese porcelain in Europe

We still do not know exactly which sorts of porcelain were made by the Chinese for themselves and which for Europe. It can no longer be maintained that porcelain decorated with representations of the five-clawed dragon[1] or on which the imperial reign-marks occur was made strictly for the royal house. The porcelain painted in the so-called 'Chinese taste' was not meant for export; but a few pieces must have reached Europe by some means at the beginning of the eighteenth century as is proved by those included in the collection of Augustus the Strong at the Johannaeum in Dresden. The porcelain made to the special order of European traders, the *chine de commande,* was the first ware deliberately made for export. But apart from this category, great quantities of porcelain were shipped to Europe, as we have seen, by the various East India Companies, of which the English was one of the biggest. Much of this must have been made for the Chinese rather than the European market in the first place, as this chapter will show. Certainly the masters bought and ordered at Canton as much porcelain as possible which came up to the requirements set out in the 'demand notes' and suited the taste of their customers. For the last quarter of the seventeenth century and during the eighteenth century, this was made in private factories, especially at Ching-tê Chên. But at other places, too, porcelain for export was made, such as Têhua, Yi-hsing and Shaokiang (or Shao King), lying to the west of Canton.

Some indications of the kinds of ware shipped to Europe may also be found in the porcelain salved from wrecked ships such as the *Haerlem* lost in 1648 and the *Jong Thomas* lost in 1763, both in Table Bay, and from the *Göthenborg* sunk in 1745 near Gothenburg.[2] The large quantity of cargo salvaged from this ship contained *blanc de chine* and porcelain with blue and sepia decoration. Evidence found in the subjects of paintings by European artists has already been mentioned. Up to 1670 this evidence is found mostly

[1] J. Fontein, 'Chinese Ceramiek', *Sprekend Verleden* (Amsterdam, 1959) p. 207.
[2] Stig Roth, *Chinese Porcelain,* fig. 7, p. 15.

on still-life paintings and after the first half of the seventeenth and during the eighteenth centuries on paintings of interiors. In the latter case the porcelain was used mainly as 'stage property'.

In this connection the paintings, drawings or prints by Cornelis Troost (1697–1750) are instructive. His *Ontdekking van Jan Claesz* and *Episode uit Hopman Ulrich* in the Mauritshuis at The Hague (both 1738) show how in the eighteenth century porcelain was used as decoration of cabinets.

The innumerable imitations of Far Eastern porcelain made at Delft and elsewhere in the Netherlands proves how highly it was valued. The decorations borrowed from Chinese porcelain are often a nearly perfect imitation of those of the blue-and-white, *famille verte, famille jaune* and *famille noire*. This is clearly visible on earthenware of the end of the seventeenth and of the eighteenth centuries made at the factories of Hoppe-steyn already mentioned, L. v.d. Eenhoorn, P. A. Kocks and De Roos. The earthenware of that period made in France, Germany and England also in some measure came under the influence of the Far East.

After the first decade of the eighteenth century the decoration on Chinese and Japanese porcelain was also imitated on European porcelain, first at Meissen and after-wards on that made in many other European factories. At Meissen and at St. Cloud the white Têhua porcelain was imitated in the first half of the eighteenth century. Porcelain imitating Chinese blue-and-white and polychrome wares, as well as Japanese Kakiemon and Imari wares was made, not only at Meissen but also at St. Cloud and Chantilly in France and at Chelsea, Bow and Worcester in England. The painters of 'Haags' (c. 1704) and 'Oude Amstel' (1770–80) porcelain applied the Imari decorations. It is obvious that European porcelain with decoration borrowed from the Far East may be indicative of the kinds of porcelain shipped from China and Japan to our part of the world. European porcelain, however, is of little use in dating as, in general, it is not accurately known when it was made. In this respect the porcelain collection of Augustus the Strong (1670–1733) formed between 1715 and 1727,[1] is useful, the more so as it was inventoried in 1721. The items in the inventory, letters followed by numbers, were painted on or engraved into the bottom of the pieces.[2] After the auctions of 1919 and 1920, mainly of duplicates, the collection still contained many first-class pieces of Chinese and Japanese porcelain, most of it acquired through the Dutch East India Company. An important part of it, however, was obtained by bartering 600 Saxon Dragoon non-commissioned officers and privates for a collection of Chinese porcelain in the possession of Friedrich Wilhelm, King of Prussia (1713–40). This collection of 117

[1] P. J. Donnelly, *Blanc de Chine* (London, 1970) p. 53, note 1.

[2] R. Soame Jenyns, *Later Chinese Porcelain*, pp. 4, 35. A cross means Japanese, an aslant H *blanc de chine*, P black Indian. Since these scratched marks could be easily imitated, they were later put on porcelain which was never part of this collection. So these marks are no assurance that the porcelain belonged to Augustus the Strong.

pieces was originally in the palaces of Charlottenburg and Oranienburg. Among the items were eighteen monumental vases, sometimes called the Dragoon Vases.[1]

Among the oldest collections of Chinese ceramic wares is the Hainhofer Cabinet at Uppsala which came into the possession of King Gustavus Adolphus in 1632. His daughter Queen Christina owned a collection which contained about three hundred pieces of blue-and-white. Besides many other large and small collections there is the one owned by Queen Mary II, wife of William III, formerly at Hampton Court, which contains interesting pieces of both Chinese and Japanese porcelain.

It is quite understandable that the collectors of Chinese and Japanese porcelain wanted to exhibit their possessions to full advantage. In making up their collections the purpose of most collectors was to own porcelain suitable for display and not to own uncommon pieces or to bring together a collection showing the development of Far Eastern porcelain. The idea of filling a room exclusively with porcelain was probably born in the Netherlands.[2] It is self-evident that because of their interest in the Chinese and Japanese wares the Dutch of the time made large collections. In order to exhibit this porcelain according to the fashion of the period, interior decorators designed panelled rooms of which porcelain was to be an integral part. One of the first halls with wainscoting specially designed for the exhibiting of porcelain was built in the Oranienburg palace, north of Berlin, between 1688 and 1695. The porcelain collected by Louise Henriette, wife of the Grand Elector, between 1652 and 1667, was placed here. Their son, Frederick of Brandenburg, from 1701 King of Prussia, had the Charlottenburg palace built for his wife Sophie Charlotte (1668–1705) and for this Eosander von Göthe[3] designed a porcelain hall, which remained in its original state until the last war. The collection consisted of eighty pieces of Delft ware and four hundred Chinese porcelain dishes, vases, etc. It was placed in niches, above the doors, on and under the mantelpiece and as a frieze around the ceiling.

The interior decoration of the time was greatly influenced by the Huguenot architect Daniel Marot (1661–1712) who designed several plans for rooms, sometimes with lacquered panels and walls with chimney pieces[4] specially drawn up for the exhibiting of porcelain. Examples showing a harmonious composition of wainscoting and porcelain can be seen at the palaces of Hampton Court or at Honslaardijk near The Hague.

The interior of a doll's house in the municipal museum of The Hague (Plate 58) shows Chinese porcelain in miniature, so-called '*poppegoet*'[5] (Plate 59) in show-cases

[1] G. Weiss, *Ullstein Porzellanbuch* (Berlin, 1964) pp. 68 ff.

[2] Arthur Lane, 'Queen Mary II's Porcelain Collection at Hampton Court', *Trans. O.C.S.* 1949–50, p. 21. Hugh Honour, though, in *Chinoiserie, the Vision of Cathay* (London, 1961) p. 68, thinks France is the probable birthplace.

[3] The plans for this were reprinted at *Theatrum Europaeum*, 1718.

[4] *Nouvelles Cheminées* published 1700.

[5] T. Volker, *Porcelain and the Dutch East India Company*, p. 145.

and on consoles. It gives a good idea of an early eighteenth-century porcelain room.[1]

Most of the porcelain in Dutch museums that originally came from old estates was shipped to the Netherlands shortly after it was made. It is not, in general, of very high quality. Much of the first-class porcelain in the so-called 'Chinese taste' came to the West only in the present century. With a few exceptions it would not have graced the porcelain cabinets of our ancestors.

In the sixteenth and seventeenth centuries, when porcelain was mounted, silver or silver-gilt was used. During the eighteenth century, copper-gilt and bronze mounts were used. In France such mounts were designed by A. J. Caffieri (1678–1755) and P. Couthière (1732–1813) in the Louis XV and Louis XVI styles, mostly for celadon.[2]

As mentioned in the Introduction, estate inventories and sales catalogues sometimes give indications concerning Chinese and Japanese porcelain. There is one difficulty, however; it is frequently impossible to ascertain which kind of porcelain is meant. One of the oldest inventories in the Netherlands (1632–33) mentioning Chinese porcelain is the one dealing with the furnishings in the Stadtholder's Quarters at The Hague.[3] It refers to a 'cabinet' with shelves on which various models are placed, such as fifty small butter-dishes or plates, seventeen cups of divers shapes and sizes and forty-two porcelain small dishes for preserves or fruits.

The library of the Ottema-Kingma foundation at Leeuwarden has various sales catalogues such as that concerning the estate of Jan Bisschop of Rotterdam, sold in July 1771, that of the collection of Gerrit Braamcamp of Amsterdam, sold in August 1771 and of the collection of Martha Raap of Amsterdam[4] sold in August 1778. From these catalogues Ottema has taken old names for types and shapes of porcelain and though these are without any scientific basis some are still used in the trade.[5]

[1] H. C. Gallois, 'Van een oud Poppenhuis' in *Mededeelingen van de Dienst van Kunsten en Wetenschappen*, 1919–25, Vol. I, pp. 179 ff. See also Chisaburo Yamada, *Die Chinamode des Spätbarock* (Berlin, 1935).

[2] Little or no celadon was exported to Holland in the seventeenth and eighteenth centuries.

[3] Published by S. W. A. Drossaers in *Oud Holland*, 1930, p. 228.

[4] Martha Raap, sister of the porcelain trader Daniel Raap, was married to Cornelis Kleerbesem who had a porcelain shop at Amsterdam. This shop appears on a painting of 1753 by Jan ten Compe (1713–61). Behind the windows Chinese porcelain cabinets are visible.

[5] N. Ottema, 'Handelstermen' in *Oude Kunst*, 1917, pp. 209, 327 and 368 and idem, *Chineesche Ceramiek*, pp. 188 ff.

9 · K'ang Hsi and eighteenth-century porcelain with Chinese decoration

The porcelain of the Ch'ing dynasty (1644–1912) attained a high degree of perfection both in the material used and in its decoration. Various techniques, applied and experimented with for the first time in the Ming period, were now perfected. Painting with enamel colours, including 'the colours of the foreigner' (see page 34) was fully developed. During the reign of Emperor Ch'ien Lung, Sung and Ming porcelain was copied so faithfully that it is sometimes difficult to be certain whether a piece is an original or a copy. After the first quarter of the century, in contrast to Ming wares, there is often little or no connection between the object and its decoration.

How did the interest in porcelain of the Emperors and other eminent Chinese come about? They had little regard for its beauty, and saw porcelain as a material which was especially suitable for the making of articles of daily use. Emperor K'ang Hsi and especially Ch'ien Lung[1] appreciated it artistically, and through the interest of the latter the Ching-tê Chên factories were enlarged and flourished because of his large commissions.

During the eighteenth century the interest in blue-and-white gradually diminished, giving way to the fashion for *famille verte* and *famille rose*. Between 1725 and 1730, *famille verte*, so popular during the last two decades of the seventeenth century, was superseded by *famille rose*, and before long the latter had conquered the European and Chinese markets. With considerable artistry and feeling for colour the painters depicted their subjects sometimes on the thinnest of material. The great diversity of design and colour is quite remarkable. But in the course of the eighteenth century, the shapes lost their strength and the decoration its freshness.

SHAPES

At the beginning of the dynasty, the shapes appearing in porcelain were still modelled

[1] J. Fontein, 'Chinese Ceremiek', in *Sprekend Verleden* (1959) p. 205.

on those of the Ming period: K'ang Hsi vases, for instance, are strongly and harmoniously shaped. In the course of the eighteenth century the shapes became more elegant, and exaggeratedly slender and mannered vases appeared. The different parts, body and neck, flow into one another without clear division, and eventually this resulted in a weak shape and a loss of balance. And at times excessive decoration and variegated colours blur the shape.

Under European influence the number of shapes increased in the course of the century and, after K'ang Hsi, early bronzes were used as models for both shape and decoration, though sometimes the moulders of porcelain apparently forgot that metal cannot always with impunity be imitated in porcelain. Pieces with shapes derived from metal were exported to the Netherlands in great quantities, especially the *rolwagen* (Plate 60), a cylindrical vase with neck and foot slightly flaring, made in many sizes; the *bussepot*,[1] a large or small ribbed oviform pot, with a somewhat flattened dome-shaped cover (Plate 78); and the round or square beaker (Plate 101), occasionally found as part of a *garniture de cheminée*. Small globular flasks with elongated slightly narrowing necks are called *puntflesjes* (Plate 320). The vase of Plate 71, existing in many related shapes, has no special name. The single or double gourd-flask was called *knobbelfles* (Plate 49). The pilgrim bottle was in use from ancient times, both in Europe and in China, but though they had probably a common ancestor[2] they developed differently. In China in the eighteenth century they were copied from fifteenth-century models. There are various types, painted with Chinese as well as European decoration. Those with a flattened cylindrical body (Plate 223) and those with an oviform shape and neck with knob painted with western scenes were exported to Europe.

DECORATION

The decoration painted on porcelain by the artists of the Ch'ing dynasty can be divided into two groups, the Chinese and the Western. In the second group, which is dealt with in detail on pages 97-99, and 126ff., there are also Chinese elements.

The traditional decorative motifs (described in Chapter 23) played an important part in this dynasty as sources of inspiration for decoration on blue-and-white and on polychrome porcelain. But as well as these there are decorations which were first used in the Transitional period, thereafter also on K'ang Hsi wares, and then on eighteenth-century porcelain. These are based on fairy-tales, sagas, legends and short stories, and show heroes from ancient times, scenes with processions, or audiences granted

[1] N. Ottema, *Chineesche Ceramiek,* Plate 210. These pots are called ginger—hawthorn or prunus—jars. They were filled with ginger, other sweets or tea for presents at New Year. They are represented on a painting by A. van Ostade in the Louvre and on a still-life by Kalf. See Dr. H. E. van Gelder, *W. C. Heda, A. van Beyeren, Kalf* (Amsterdam, 1941) p. 49. See also A. Spriggs, 'Transitional Porcelain Ginger Jars', *Oriental Art,* XI, 1965, and T. Volker, *Porcelain and the Dutch East India Company,* p. 39.

[2] Basil Gray, *Early Chinese Pottery and Porcelain,* pp. 6, 11.

by emperors or personages of rank (Plates 52, 74). Under Ch'ien Lung decorations were frequently based on archaic bronzes, often with dragons and meanders. Slender Chinese ladies (*mei-jên*), with and without children (Plates 85, 89), appear playing with birds and butterflies. Poems, in which love and intrigue play their part, also provide themes, as do flowers and beasts. These porcelain painters had access to paintings on silk and to illustrated books, especially *Shih-chu chai shu-hua p'u* (*Ten Bamboo Studios*) by Che Chu, 1633, and *The Mustard Seed Garden*[1] which are both illustrated with coloured woodcuts. Other sources were the books republished under the auspices of Emperor K'ang Hsi, about agriculture and silk-culture (*Kêng-Chi-t'u*), in which the influence of European perspective is clearly seen. These were reprinted up to the nineteenth century. There were also painter' manuals, such as *The Art of the Drawings* (*Hua Chuan Sŭ Chi*) by Ting Kao or *The mountains of China and the mythical animals* (*Chan Hsi King*). These textbooks, of which there are a number in the British Museum, include drawings of trees with twigs and leaves, bushes, bamboos, and mountains showing various rock types in great diversity. They provided painters with a wide choice, and were much used by artists as well as porcelain painters. Chinese artists gave careful thought to detail, and whether they were concerned with figure, animal or tree the painters knew how to make a balanced composition from their theme. They seldom painted from nature: when the painter came home to his studio after a walk he put on to his paper or silk a synthesis of the landscape he had seen. In this no use was made, for instance, of shadow, light and dark, or the reflection of trees in water. Nature is pictured as the artist wished to see it. With people, the structure of the body can scarcely be discerned beneath the clothing. Nevertheless the painter knew anatomy from the six canons of the art of painting.[2] In the portrayal of human figures the face was seldom shown in profile, but preferably three-quarter or full face.

Just as our painters of the middle ages portrayed several episodes from one story on a single panel, so the Chinese painters, for instance on vases, sometimes showed a number of scenes from one episode of history.

PERSPECTIVE

The Chinese, who only learned of our European perspective at the beginning of the

---

[1] *Chieh-tzŭ yüan hua chüan:* appeared in five parts, the first in 1679, the second and third in 1701. The garden of the writer was situated in Nanking. R. Goepper, *Chinesischer Blütenreigen*. In this connexion reference should also be made to the so-called Kaempfer coloured woodcuts now in the British Museum, which we come across in Japan at the end of the seventeenth century, where they had much influence on the development of the colour woodcut. These were acquired by Engelbert Kaempfer (1651–1716) in 1691/92 in Nagasaki in Japan and taken by him to Europe.

[2] Formulated by Hsieh Ho, c. A.D. 500. Margaret Medley, *A Handbook of Chinese Art* (London, 1964) p. 122.

eighteenth century, from Jesuit painters such as Castiglione (1688–1766), made use of three perspective schemes:[1] the knowledge of height (*kao yuan*), width (*ping yuan*) and depth (*shen yuan*). In the last, the landscape has a high horizon; in *kao yuan* the horizon is low and the spectator looks for example from below up to high mountain tops; in the *ping yuan* the horizon is placed about the middle of the picture.

PORCELAIN WITH BLUE-AND-WHITE UNDERGLAZE DECORATION

Only the blue-and-white porcelain which was exported to Europe will be dealt with here. During the reign of Emperor K'ang Hsi, the blue-and-white reached its peak of technical achievement; aesthetically this is the finest blue that was ever manufactured. The beautiful white porcelain is of a fine texture and has a shiny, sometimes slightly bluish glaze. Father Louis le Comte wrote in his book *Memoirs and Observations made in a late journey through the Empire of China,* the English edition of which appeared in 1698, that the blue-painted china was manufactured most, and the quantity of blue-and-white that exists in the Netherlands also testifies that much was made for export. In general even the simplest blue-and-white has its particular cachet. Figures, animals, landscapes with trees and plants and flowers, are evenly distributed over the background and carefully painted. The outlines are more finely drawn than on Ming porcelain, and the spaces filled in with blue wash. The uneven thickness of the cobalt lent the painting a certain liveliness. In the course of the eighteenth and in the beginning of the nineteenth century, blue-and-white became mass produced, at the cost of quality of material and originality of the painting, though this was partly offset by the great craftsmanship of the porcelain painters. As has been said, the ceramic wares made at Delft and elsewhere in the Netherlands gives an indication of what Chinese porcelain was exported to the West. Blue-and-white K'ang Hsi porcelain was imitated at Delft; the potters and earthenware painters even replaced a cover missing from a Chinese vase, or made a duplicate[2] vase.

The cargo of a ship sunk in Table Bay near Capetown (London, British Museum, recovered in 1853) gives some indication of the blue-and-white porcelain shipped to Europe. Among it is a plate of which the rim has diaperwork with reserve panels containing flowers. In the centre, which is separated from the rim by an undecorated band, is a landscape with an elongated Chinese lady. Plates with similar 'Long Elizas' decoration painted in deep blue occur in many variations. One is decorated with two Long Elizas on a terrace (Plate 66) and another with two Chinese men beside a river flowing among mountains. An alternative treatment of the rim (Plate 63) recalls those of certain Wan Li dishes. Broad panels are separated from each other by narrow ones with a

[1] William Willets, *Chinese Art* (Harmondsworth, 1958) pp. 615, 616.
[2] Dr. C. H. de Jonge, *Oud Nederlandsche—Majolica en Delftsch Aardewerk* (Amsterdam, 1947) ill. 213.

meander ornamentation, the broad panels alternately filled with plants and two seated Chinese ladies. As with the Wan Li plates the rim decoration here also extends into the well, the centre of which is painted with a scene of slender Chinese ladies. A decoration which occurs in many variations is 'Joosje on horseback',[1] in which a Chinese man and his wife hunt a rabbit. It is found on plates and also on *rolwagens* (Plate 60), as the example here from the Zeeuws Museum at Middelburg shows; the upper part is decorated with flowers in a rectangular vase. Under K'ang Hsi, plates and dishes were also painted with trees, bushes and flowers (Plate 69).

Plates, often parts of services, may be round or octagonal. Deep dishes and bowls may have straight sides (Plate 64), or gadrooned sides and scalloped rim (Plates 62, 65). The latter are often decorated with the eight Immortals, sitting, or standing on a cloud, on their journey to the Islands of the Blessed (Plate 62). The straight-sided bowl (Plate 64) is painted with a landscape filled with running and sitting animals. Other common decorations are a river with water-plants and a boat moving through it, a Chinese interior, Buddhist symbols or flowers, and, more rarely, the female figure of Hsi Wang Mu, carrying on her shoulder a wooden stick from which hangs a flower basket. In addition to plates, dishes and bowls, K'ang Hsi blue-and-white includes different kinds of long-necked vases (Plates 67, 70), and also ginger jars, *kêndis* (the one shown in Plate 73 is painted with a Chinese mountain landscape) and barrel-shaped jars such as that decorated with Chinese ladies, with two handles in the form of a lion's head (Plate 75). The lid of this is surmounted by a sitting lion.

Big vases with lids are also known: these must have been kept in the fireplace, as shown in an interior with the Tolling family by Cornelius Troost (dated 1742). A similar vase—probably used as a water pot—painted in blue with a decoration of Chinese ladies, is to be found in the Frans Hals Museum at Haarlem (Plate 71). By boring a hole in the body, in which a tap could be fixed, these could be used as water-holders.[2] Other large pieces, varying in height from 80 to 100 cm., have dome-shaped lids, such as the one of Plate 74 in the Princessehof at Leeuwarden. This, which shows an audience with a high-ranking personage, is one of the so-called Dragoon vases (see p. 69). A peculiarity of this vase is that it has a European coat of arms in underglaze blue, without doubt that of the person who ordered the piece (fig. 7).

A curious piece is the 'surprise cup', known in the Netherlands as 'Hans-in-the-cellar'. This is a cup—sometimes on feet—in which there is a small inverted cup with holes on the side and top, and through this latter opening a figure appears when the cup is filled with water. Probably, similar 'surprise cups' were being made as early as the

[1] The term 'Joosje' is derived from *yoshi* or 'joss', a good luck figure. In reality a Manchu or other Asian horseman.

[2] Dr. J. de Hullu, 'De porseleinhandel der Oostindische Compagnie en Cornelis Pronk als haar teekenaar', *Oud Holland*, 1915, p. 60.

K'ang Hsi and eighteenth-century porcelain

7. European coat of arms in underglaze blue on a so-called 'Dragoon' vase. Ht. 88 cm. *Princessehof Museum, Leeuwarden.* See Plate 74

Sung dynasty (900–1279) in Chün ware.[1] The one shown here (Plate 96) from the De Sypesteyn Museum at Loosdrecht, was made in the first half of the eighteenth century.

PORCELAIN MADE FOR EMPERORS YUNG CHÊNG, CH'IEN LUNG, AND THE PALACE HOUSEHOLD

Towards the end of the reign of K'ang Hsi, and even more so under his successors, fine porcelain came to be manufactured under royal control. The fact that T'ang Ying devotes three out of the twenty illustrations in his book[2] to blue-and-white, demonstrates that he found it important. In addition, it appears from the so-called Yung Chêng list (see page 35) that for this emperor copies were made of Ming pieces, for instance Chia Ching (no. 42 of the list, Mohammedan blue), and Ch'êng Hua (no. 43, pale blue). These pieces were copied from originals in the royal collections, and were so well made, and the *nien hao* so carefully reproduced, that they were often taken to be original Ming ware. Porcelain also exists which has the Yung Chêng mark on the base.

BLUE-AND-WHITE EXPORT PORCELAIN AFTER K'ANG HSI

The blue-and-white export porcelain made during the reigns of Yung Chêng and Ch'ien Lung at first resembled K'ang Hsi wares in their decoration. On the whole the later porcelain is somewhat inferior in quality, rather coarse and heavy. The decoration, which by the second half of the eighteenth century often covers the whole of the paintable area, is rather carelessly drawn, and thus the porcelain loses its distinguished

[1] S. Yorke Hardy, *Illustrated Catalogue of Tung, Ju, Kuan, Chün, etc. in the Percival David Foundation in London*, p. 47. *Illustrated Catalogue of Ming Polychrome Wares in the Percival David Foundations*, p. 721. M. H. Gans and Th. M. Duyvené de Wit-Klinkhamer, *Dutch Silver*, pl. 29.

[2] See p. 26, n. 2.

character. Nevertheless, from time to time fine pieces do occur. A very popular decoration was of a river landscape with mountains in the background, almost filling the centre of the plate (Plate 61). Trees, bushes and flowers were still used for decoration after the death of K'ang Hsi. The dish shown here (Plate 68), in the Frans Hals Museum at Haarlem, has an asymmetric pattern of fantastic trees. The tea tree pattern was also fashionable, and was imitated, among others by J. van Duyn, on Delft plates. Late eighteenth-century blue-and-white was given the name Nanking China, because it was shipped there from Ching-tê Chên, and then transferred to sea-going junks for Canton.

POWDER-BLUE DECORATION
(Technique, page 33)

Porcelain with decoration painted in reserve panels against a powder-blue stippled background was exported to Europe, as can be seen from a painting by W. Kalf showing a ginger jar. On two similar pots, originally in the collection of Augustus the Strong (Plate 78, on the bottom the engraved and painted inventory number; fig. 8) the reserve panels are decorated in blue with some of the Hundred Antiquities. The powder-blue ground was sometimes embellished with gold decoration, as on the dish of Colour Plate A, though here the gold has been almost entirely rubbed off. The plants growing out of the rocks are in green, blue, lilac, and red enamel heightened with gold. A cylindrical vase (Plate 77) in the Rijksmuseum with similar ground shows in the reserve panels a decoration of twigs and flowers among which a bird perches, the colours painted in *famille verte*. Vases of this type were exported to the West, as is shown by a Delft imitation in the Cinquantenaire Museum at Brussels.[1]

8. Inventory mark of the collection of
Augustus the Strong. Dresden, on bottom of
covered pot shown in Plate 78

There is also porcelain in which the decoration is outlined on a blue background. Plate 76 shows a cylindrical vase with 'Dragon on Band' decoration, c. 1700. Here the decoration is combined with underglaze blue decoration painted on the white body.

[1] J. Helbig, *Faïences Hollandaises XVIIe–XVIIIe–debut XIXe siècle* (Brussels, n.d.) pl. 15 E.

K'ang Hsi and eighteenth-century porcelain

'STEATITE' (Soft paste porcelain)
(Technique, page 35)

Towards the end of the reign of K'ang Hsi, 'steatite' porcelain was made for the first time, in general for small articles. Special mention must be made of small flasks (Plate 72) and cylindrical vases, varying in height from six to eleven centimetres, painted with landscapes, *mei-jên*, boys, and so forth. The decoration, in underglaze blue, of landscapes, trees and bushes is mostly finely drawn, though somewhat hazy. A splendid example is the plate shown in Plate 61 from the Groninger Museum. The rim is decorated with posies of flowers; the centre shows a delicately painted mountain which, characteristic of the second half of the eighteenth century, reaches almost to the edges of the well. In the foreground is a walled villa, past which a river flows.

WU-TS'AI
(Technique, page 34)

A series of plates decorated with this technique, and made at the end of the Ming dynasty, or at the beginning of the reign of K'ang Hsi (before 1683), have a groove in the circular base, and because of this Ottema[1] gives them the name groove-rimmed plates. The decoration, in red, green, yellow and aubergine enamels, consists of stylized and naturalistic plants with tendrils and flowers and sometimes a bush. They were most probably made for export, among other places for Indonesia. The Princessehof Museum has an extensive collection (Plate 81). These plates could not be counted on as coarse porcelain.

FAMILLE VERTE

Famille verte porcelain, in which green enamel predominates, was probably made in private kilns at Ching-tê Chên. From the last decade of the seventeenth century it was shipped to Europe in large quantities: for the Day Registers of the castle of Batavia for 1664 mention 'five-coloured porcelain', in Chinese called *wu-ts'ai* (see page 35). It seems that Europeans did not know the difference between *wu-ts'ai* and *famille verte*. The collection of Augustus the Strong[2] gives more evidence of its being shipped to Europe. In this collection are various pieces of *famille verte* porcelain with engraved inventory numbers. Honey[3] points out that the *famille verte* intended for export is difficult to distinguish from that meant for the Chinese market. The writer presumes that dishes painted with flowers, kylins and phoenixes were made for the West. In

[1] *Chineesche Ceramiek*, p. 182.
[2] W. Bondy, *K'ang Hsi* (Munich, 1923) ills. 121, 124, 125, 136, 138, 139, 141, 143, 148 and 149.
[3] W. B. Honey, *Guide to the Later Chinese Porcelain* (Victoria and Albert Museum, London, 1927) p. 49.

France at the beginning of the eighteenth century *famille verte* was often mounted in gilded metal.

In general the shapes and decoration are similar to those of blue-and-white wares. Chinese type decoration appears on porcelain both in Chinese and in Western shapes, as for example the beer-mug (Plate 103), and was painted on glazed porcelain or biscuit.

Characteristic decoration on plates includes landscapes, birds on a branch (Plate 80), a vase with flowers, or scenes on or below the terrace of a house, showing for instance an audience with an emperor or dignitary, or boating on a lotus pond (Plate 82).

Scallop shells of rather thick porcelain, such as that shown in Plate 119, are usually decorated in *famille verte,* or sometimes in Imari. In a few cases the decoration is executed in panels on a powder blue or *café au lait* background; or on a background strewn with flowerets or symbols in different coloured enamels. Proof of great technical skill is the speckled green background called frog's spawn, that came into use around 1700. Sometimes decoration in iron-red was executed against a plain background.

FAMILLE ROSE
(Technique, page 34)

It seems probable that real success in the decoration of porcelain, using the rose colour made from chloride of gold, did not occur until after 1720. The early pieces painted in *famille rose,* and dateable from their decoration of coats of arms, are of poor quality.[1] The rose-red colour had originally come from Europe, where it was used from the second half of the seventeenth century, and it was therefore known in China as *yang ts'ai* 'foreign colour'.[2] T'ang Ying explained the term as 'painting of white porcelain with enamel in the way of the Westerners'. The colours on *famille rose* were almost always opaque: the painters achieved this by mixing the rose-red and other enamel paints —blue, red, purple, light green, yellow and black—or with arsenic white as mentioned in Chapter 3. On early pieces the green was still transparent, but this too soon lost its translucence. In the Yung Chêng period the *famille rose* was generally of a very high quality. During the reign of Ch'ieng Lung it was still made in large quantities, but after about 1740 it lacks the freshness and artistry of the Yung Chêng wares. All the same, it is difficult in many cases to decide exactly when a piece was made.

During the directorate of T'ang Ying the porcelain painters and enamellers were able to develop a perfect technique, but this often led to over-enthusiasm. It is understandable that T'ang Ying was proud of his achievements, being able to imitate everything in porcelain, bronze, gold, silver, stone, lacquerwork, wood, etc. In the Groninger

[1] Sir Harry Garner, 'The Origins of *famille rose*', *Transactions of the Oriental Ceramic Society,* 1967–9, pl. 12.

[2] H. Hansford, *A Glossary of Chinese Art and Archaeology* (London, 1961): 'Painted enamel, as made in Canton and Peking is named *yang t'sai*'.

Museum there is a piece of porcelain, the decoration of which is an imitation of wood. This was also shipped to Europe in the eighteenth century and imitated there.[1]

Famille rose in the Chinese taste

The *famille rose* in the so-called Chinese[2] taste belongs to the finest Chinese porcelain of the eighteenth century. It was above all set apart for the Imperial court. Dishes and bowls, often of eggshell thinness, are subtly painted in soft fine colours with birds on a branch, silver-pheasants, quail, parrots, or flowering plants such as peonies, asters, chrysanthemums, small nosegays, an insect on a fruit, or peaches on their branch (Plate 84), all contrasting beautifully with the clear white porcelain. Sometimes the decoration has a background of ruby-red. Many dishes also have a 'ruby back' (Plate 85). The decoration is never excessive nor is the colour; they are simply and harmoniously composed. Plates and dishes with a broad flat rim do not occur, while those with a narrow rim do. The Emperor Ch'ien Lung had a weakness for *famille rose*, and especially for the kind decorated with a cock; he even made poems on the subject. In one of them the Emperor lauded the manly beauty of the cock and the artist who portrayed the pride and splendour of the bird.

PAINTING

During the reigns of Yung Chêng and Ch'ien Lung most of the porcelain was shaped, painted, fired and muffled at Ching-tê Chên, but large quantities were carried away to Canton to be enamelled there. Witness to this is an inscription on a small dish in the British Museum[3] reading 'painted at Canton'. The Cantonese painters were considered inferior to those of Ching-tê Chên. This enamel painting at Canton was done by the artisans who decorated metal objects with enamel as they were accustomed to handling enamel paints. It is possible to find the same subject on both porcelain and on enamelled metal objects.

INFLUENCE OF THE WEST

In the third decade of the eighteenth century the influence of the West increased. English, French, Dutch and Italian works of art were shipped to China, there to adorn the palaces of Emperor and courtiers and the houses of people of note and standing. The Chinese were very fond of clocks, watches and miniatures, notably those made in England and France, and of Limoges enamel. The Emperor Ch'ien Lung was presented

[1] It was imitated again in earthenware at Niederwiller; see Arthur Lane, *French Faience,* ill. 78b and 79.
[2] Here can be included the plates made in honour of the sixtieth birthday (1713) of Emperor K'ang Hsi.
[3] Another dish bears the signature of the Hermit of the White Rocks, dated 1734.

E. Plate with *famille rose* decoration and *bianco-sopra-bianco* rim.
Third quarter eighteenth century

with dinner services of Sèvres porcelain. For this western influence China was indebted to the Jesuits, Gherardini and Attiret, and above all Castiglione,[1] all of whom were employed at the palace academy of painting established by K'ang Hsi. Castiglione, whose Chinese name was Lang Shih-ning, aimed at combining the Chinese and the European conceptions of the art of painting. He was very well versed in both Chinese and western techniques. It is said that he also painted on porcelain. To the great influence of Castiglione Nien Hsi-yao (p. 26) bears witness. In his book *Shih Hsüeh* (Foreign perspective, 2nd edition published in 1755) he calls himself a pupil of Lang, and mentions that Lang has taught him western perspective. The name of Lang and his pupils is also connected with the *Ku Yüeh Hsüan* porcelain,[2] made for the emperor and highly placed persons. According to T'ang Ying it attained its highest degree of perfection between 1727 and 1753, and it went on being made until the reign of Emperor Chia Ch'ing (1796–1820).

The decoration was painted on the porcelain in a delicate manner and includes birds perched on branches, plants and leaves, flowers, and bamboo growing between rocks, elegant Chinese ladies (Plate 91), and lovely young shepherdesses with sheep or dogs. The attitudes of the figures, the perspective and the shading indicate a European conception. It is said that these representations found on vases and snuff-boxes, clearly showing western influence, were painted by Lang.[3]

PORCELAIN FOR EXPORT

Porcelain made for the Imperial court but influenced by the West became known in Europe only in this century. Western influence of another kind can also be detected on porcelain of the same period destined for export. In contrast to 'Chinese taste' porcelain it is excessively decorated, the central part and rim often both entirely filled. Crowded though it be, it has harmony of composition and colour.

Western influence finds expression in the way elegant fashionably-dressed ladies and playing children are rendered on dishes and plates. There are variations on this theme, but the lady is always represented seated. Usually two playing Chinese boys and occasionally a lady's maid are with her, and the scene generally includes such objects as a few large porcelain pots for preserves, a table with a mirror, a vase with peacock's feathers, or a *ling chih* (symbol of longevity). The central composition is in general surrounded by a diaper border.[4] The flat rim is decorated with diaperwork

[1] Castiglione arrived in China in 1715 and died there in 1766. For forty years he worked at the imperial court. He was commissioned by Ch'ien Lung to portray this emperor while receiving tribute from the Tartars. He also painted the imperial concubine Hsiang Fu in European armour.

[2] This 'ancient moon terrace' porcelain was made at Ching-tê Chên and sent to Peking to be painted there.

[3] W. B. Honey, op. cit., pl. 137A.

[4] W. B. Honey, *German Porcelain* (London, 1951) p. 15, ill. 13A. At Meissen this decoration first appears in 1760 and later on various other kinds of European porcelain.

interspersed with oblong panels of flowers and other ornaments. Those which are the most abundantly decorated are sometimes called 'seven bordered' plates (Plate 85), with eggshell body and ruby back. The colours are rose-red, yellow, blue, green, brown and red. They give evidence of an exceptionally high technical ability, figures and ornamentation both being painted with extreme skill. The outer border of some of the pieces is covered with silver which in the course of time has become black. Others have intricate borders and a central part showing *fêng huang* and quail. Though most of them were made in the Yung Chêng period they were still produced in the second half of the century. A few museums in Holland have examples: because the same composition occurs often, identical in its details, one wonders if a stencil of some kind was used. The well-known porcelain, plates and small saucers, cups, some octagonal, teapots, vases and garnitures decorated with cocks (Plate 83), flowers such as peonies and asters, and insects with rocks as a background are far less excessively decorated.[1] The most beautiful of this porcelain is the eggshell porcelain of the Yung Chêng period; the representation, however, was also used on more common wares. The composition on the dishes has a narrow border with a cell-diaper pattern. Under Ch'ien Lung it becomes more intricate and is sometimes surrounded by diaperwork (Plates 90 and 136). This porcelain was exported to Europe in various qualities; most in demand are those where the breast and tail of the cock are in black enamel, the feathers of head and neck in yellow, and the head itself in purple.

In general the porcelain exported to Europe in the eighteenth century is of lower standard than the kind just discussed, but there is nevertheless considerable variation in its quality. Sometimes the porcelain and the painting are both good, but frequently the body is rather coarse and thick-walled, and the painting second or third rate.

Only a very few of the many motifs occurring on *famille rose* porcelain exported to Europe can be described here. Popular themes are those which show flowering branches (Plate 87), or small bouquets, and an urn or basket (Plate 86), occurring on the central part as well as on the rim. The central decoration may be clearly separated from the border by an area of white (Plate 88). Besides floral decoration one finds Chinese ladies, with or without children, inside a house or on an outdoor terrace (Plate 89), mountain-landscapes with trees and animals, and ducks swimming in a pond with aquatic plants. Sometimes the border is decorated with a *bianco-sopra-bianco* decoration with widely spaced scroll-edged medallions (Plate 86).

Whilst during the K'ang Hsi period the borders frequently have regularly shaped panels or medallions, these become more complicated in the course of the century, resembling a leaf or mushroom. The rims often have three or four small bouquets (Plates 87, 89), and sometimes the border is broken up by an undulating outline separating diaperwork from bouquets (Plate 90). These plates sometimes have well-borders

[1] The small plates decorated with cocks made at Delft prove that this kind of porcelain was exported to the Netherlands in the eighteenth century.

ornamented with diaperwork. It is noticeable that, apart from small bouquets or flowers in medallions or panels, the other characteristically Chinese rim-ornaments do not occur in export porcelain in the stricter sense. On the other hand various rim-decorations occur which are not seen on porcelain with purely Chinese ornamentation.

After K'ang Hsi the so-called Dragoon vases, which remained in fashion in Europe during the century, were also painted with *famille rose* decoration (Plate 79).

FAMILLE NOIRE

At this time the *famille noire* class of porcelain (technique page 34) was one of the costliest of wares. The painting—with a black enamel covered by a green one which produced a vivid effect—caused many difficulties as a result of which failures were frequent. The best *famille noire* was made in the reign of K'ang Hsi. That it was exported to the West is shown by the cups and saucers in the collection of Augustus the Strong. The 'black Delft', which is an imitation of it, proves that it was exported at the end of the seventeenth and the beginning of the eighteenth centuries. Vases on a square or a round base, covered pots, writing things, pieces intended to be placed on brackets, teapots, and many other objects were decorated in *famille noire*. The ornamentation consisted of rocks, plants, flowers, flowering plum trees, or birds, in the colours of the *famille verte* set against the black ground.

Sometimes the black enamel was applied to a body already glazed (Plate 93). The decoration of red-flowered branches with gold has a background of black painted on a glazed body. In contrast to these cups and saucers, made first for the Chinese market and afterwards for export, there is a tea-and-coffee service, the shapes of various parts of which, such as the covered jug, in Plate 92, are borrowed from the West. Against a black-enamelled background, a Chinese trumpeter drawn in western style is painted in yellow and green. (This set was probably made for the market in India.) In the eighteenth century people were fond of similar exotic representations. When one sees various objects decorated in this way the question arises whether the black, which is often sloppily painted, was perhaps applied later in the Netherlands and by the same painters who decorated the 'black Delft'. Another possibility is that the black may have gone wrong during the firing.

LAKMOES

During the eighteenth century the Chinese porcelain painters invented a simpler method of making *famille noire* decoration. The black pigment was mixed with enamel before being used, though as a result the translucence of the enamel was lost. An overloaded decoration of plants and perhaps a small figure similar to the one shown on the jug of

Plate 94, is characteristic. This variety of *famille noire* is fairly frequent in the Netherlands and is called '*lakmoes*'.

EUROPEAN GREEN

About 1750 a new kind of opaque hard turquoise-green enamel came into use, and was used among other things for the inside and the bottom of vases with *famille rose* decoration.

OPENWORK

In the reign of K'ang Hsi the number of objects decorated with the openwork pattern was considerably increased. Besides bowls (Plate 97), one comes across vases, teapots and cups. The rims of plates and small saucers were sometimes ornamented with it. Nien Hsi-yao was famous for his openwork porcelain, the meshes being so fine that the pattern was like lace, and even after the firing the openings were as large as before and the porcelain in between had retained its original thinness. Lanterns with openwork decoration were much sought after: they were exported to the Netherlands as may be seen on a painting of the Verbrugge family by H. Lapis (1723–98), painted in 1773. Two lanterns on brackets are visible on either side of the painting over the mantelpiece. They are executed in openwork pattern with a *famille rose* decoration (Plate 95).

10 · Garniture sets for cupboards and cabinets

A feature of many old Dutch interiors during the seventeenth century and later was the *garniture de cheminée* or cupboard set. This was a set of a fixed number of pieces of porcelain to be put on cupboards, cabinets, etc. On paintings of interiors one sees cupboards, cabinets, mantelpieces, door-lintels, and frames of closet-beds embellished with covered pots, plates (on a family group by A. van Ostade, 1664, Louvre, Paris), or bowls (on an interior by P. de Hoogh (1629–83), Rijksmuseum, Amsterdam). Sometimes bowls alternate with plates as shown on an interior by Jec. Vrel (active during the second half of seventeenth century) and Nic. Muys (1740–1808). In the third quarter of the seventeenth century vases alternating with bowls were put on top of cupboards;[1] they are represented on paintings by de Hoogh and on a tableau of tiles by G. Verhaast.

The garnitures consisting of beakers, and a varying number of vases, probably became fashionable in the last quarter of the seventeenth century. The sets as such have a Chinese origin: they were put in the reception hall[2] or on an altar.[3] They consisted of five pieces, the middle one with a narrow neck flanked on either side by first a covered vase and then a beaker. At the time when the Dutch Company was shipping these vases to Europe, either singly or in pairs they were considered eminently suitable to embellish cupboards and mantelpieces, or to be put on the hearth in the chimney in summer-time. In this position they appear on a print showing a wall of the porcelain-room of the palace Charlottenburg in 1705.

In Europe there are sets of three, five and seven pieces. As in China usually a covered,

[1] F. W. Hudig, *Delfter Fayence* (Brussels, Musée de Cinquantenaire) Plate 117. It is difficult to say whether gourd-flasks have been regular parts of cupboard sets as such, but they *are* represented on the painting by C. Troost, the *Ontdekking van Jan Claesz* of 1738, in the Mauritshuis at The Hague.

[2] W. B. Honey, *Guide, etc.*, p. 65.

[3] Ibid. *The Ceramic Art of China and the Far East*, p. 205.

9. *Garniture de cheminée,* 1st half eighteenth century, taken from *The Feast of S. Nicholas,* a painting by C. Troost

somewhat bellied, pot in the middle was flanked first by a beaker on either side, and then by a covered vase—or the other way round (see figure 9).

The vases to the right and left of the central one are usually smaller, but it is not unusual to find that the central and end pieces are different in both size and shape. This is shown by the sets made at Delft[1] and elsewhere in the Netherlands. The Dutch sets made until well into the nineteenth century are often copies of Chinese models, but it is remarkable that the shape of the Chinese cupboard set has never been influenced by the West. The vertical flutes and ribs with which the Delft sets are sometimes provided are absent on the Chinese ones. It is not certain whether the hexagonal vase on the painting *Leren Lopen* by de Hoogh (Lügschena, Frelherr Speck von Sterburg)[2] between 1668 and 1673 was also used as part of a garniture, though this shape appears in Delft sets. It is probable that the squat or thick-set, covered, pear-shaped pots which were current in Ming times formed, completed with beakers, the oldest garnitures in Holland (fig. 10). This type of ware was still in use during the K'ang Hsi period,

10. Covered pot and beaker, blue-and-white, with decoration of Chinese lady musicians in garden. Late seventeenth century. *Auction sale, Frederik Muller, Amsterdam,* 15–19th November 1904

[1] Dr. C. H. de Jonge, *Oud-Nederlandsche Majolica en Delftsch Aardewerk,* p. 205.
[2] W. R. Valentiner, *Pieter de Hoogh* (Berlin, 1929) pl. 90.

11. Baluster-shaped covered vase, with *famille verte* decoration of Chinese landscape and *ch'i-lin. British Museum, London*

though the individual pieces were somewhat more slender. In the time of K'ang Hsi, the usual sets consisted of a more slender covered vase, with only a slight affinity with the baluster vase, and a beaker with a bulge below the middle, often with a decoration of tendrils, leaves and flowers within lozenges (Plate 98). Occasionally a vase shaped like the covered pot of Plate 74 was used as part of a set, but, instead of its having a flattened dome-like cover it now has a cover with a knob. Similar vases, but more slender, appear on an interior by de Hoogh of c. 1665 in the Cleveland Museum in America.[1] During the reign of K'ang Hsi, besides the round baluster vase, the same vase but on a square or polygonal base, derived from metal prototypes, came into fashion (fig. 11). The beakers that go with it are pear-shaped (fig. 12). Both these shapes are frequently met with during the eighteenth century, with either blue-and-white or polychrome decoration (figs. 13, 14 and Plate 99).

In Yung Chêng's time the bulge on the beaker appears only sporadically. The number of pieces in the garniture is now sometimes increased to seven and the sets occur in several sizes. Sometimes the central vase is the biggest, as in the case of Troost's painting

12. Beaker and covered vase, turquoise-blue glaze, engraved with flower ornament. About 1700. *Johanneum, Dresden, Germany*

[1] A. Staring, *The Dutch at Home*, ill. X.

13. Two vases of set of five decorated in *famille rose* with coat of arms, branches and birds. *Helena Woolworth MacCann collection, New York*

of 1738 *Episode uit Hopman Ulrich* already mentioned. They are frequently decorated in *famille rose,* with either trees and bushes, branches with leaves, and flowers on which a bird is perched (Plate 100), or with some of the 'Hundred Antiquities' or with a tobacco leaf. Sometimes they have a frieze of false gadroons round the foot and on the shoulder the well-known cloud motif. Similar shapes are seen in a very tall *garniture de cheminée* of 1740, decorated in *famille rose* with the coat of arms of Albert Sichterman (1692–1764) (a squirrel on a field of gold) in the Groninger museum (Plates 101 and 102). The Yung Chêng sets, the vase of which developed from the K'ang Hsi type, are very pretty.[1] They have a new and characteristic foot often embellished with a broad band of diaperwork; the matching beaker, with the same kind of foot, reminds one a little of the albarello. They were imitated at Meissen c. 1726, which means that the Chinese model must have been imported into Europe before that time. After the middle of the eighteenth century, vases and beakers lose their strong outline, as a result of which the various parts flow into each other without marked division. An excessive decoration, sometimes very gaudy, as in the 'Mandarin' porcelain which also has decorations in relief, makes the vases and beakers decidedly unattractive (Plate 339).

14. Painted garniture from the isle of Ameland with decoration of plants in blue, red and gold. Based on a silver or pewter model. Eighteenth century. Ht. 36 cm. *Nederlands Openluchtmuseum, Ameland*

[1] See R. Soame Jenyns, *Later Chinese Porcelain*, pl. 53, 1 and 2.

11 · Eighteenth-century export porcelain with western shapes

As in the Transitional period, Chinese porcelain makers of the eighteenth century imitated western shapes when fulfilling orders from Europe and they, too, used wooden models sent to China.[1] Earthenware, porcelain, glass, and metal patterns and perhaps even silver ones[2] were also sent from Europe. Various articles of daily use made in China, such as diverse parts of dinner-sets, have become so integrated that one hardly recognizes that in shape they are not Chinese but European (cf. Chapter 14).

Sometimes objects were demanded which it was hardly possible to make in porcelain. In his letter of 1712 Père d'Entrecolles writes that the foreigners liked new, often strange objects, which if they were faulty in any way were not accepted by the customer. The *T'ao-lu*[3] speaks of the usually strange shapes made for the oversea trade.

On the whole the porcelain made to order is easily recognizable because of either the western shape or the western decoration.

In contrast to the seventeenth century, when the Dutch East India Company was the principal buyer of Chinese porcelain, in the eighteenth it is in many cases impossible to decide from which country the orders had come. This is the more understandable as, since the end of the seventeenth and especially during the eighteenth centuries, the French styles of the time were widely followed on the Continent and to some extent also in England, and influenced the plastic arts in general.

When in the course of the eighteenth century England became the foremost customer

[1] In the Openlucht Museum at Arnhem there are some turned wooden, polychrome painted vases. It is possible that things like these were sent to China as models for porcelain. Cf. J. de Kleyn, 'Een zeldzaam houten kaststel uit Ameland' in *Nederlands Openluchtmuseum, Bijdragen en Mededelingen*, 1961, p.47.

[2] J. A. Lloyd Hyde, *Oriental Lowestoft* (Newport, 1954) p. 51 mentions a silver Queen Anne tea-pot found in Canton in 1930.

[3] *Ching-tê Chên T'ao-lu*, etc. Being a Translation with notes and an Introduction by G. R. Sayer, p. 19, nr. 29.

in Canton, this resulted in typically English shapes and decorations being imitated. At the end of the eighteenth and the beginning of the nineteenth centuries the makers of porcelain for export also paid much attention to the taste of the American public.

It quite often happened that after a certain piece had been made for one of the Companies, or for some private person, and had been sent to its destination, it was seen and ordered by others than the original customer. The resulting copies were sometimes painted with the same decoration as the original piece, or in a style more to the taste of the public in the country concerned. The magnificent Chinese imitations of Louis XV and XVI vases[1] and parts of sets, exaggerated in shape and richly decorated, were not much in demand in the Netherlands, probably because the Dutch in the main felt more drawn to simple articles of daily use than to this magnificence.

Often it is impossible to ascertain of which material the models sent to China were made, the more so as it was in general not known which was there first: the metal or the ceramic one. With expensive articles, as for instance the sugar caster, the one made of silver was very probably the original one, and there are some Chinese shapes which are clearly derived from a pewter ancestor. This is the case for instance with the English 'monteith' silver punch-bowl and the pewter high relief '*temperantia*' dish. The latter, in *blanc de chine,* in the Princessehof Museum is a true copy of the pewter dish[2] made by François Briot (between 1585 and 1590) or by Caspar Enderlein in 1611. In the Groninger Museum there is a porcelain copy of a 'monteith' silver bowl,[3] decorated in *famille verte,* which was in use between 1680 and 1705. Earthenware samples must have been sent to Canton more often than silver ones,[4] simply because the latter were too costly. For the candlesticks of Plates 115 and 117 a pewter[5] or Delft original[6] must have served as the model, rather than the silver[7] Louis XIV one, in use since 1720. The decoration of the latter, either in blue or in polychrome, is the same as that of the parasol sets (Plate 193 ff.). It is rather striking, and this goes for the candlestick as well as for the sugar caster, that it is always a Louis XIV shape which was used as a model. The question may arise here, did the Chinese porcelain makers think the Louis XV style too

[1] Several of these pieces are reproduced in M. Beurdeley, *Porcelaine de la Compagnie des Indes.* See also J. A. Lloyd Hyde, *Oriental Lowestoft.*

[2] A. J. G. Verster, *Tin door de Eeuwen* (Amsterdam, 1954) pl. 52.

[3] Gerald Taylor, *Silver* (Harmondsworth, 1954) p. 194, pl. 22a.

[4] W. B. Honey, *The Ceramic Art of China,* pp. 157-8, is of the opinion that first silver and afterwards earthenware models were sent to China.

[5] Several of the pewter objects mentioned in this chapter are reproduced in A. J. G. Verster, op. cit.

[6] F. W. Hudig, *Delfter Fayence,* pl. 194. Several of the earthenware objects mentioned in this chapter are reproduced in the books on Delft ware and majolica listed in the bibliography.

[7] Several silver objects mentioned in this chapter are reproduced in C. J. Hudig, *Zilver van de Nederlandse Edelsmid* (Amsterdam, 1951). Th. M. Duyvené de Wit-Klinkhamer, *Catalogus van Goud-en Zilverwerken,* Rijksmuseum Amsterdam, 1952; and Id. and M. H. Gans, *Dutch Silver* (London, 1961) translated from *Geschiedenis van het Nederlandse zilver* (Amsterdam, 1958).

intricate, or did the public of the time prefer silver rococo candlesticks and casters to Chinese porcelain ones? Because both shapes were made till the sixties of the eighteenth century it may be concluded that the Louis XIV model had captured the popular fancy. For the candle stand, such as that shown in Plate 113, wooden ones were probably used as models. This one (in the Princessehof Museum at Leeuwarden) is attached to an oval plate that ends in a point. The decoration includes *ju-i* motifs in blue, green, lilac and yellow enamel. Unfortunately, the candle-holder and the snuffer are missing here. A complete example is in a private Danish collection.

The cylindrical caster of Plate 118 must have been made from a late seventeenth-century silver model of the type that only came into fashion c. 1680; this and the Louis XIV-shaped caster of Plate 116, are frequently found in Chinese porcelain. It is quite possible that pewter, earthenware (e.g. Rouen[1]), or porcelain casters, which in turn were based on silver ones have served as models. The silver caster with a round body became common after about 1730 and the one with a many-sided body after 1740. The Chinese porcelain ones were therefore probably made after these dates. The top is fastened to the body with a bayonet-catch (Plate 118). There are also Chinese porcelain casters which have the top standing on the body, but quite separate from it. In these cases the Chinese porcelain makers apparently knew no solution for the locking. Writing materials too, such as square, hexagonal or cylindrical ink-pots (Plate 120), and pounce-pots (Plate 110), sometimes as a set on a small porcelain tray, were probably made from pewter models. A decoration with small flowers in blue or polychrome was generally used.

In former times the ewer with saucer or basin[2] was an indispensable object of daily use, which in the first place served to wash the hands after a meal. They are represented several times on paintings by Vermeer (1632–75) and Gerard Terborgh (1617–81). They were first made of silver, pewter or earthenware, and it is quite understandable that people wanted them too in Chinese porcelain in western shape. Well known is the splendid silver set, which Joh. Lutma made in 1655 for the new town hall in Amsterdam (Rijksmuseum).[3] To prevent the ewer from slipping the tray had a projecting ring in the middle, fitting the ewer. In the collections of the Rijksmuseum of Amsterdam there is a fine one (Plate 106) decorated in blue and of K'ang Hsi date. On the ground of its great similarity to a silver set made by Frans Maerschalck in 1641, now at the Lakenhal Museum at Leiden, and considering the K'ang Hsi blue-and-white decoration, this porcelain one must have been made in the last quarter of the seventeenth century.

Besides these shapes there are also silver and pewter inverted helmet-like jugs. They

---

[1] Arthur Lane, *French Faience*, ill. 186.

[2] A. Westers, 'Een Lampetkan van Delfts Aardewerk', in *Bulletin Museum Boymans-van Beuningen*, 1961.

[3] M. H. Gans and Th. M. Duyvené de Wit-Klinkhamer, *Dutch Silver*, pl. 36.

Eighteenth-century export porcelain with western shapes

were made of earthenware at Rouen[1] about 1700 and had French silver or pewter ancestors. They were imitated in China with *famille verte* decoration as well as in Imari and *famille rose*. The French 'lambrequin' decoration of the Rouen jugs is replaced by a Chinese one of flowers and leaves. Sometimes the French *mascaron* in relief was copied.[2] They were made in China, possibly at the end of the seventeenth century and certainly after the first quarter of the eighteenth. The ewer of Plate 104 was made for the Portuguese Ataïde family probably at the beginning of the eighteenth century.[3] The plate shown here (fig. 15) with the scalloped rim, was derived from a silver or pewter pattern. Most probably it was ordered at the time by the governors of the St. Sebastian's doelen at Middelburg. The barber's bowl (Plate 314), so popular in these centuries, was made in Chinese porcelain after wooden, pewter and earthenware models, but not after silver ones.

A common feature of eighteenth-century houses was the detachable wash-basin, consisting of some kind of water holder with faucet, and a basin placed under it. In Europe they occur in pewter, copper, painted lead and earthenware.[4] These articles of daily use were also copied in Chinese porcelain decorated in blue,[5] *famille verte*,[6] and *famille rose* to the order of western customers, at the end of the seventeenth and the beginning of the eighteenth centuries. A very fine specimen is in the palace Huis ten Bosch at The Hague (colour plate B). Sometimes the Dutch East India Company gave instructions concerning the shapes: 'Ewers with basins below them, the basins should be like a shell with three little feet, but not such clumsy high feet and heavy basins as

15. Dish, scalloped rim, with Imari-style decoration of plants in red and gold. Late seventeenth century or early eighteenth. D. 35 cm. *Hotel De Burg, loan St. Sebastiaans doelen, Middelburg*

[1] Arthur Lane, op. cit., pl. 19a.

[2] K'ang Hsi jugs decorated in *famille verte* may be found in the Rijksmuseum at Amsterdam and the Victoria and Albert Museum at London.

[3] M. Beurdeley, *Porcelaine de la Compagnie des Indes*, p. 77, fig. 49.

[4] Rouen, Moustiers and Marseilles.

[5] De Chinese porseleinkast, exhibition catalogue, *Vrienden van de Nederlandse Ceramiek, Mededelingen-blad*, nr. 52.

[6] R. Picard, etc., *Les Compagnies des Indes, Route de la Porcelaine* (Paris, 1966) pl. 73.

those shipped in the year 1756, which take up too much room in the chests.' Very probably the basin meant here was like that of Delft earthenware in the Rijksmuseum at Amsterdam.[1] In the Rijksmuseum at Amsterdam there is a very fine wash-basin set consisting of a water holder in the shape of a baluster pot and an oval basin (Plates 122 and 123). It is difficult to say whether the basin has a western or a Chinese origin.[2] The decoration, consisting of festoons painted in *famille rose,* is a combination of Chinese and European elements. Wholly European is the baroque cartouche painted on the body of the vase, which at its bottom ends in a satyr's head and at its top in an acanthus leaf. This leaf also appears as an ornament on Delft ware. The Chinese archer in the cartouche is so little Chinese that he must have been modelled after a European drawing, perhaps by Pronck. The frieze of fleurs-de-lis round the foot and the butterflies on the inside of the neck, as well as the leaf motif round the foot of the basin and the festoons, are borrowed from the West though both the latter clearly show Chinese influence. The decoration is in green, yellow, red, violet, rose and black and is embellished with gold. Another type of wash-basin set ordered in China had a bottle-like ewer that reminds one of the seventeenth-century medicine bottle, with the difference that the thickened ring on the neck now only serves as a decoration and has no practical use. The set illustrated (Plates 125 and 126) was made between 1760 and 1780 and is decorated with a combination of European and *chinoiserie* elements.

Other parts of the toilet-set, such as pomade boxes, chamber-pots, and bourdaloues, were also imitated in Chinese porcelain. The bourdalou is a small oblong chamber-pot with or without a lid, often decorated in *famille rose.*[3] The name comes from the French cleric Bourdaloue (1632–1702). Objects such as the beer-mug of Plate 103, the goblet, the flower-holder, the fruit or cake stand on a short stem of fig. 17, and the spittoon of Plate 109, are clearly based on European models, but it is difficult to know whether the original was made first in metal or in earthenware.

In the Zeeuws Museum at Middelburg there are two jugs shaped like beer-mugs (fig. 16). They show the impaled arms of Leendert Bomme (1683–1760; mayor of Middelburg) and Suzanna de Haze (1693–1743). As the jugs were probably ordered on the occasion of their marriage in 1734, and certainly before her death in 1743, they must have been made between those dates.

The eighteenth-century dish on a stem,[4] usually with a Chinese floral decoration in blue, is of a shape that may have been taken from Dutch delftware: on the inside of the

[1] J. G. A. N. de Vries, *Porselein,* p. 24. F. W. Hudig, op. cit., ill. 231.

[2] One is tempted to connect this basin with the goldfish-bowls so much the fashion in China. Cf. T. Volker, op. cit., ill. 24 and M. Beurdeley, op. cit., fig. 3 and 4 (The Hague, Gemeente museum) though both these basins are less bulging and deeper. It is therefore difficult to say whether we have here a sinified European prototype or a westernized Chinese one.

[3] M. Beurdeley, op. cit., p. 87.

[4] Dr. C. H. de Jonge, *Oud-Nederlandsche Majolica en Delftsch Aardewerk,* p. 269, also T. Volker, *Porcelain and the Dutch East India Company,* p. 62. 'Fruit dish on foot.'

16. Jug with handle and polychrome decoration of tendrils and impaled arms of Leendert Bomme (1683–1760) and Suzanna de Haze (1693–1743), 1735–42. Ht. 25 cm., D. 16 cm. *Zeeuws Museum, Middelburg*

hollow foot of the example shown in fig. 17, there is a mark A K, initials copied from delftware probably made in the factory of Adriaen Kocks, who died in 1701. There is some similarity to the fruit-dishes painted, usually in polychrome, on mid-seventeenth-century Dutch tiles.[1]

The spittoon came into fashion as smoking increased in the course of the seventeenth century. By the end of that century and the beginning of the eighteenth, round (Plate 109) and polygonal cuspidors or spittoons were being ordered from China.[2] Some were decorated in blue-and-white, and from Yung Chêng times onwards examples painted in *famille rose* also appear.

Other European shapes are the square, round, and oval butter-dishes, the latter with a dog on the lid (Plates 111, 168, 170 and 174), the jug (Plate 105), and the so-called tulip-vase. The butter-dishes in blue and *famille rose* are common, but the other shapes mentioned above are less frequently found. In the Princessehof Museum there is the

17. Fruit or cake dish, with blue-and-white decoration of flowers. Marked inside the foot with initials A K (Adriaen Kocks). Late seventeenth or early eighteenth century. Ht. 6 cm, D. 16 cm. *Johanneum, Dresden,* c. 1928

[1] D. Korf, *Dutch Tiles*, pp. 95–98.

[2] The word derives probably from the Portuguese cuspidor. According to Willets in *Foundations of Chinese Art* the origin of the spittoon is western Asiatic, and the one of illustration 109 is closely related to those of plates 181–183 of his book, which are of T'ang date. Similar ones were exported by the Dutch Company in the seventeenth century. T. Volker, *The Japanese Porcelain Trade, etc.* On p. 28 porcelain cuspidors are mentioned under 1781, and copper ones under the year 1702.

18. Plate with gadrooned border, the centre with blue decoration of a phoenix, the rim with tree, flowers and monkeys, K'ang Hsi. D. 21.5 cm. *Groninger Museum*

puzzle-jug of Plate 105. It is a true copy of a Delft one.[1] Stranger still is the tulip-vase in the Groninger Museum (Plate 108). It is marked A.(P.)K. and, in shape and decoration, is derived from a Delft example. Most remarkable in this piece is the decoration including the standing nude-winged amors on the sides of the base: a Chinese interpretation of a Dutch pattern that was itself taken originally from a Chinese model.

Heads of walking-sticks, made by factories at Meissen, Chantilly[2] and St. Cloud, after the second quarter of the eighteenth century, were imitated in Chinese porcelain (Plate 114). Several are shaped like a capital letter 'T', the hollow, vertical part fitting the stick. Others are curved and have the hollow end shaped to fit over the stick. Plates with different types of gadrooned border were probably copied from those made at Delft and elsewhere. The example in fig. 18 (Groninger Museum) is in underglaze blue painted with a phoenix. When wigs[3] (fig. 19) became fashionable in Europe in the

19. Wig-stand with blue flower decoration. 2nd to 3rd quarter eighteenth century. *Cooper Union, New York*

[1] Dr. C. H. de Jonge, op. cit., p. 271. This kind of jug or mug is in Dutch called *fopkan*, literally 'hoax jug' (puzzle jug in English). In general, it has an openwork upper part which it seems impossible to pour or drink from.

[2] W. B. Honey, *French Porcelain* (London, 1950) pl. 51.

[3] Dr. C. H. de Jonge, op. cit., p. vii.

last quarter of the seventeenth century, wig-stands were required on which they could be placed when not being worn. In various factories, including Delft, stands were made with blue decoration. Glass was also copied in Chinese porcelain, for example the Venetian or Dutch winged glass from which the winged vase of Plate 107 was clearly derived. This has a bowl-shaped body and long neck, to which two openwork ears are attached, and is decorated with flowers in underglaze blue. Wine-cups with knopped stem were also copied in porcelain (fig. 20) and decorated with floral motifs in blue.

As early as 1639 a lot of 120 of them was shipped to Holland, probably to serve as gin bottles; indeed, it is not impossible that their shape was borrowed from glass gin bottles (Plate 215) on Jan Steen's painting *Soo gewonnen, soo Verteert* of 1661, in the Boymans-van Beuningen Museum at Rotterdam, a boy is pouring gin from such a bottle into a pewter mug.

Even wooden objects like knife-trays or -boxes were made in Chinese porcelain. Sometimes they were ornamented with sailing-boats or hunting scenes. The jar with two spouts (a shape also seen in Medici porcelain, made in Florence between 1575 and 1587) in the Princessehof (Plate 124) is what is probably one of the oldest oil-and-vinegar sets. It is decorated in blue with a floral motif, and was perhaps copied from a similar piece made at Meissen c. 1785. The true oil-and-vinegar set, often made in Delft ware, consists of two small flagons or jugs, and two round boxes connected by a handle, and this also was imitated in China. The subject of Plate 112 was decorated in the Netherlands with bushes and monkeys in Kakiemon style, in blue, iron-red, green, black and gold.

20. Cup on foot, blue-and-white. 1st half eighteenth century. Ht. 13.7 cm. *Rijksmuseum, Amsterdam*

12 · Porcelain of the K'ang Hsi period decorated with western subjects in underglaze blue

During the last quarter of the seventeenth century, drawings, prints and sometimes even coins and medals were sent to China to serve as models to be used in the decoration of porcelain. Since in China only porcelain with eastern decoration was available, for which there was much interest in Holland and other European countries, the Company ordered large quantities of this, on which they made a solid profit. The adding of western motifs to Chinese porcelain decoration had, as we have seen, started in the Transitional period, but a real demand for it only grew up at the end of the seventeenth and the beginning of the eighteenth centuries. The first porcelain so decorated is of course curious and rare. The representation borrowed from the West was usually placed in the centre of a dish or plate; but the rim was invariably painted with Chinese motifs. One of the oldest, but none the less well-known European motifs of decoration is the 'Tumult of Rotterdam', also called the 'Costerman Revolt'. Costerman was sentenced to death on September 16th 1690 because on the night of 28th August he had killed a servant of the tax collector in a fight caused by his refusal to pay excise-duty on a cask of wine. The people of Rotterdam, angered at this event, took illogical revenge on the much hated first sheriff Jacob van Zuylen van Nyevelt by assaulting and rifling his house. News of the whole affair spread far beyond Rotterdam, and inspired a certain Johannes Smeltzing (who died in 1693) to make a medal (Plate 131), which was struck in pewter, silver and gold,[1] but since by an edict of 1688 it was forbidden on pain of corporal punishment 'to make, print and retail scandalous and infamous lampoons' this medal could not be openly distributed. None the less a specimen must have been secretly forwarded to China, as a sample for the representation of this episode on Chinese plates and cups and saucers. There was apparently more than one version of the scene, for on some pieces there are three lop-sided houses next to

[1] A. C. van Kerkwyk, 'De Costerman penning' in *Oude Kunst*, 1916. P. A. van de Kamp, 'Een Rotterdams belastingdrama op Chinees porselein', *Antiek* 2, 1967/1968, p. 271.

the sheriff's house, and on others four. Costerman's head, which is on the obverse of the medal (the houses are on the reverse and are represented on the plates (Plate 132)), is painted on the bottom inside the cups. This seems to indicate that a copy of the medal itself was sent to China, rather than a drawing of the houses. Most of the pieces show the reign-mark of Ch'êng Hua (1465–87), or the character *yü*. They were made before the end of the century.

A cup and saucer set (Plate 129), perhaps made for the French market, but well-known in the Netherlands, are probably of the same date as the Costerman pieces. One of the saucers shows a ship, all sails set, and also a siren, alluded to by the in-correctly spelled inscription *gardes vous de la syrène*. The accompanying cup shows a man, Odysseus, standing on the prow of a ship, set against the sails.

The cup of the other set (Plate 130) is inscribed under the outside lip: *L'empire de la vertue est établi jusqu' au bout de l'univers*. According to an apocryphal tradition this cup and saucer set was presented to Louis XIV. On the wall of the cup on a broad panel two crowned personages are seated. It has been presumed that this picture represents either Louis XI (1226–70) being advised by his mother Queen Blanche[1] or Louis XIV (1661–1715) with his Queen. The narrow panels show alternately a small bush and a kneeling Chinese. Besides these mythological and historical portrayals there are also pieces decorated with scenes of daily life at the beginning of the eighteenth century. It seems more probable that they were taken from prints rather than from Delft ware, upon which similar scenes had already appeared.[2] Other well-known subjects, which probably came into fashion at the beginning of the eighteenth century, are the pictures of music making (Plate 133) and a dancing company. On the former[3] a lady is playing a stringed instrument (possibly a dulcimer?) which is on a table in front of her. She is accompanied by two gentlemen, one playing a flute, the other a lute. On the plates showing dancers, the Chinese porcelain painters evidently found it difficult to cope with the ladies' head-dresses with their unfamiliar high *coiffures*. Other decorations of this type show European ladies strangely Chinese in style, and Dutch landscapes.

The octagonal coffee-pot on three ball-shaped feet, of Plate 128, is of early eighteenth-century date. It is painted with a Dutch landscape against a background of trees. In the clouds one sees, remarkably enough, a not very attractive scene of 'Europa and the Bull' which must have been borrowed from a European print.

During the K'ang Hsi period one rarely encounters vases painted with European representations. There is, however, in the Sypesteyn Museum at Loosdrecht in the

[1] A. Jacquemart and E. Le Blant, *L'histoire artistique, industrielle et commerciale de la Porcelaine*, p. 386.

[2] J. Helbig, *Faïences Hollandaises, XVIIᵉ et XVIIIᵉ début XIXᵉ siècle* (Royal Museum, Brussels) ill. p. 121, plate (c. 1720) with the initials A.P.K. and decorated with a card-playing company.

[3] In the Moriaan at Gouda there is a tile with this same decoration, except that it is reversed. The musical company is here depicted on a terrace, with a half-door to the left. Probably both representations were taken from the same original. Anne Berendsen, Marcel B. Keezer, Sigurd Schoubye, Joao Miguel Dos Santos Simões, Jan Tichelaar, *Fliesen, Eine Geschichte Der Wand- und Boden-fliesen*, p. 173.

Netherlands, a large covered pot (Plate 127) ornamented in blue-and-white with Chinese tendril motifs framing four oval medallions showing European ladies in earliest eighteenth-century dress.

Occasionally *albarelli* are decorated in western style[1] like the one in the Victoria and Albert Museum (fig. 21) which is painted with a Dutchman in a cape, accompanied by two servants. This shape itself was not new to the Chinese, for in the beginning of the fifteenth century they had already made *albarelli* in imitation of Near-Eastern ones, as is shown by one in the Freer Gallery of Art in Washington DC.[2]

21. *Albarello*, decorated in blue-and-white, with three Dutchmen. Late seventeenth or early eighteenth century. Ht. 28 cm. *Victoria and Albert Museum, London*

Tiles

Influenced by Dutch tiles which, as was mentioned in Chapter 6, were sent to China, the Chinese made porcelain tiles that were exported, e.g. to the Indies, where they were used as skirting in rooms and halls. Apart from the corner ornaments, the decoration is Chinese (Plate 134). There is a different type[3] without the ornamented corners and without the double circle shown in Plate 134.

From the time of the Ming dynasty, porcelain plaques of varying size and shape were also made. They were used as decoration on wooden screens, altars, chairs and benches. The designs are in blue and in polychrome, and include western elements.

[1] *A Handbook to the W. G. Gulland Bequest of Chinese Porcelain* (London, Victoria and Albert Museum) pl. XLIII.

[2] John Pope, *Chinese Porcelain in the Ardebil Shrine* (Washington, 1956).

[3] T. Volker, *Porcelain and the Dutch East India Company*, p. 242, ill. 38. F. H. de Haan, *Oud Batavia*, p. 65, 66; album with plates, pl. 24 and 25.

13 · Tea, coffee and chocolate services

TEA

The Dutch first heard about tea[1] from the journals of Huygen van Linschoten (1596). After 1610, tea was imported from Hirado into Holland, where it was originally used as medicine. After the healthy had acquired a taste for it, the Seventeen Gentlemen (directors of the Dutch East India Company) wrote to Batavia in 1637 that, since tea was now in demand, they would expect a few casks of Chinese and Japanese in all ships. The first recorded shipment arrived in 1667, 75 baskets of tea from Hocchieu,[2] which the Company did not really know how to deal with. But it was sold, and the Seventeen Gentlemen wrote to Batavia in 1685 that the company had the right to a monopoly. In his 'Treatise on the excellent herb tea', Dr. Bontekoe wrote in 1678 that he saw no reason why 50 to 100 or 200 cups should not be drunk one after the other. In 1719, a shipload of tea was auctioned for half a million guilders. At first tea was drunk in cafés, but in the eighteenth century as the imports grew in quantity, it began to be used more and more in the home. From Holland the habit spread to France and Germany; and in the second half of the seventeenth century it was served in coffee-houses in London.

In the eighteenth century, Amsterdam was the principal tea market of Europe. From 1729 to 1734, two Dutch East India Company ships brought a yearly cargo of tea direct from China, and it had become the Company's most profitable trading article. Porcelain was used as ballast, since it had the great advantage of being without smell: tea was 'a fine maid, which should not come in contact with merchandise, which might spoil her delicate aroma'. The cargo of a ship varied from 1142 to 2579 pikols.[3]

[1] T. Volker, *Porcelain and the Dutch East India Company*, p. 48 ff. C. A. S. Williams, *Chinese Symbolism and Art Motives* (New York, 1960) p. 383. W. Ukers, *All about Tea*, Vol. I, pp. 28 ff.

[2] The word tea comes from the Fukien pronunciation of the Chinese word Tcha.

[3] Pikol was originally a shoulder-weight of c. 62 kg. There were different sorts of tea, such as *boei*, *krysou*, *souchou*, *bing*, *singlo*, *pecco*. People had tea-caddies, in which they could keep five or six different sorts.

Tea, coffee and chocolate services

In 1729 the *Coxhoorn* brought 268,479 pounds of tea packed in casks, hampers or canisters.

In China, tea had been drunk since T'ang times (618–906). Originally it was mixed with other ingredients and the whole brought to boiling point.[1] From the time of the Sung dynasty (960–1279), dried, powdered tea was infused in a bowl with boiling water—this was 'thick' tea. Only in the seventeenth century was it made from the leaves, which was the method adopted in Europe. The metal, glass and wooden articles then available in Europe for use in making and drinking tea were not considered good enough for the 'fine maiden'. Even the teacups without a handle, made at Delft[2] in imitation of the Chinese ones, did not become popular. With their thick earthenware body they were thought hardly suitable. Since tea-drinking played an important rôle in Chinese life, the wares needed for the ceremony were naturally readily available in that country: cup without handle, teapot, slop basin and tea-canister, -box, or -caddy. Teacups with handles and saucers to go with them were made especially for export to the West, though cups without handles are even nowadays occasionally used in Europe. The teapot of red stoneware was the most popular in China and, with the growth of the tea-drinking habit, similar pots were exported to the Netherlands in great quantities (Plates 146, 321 and 322). The demand for these pots, which were costly, became so strong that they were imitated in the Netherlands with some success at Delft before 1680, and after this in England and at Meissen in Germany. As tea was still very expensive small pots only were made (see p. 167).

An early export to the West was the porcelain teapot with a spout and fixed hoop handle (Plate 18), of a shape originally used in China as a wine-pot. This was also the shape for the pots made of white porcelain at Têhua for home use, one of which (Plate 137) is represented on a still-life painting by P. G. van Roestraten (c. 1630–98). Another painting by the same artist (Plate 146) shows a metal-mounted, red stoneware teapot in the popular pear shape. Octagonal, globular, cylindrical and square pots also occur as well as those made in the shape of a fruit, or as if fashioned in sections of bamboo. As to the porcelain pots which were not made as wine-pots first, but as proper teapots, the globular one with a flat bottom and without a footrim became the most popular. Some have curved spouts (Plate 136); others the straight spout (Plate 139), which first appeared between 1730 and 1740. The handle is always opposite the spout. About the middle of the eighteenth century teapots occur with decoration, and an openwork foot (Plate 135). Sometimes the body is ornamented with tendrils in relief.

[1] Ir. G. Knuttel, Jr., *Japans Aardewerk* (The Hague, 1948) p. 38, 39. Francesco Carletti, *Voyage around the World 1594–1606.*

[2] It is probable that already at the end of the seventeenth century teacups with Chinese and with Japanese decoration were made at Delft. Dr. C. H. de Jonge, *Oud Nederlandsche-Majolica en Delftsch Aardewerk,* ill. 239 and 277.

Tea, coffee and chocolate services

The first teapots made in conformity with the wooden models sent from the Netherlands were ordered in 1639, when the order to the Chinese merchant Jousit was for '200 teapots with covers and handles, also with ribs according to no. 4 sample'. A similar ribbed teapot decorated with leaves and flowers in red, blue and gold,[1] but from the first half of the eighteenth century with decoration in Imari style, is shown in Plate 139. This proves that the Dutch now wanted teapots made to their own taste and from their own models. The teapot with oval base, straight spout, and oval handle of intertwined stalks, based on the silver pots which originated in England in the second half of the eighteenth century,[2] also occurs in Chinese porcelain.

Teapot, teacup, *sucrier* or sugar basin, milk-jug and other tea wares, were, just like other Chinese porcelains, decorated in underglaze blue, blue, red and gold, or in *famille verte, famille rose* or *encre de chine*. After tea had come to stay in the Netherlands, the Company ordered teacups in quantity, with or without round or octagonal saucers. By 1644 the large amount of 80,000 cups-and-saucers of various sizes (including 3906 openwork cups) and 7600 octagonal cups were ordered.[3] It is not impossible that these cups were also used for drinking other liquids, for instance gin. In the order for that year 24 teapots, probably Yi-hsing ware were also listed (Plates 321, 322 and see also chapter 18). In the same year, 33,020 'red' teacups and 330 large teacups were shipped to the Netherlands.

During the seventeenth century, people were contented with a tea-set consisting of pieces of different materials and shapes. During the eighteenth century, on the other hand, people wanted a tea service the component parts of which were matching in decoration and harmonious in shape. As a result of the increased tea-drinking habit, the composition of the tea-set became wholly western, and the breakfast-set[4] came into being: either for one person, called *solitaire* or for two, called *tête a tête*. They consisted of a tray, tea- or coffee-pot, milk-jug, *sucrier* and slop basin, an oblong small tray (Plate 149), possibly used for spoons or to go under the pot or jug, a tea-caddy and one or two cups (also used for drinking coffee). As the fashion for these sets spread, special pieces were ordered, and in the course of the eighteenth century chocolate-cups and jugs were added.

Schotel's[5] description of a tea service is interesting—he refers to a complete service

[1] At Delft too teapots with ribbed body were made as is shown by one in the Rijksmuseum at Amsterdam. F. W. Hudig, *Delfter Fayence,* ill. 146.

[2] Similar handles appear very frequently on English pottery after 1760. See D. Towner, *English Cream-coloured Earthenware* (London, 1957) ill. 13b, 14a, 15a, etc.

[3] In the Day Register the word teacup appears at least as early as 1629. According to T. Volker, op. cit., p. 49, this was only a trade-name for a special kind of cup. Very probably cups used in China as wine-cups were also exported as teacups.

[4] Schnorr von Carolsfeld, Ludwig Köllman, *Porzellan der Europäischen Fabriken* (Braunschweig, 1956), p. 114.

[5] *Het Oud-Hollandsch Huisgezin der Zeventiende Eeuw.*

containing among other things, tasting pots and larger teapots, big and small covered and uncovered cups, cup-holders and saucers, *sucriers* and sweetmeat dishes with small golden forks. The teapots were of various shapes, including double-spouted pots, one spout being used for filling and the other for pouring out. From this description it is known that the eighteenth-century tea service (Plate 349) also included one, two or more tea-caddies with lids, for the different kinds of tea, a milk-jug and a small tray. This last was a round, hexagonal (Plate 149) or lotus-shaped tray placed under the teapot to catch any drops; a use confirmed by the reference to a teapot with tray in a sale catalogue of the late eighteenth century. It may well have been an innovation of the Dutch house-wife, so renowned for her neatness. These articles, except for the milk-jug, are all depicted in the Mandarin service in the still-life painted about 1775 by J. E. Liotard (1702–89).[1]

Bills of lading from the eighteenth century show us that tea utensils were shipped in far larger quantities in that century than in the preceding one. In 1730 for instance the *Coxhoorn*[2] carried 100 teapots, 124,595 cups and saucers, of which 13,805 were brown-and-blue, 490 tea services, of which 324 were enamelled and 176 wholly white.[3]

In 1758, a total of 24,958 sets of large 'Dutch tea- or single coffee-things' was brought by the ship *Sloten* to the Netherlands, 19,538 of middle size, 19,471 of small size and 100 tea services.[4] These numbers provide evidence that there was still a strong demand for Chinese tea wares in Europe, which is not surprising as European porcelain services were as yet rather rare and therefore expensive. The first were made at Meissen and Vienna, and were used by the nobility and well-to-do commoners. Even as late as 1780,[5] 50,000 pieces were ordered in China, among other things. Fairly large porcelain tea-trays, on which to put all the tea things were also ordered in China, as is shown by the 'Feith' service in the Groninger museum.

In the bills of lading a distinction was made between single teacups and tea-sets. It is quite possible that the latter were used by the well-to-do and that the single cup-and-saucer was either a mass-produced article, meant for the common people, or to be used with the silver tea things as is shown by a painting by an unknown artist in the Victoria and Albert Museum.[6] On this painting a lady and gentleman are shown drinking tea from Chinese handleless teacups. As mentioned already, the teacup and saucer was new to western society. The Chinese teacup was very probably used in the Netherlands for various other purposes before the people of that country knew about its use for tea in China (p. 102, n. 3). Cups with slightly curved sides, and with Wan Li

[1] N. Ottema, *Chineesche Ceramiek Handboek*, pl. 263.

[2] Dr. J. du Hullu, 'Over den Chineeschen Handel der Oost-Indische Compagnie, etc.', *Land-en Volkenkunde*, Vol. 73, 1917.

[3] They were probably painted in Europe and fired in the muffle kiln.

[4] Dr. J. du Hullu, 'Instelling van de Commissie voor den handel der Oost-Indische Compagnie op China in 1756', *Taal, Land-en Volkenkunde*, etc., Vol. 79, 1923, p. 545.

[5] Dr. J. du Hullu, 'De Porseleinhandel der O. I. Compagnie, etc.', *Oud-Holland*, 1915, pp. 54, 55.

[6] Günther Schiedlausky, *Tee, Kaffee, Schokolade*, ill. 12.

decoration, were being imported into the Netherlands by the beginning of the seventeenth century, and these had probably been used in China as teacups. A cup and saucer ordered in 1643 would probably have been of the blue-and-white variety, which is shown by paintings of Roestraten (Plates 137 and 146), Fr. Mieris de Oude (1653–81) and others, painted between 1650 and 1670. Such bowl-shaped cups with footrim (Plate 137) were in frequent use at that time, both the rather thick-walled coarser kinds and the thin-walled cups-and-saucers of finer quality. During the reign of K'ang Hsi, deep cups with two handles were made (Plate 140).

There are a number of different shapes of cups: octagonal (Plate 143), those with walls curved or lightly moulded into an elongated S line (Plates 130, 328) and those with almost straight sides. These last are usually decorated with two cuckoos (Plate 147), or with fools, 'long Elizas' (Plate 142), or a vase with flowers (Plate 144). The cups illustrating the 'Riots in Rotterdam' have slightly curved sides. There are also cups with flared lips (Plate 129) and with scalloped rims (Plate 141). All these cups have footrims and are without handles. The finest are the slim, fairly deep cups with the elegant S-shaped sides (Plate 130) already mentioned. This shape continued to be made right up to the eighteenth century. Sometimes the cups have lids, such as the one with 'l'empire de la virtu' decoration (Plate 130). Others have saucer-shaped lids which rest on a rim in the cup.

Cups with single handles were ordered and made in the course of the eighteenth century, as is shown by the one with polychrome decoration of two Chinese (Plate 145). It is quite possible that this kind of cup was first meant for coffee. Cups without handles were also made in great quantity for the European market.

Paintings of the period show how people drank tea in the eighteenth century. Cups were not held by the body but by the footrim and it seems that tea was also drunk from the saucer. This is shown in a painting of about 1700 by Nicolass Verkolje (1673–1741).[1]

Tea-jars or -caddies[2] were made in various shapes. The oldest kind is probably the

22. Ribbed tea-jar, with dome-shaped cover. Eighteenth century. Ht. 16.5 cm. *Collection Bal, Zeeuws Museum, Middelburg*

[1] A. Staring, *The Dutch at Home*, pl. XIX. Anthony Du Boulay, *Chinese Porcelain* (London, 1963) ill. 117.

[2] The English name 'caddy' is derived from the Chinese *catty*, equivalent to 625 grams.

23. Tea-jar, blue-and-white, with decoration of Chinese ladies and flowers. Eighteenth century. Ht. 6.5 cm. *Collection Bal, Zeeuws Museum, Middelburg*

hexagonal one, a specimen of which in blue-and-white was salved from a ship lost in the last quarter of the seventeenth century, in Table Bay off Capetown. Similar tea-jars with cap-shaped covers[1] were made at Meissen between 1719 and 1730. The most common type is the one of fig. 22, in the shape of a covered vase with cylindrical neck, either with or without vertical ribs. Sometimes these jars have an openwork foot (Plates 151 and 209). Other shapes are the oval jar of fig. 23, the rectangular one of fig. 24, and occasionally the square one of Plate 150, which was also made at Delft. The rectangular tea-jars about ten to twelve centimetres high, probably copied from Chinese models, occur in Europe made of porcelain and earthenware as well as of silver or pewter. Those made of Chinese porcelain were decorated with Chinese as well as with western decoration. The cap was sometimes used as a measuring cup for the quantity of tea to be put in the teapot. After the middle of the eighteenth century, and in imitation of western models, these jars were made with curved shoulders as shown in Plate 152.

In England silver-covered boxes seem to have been first used for sugar about 1685, and at Rouen a pottery sugar bowl of *pâte tendre* was made near the end of the seventeenth century.[2] By the twenties of the eighteenth century the sugar bowl was in general

24. Rectangular tea-caddy with blue-and-white decoration of Chinese ladies. Eighteenth century. Ht. 8.5 cm. *Collection Bal, Zeeuws Museum, Middelburg*

[1] Meissen tea set with Chinoiserie in the style of J. G. Herold in the Munich Residenzmuseum, L. Schnorr von Carolsfeld, *Porzellan*, pl. 6.
[2] W. B. Honey, *French Porcelain*, pl. 1a.

25. Milk-jug painted in *grisaille* with arms of
town of Kampen. Ht. 10.5 cm. *Museum De
Broederpoort, Kampen*

use for the *Coxhoorn* mentioned earlier had 251 covered sugar bowls in her cargo. The
sugar bowl with cover and two handles (like those shown in Plates 148 and 296)
appears from the middle of the century onwards, and seems to have been used for sugar
candy as well as loose sugar.[1]

It is not known when the milk-jug came into use. According to some authorities it
was in 1680, but others believe that it was not before about 1730.[2] The little bulging
jug on three feet, and with broad lip, came into use in the middle of the eighteenth
century in Europe and is frequently found in *chine de commande*. It was still in use in
1776, as is shown by the specimen of Plate 153. It occurs in silver, in Delft[3] ware, and
in porcelain. Also copied from silver is the pear-shaped jug with handle and pouring
lip (Plates 92 and 151), which was probably used as a milk-jug from the beginning of the
eighteenth century. There are also tea- and coffee-sets, first made in China between
1750 and 1760, with a milk-jug like that of fig. 25, in shape not unlike the ewer of
Plate 104. These jugs are known with *en grisaille* as well as with an underglaze blue
or a mandarin decoration.[4]

COFFEE

The first European reference to coffee was in the description of a journey to Jerusalem
by the Augsburg physician Leonard Rauwolf, published in 1582. At the beginning of
the seventeenth century Pieter van den Broecke (1575–1641) found the plant growing in
Abyssinia. The bush grown at that time, in the botanical gardens established at Amsterdam by Willem Wissen, was the ancestor of the coffee in South America, planted
in Surinam at the beginning of the eighteenth century. Controversy among the

[1] Raw sugar was imported by the Dutch Company about 1616 from China, Formosa, Siam and
Bengal, and refined at Amsterdam from the first half of the seventeenth century. After 1637 cane-sugar
was planted in Java. The West Indian Company imported sugar from Brazil.

[2] C. H. Wylde, *Continental China* (London, 1907) p. 143.

[3] Dr. C. H. de Jonge, op. cit., ill. 218, 1771. B. Jansen, *Catalogus v. Haagse Zilverwerken*, nos. 65, 93.

[4] J. G. Phillips, *China Trade Porcelain*, p. 80, tea service with milk-jug decorated with the arms of the
Hammond family, made between 1785 and 1800.

Tea, coffee and chocolate services

26. Coffee-pot with handle and spout.
Decoration in *famille rose* of flowering
branches. 2nd quarter eighteenth century.
Height 18 cm. *Princessehof Museum, Leeuwarden*

physicians of the time concerning the effects of coffee, whether noxious or beneficial, without doubt did much to make people better acquainted with it. The drink had become famous by 1760 through the Greek-owned Café Greco. In 1711 the first cargo of Java coffee[1] arrived at Amsterdam. Besides porcelain tea-sets, porcelain coffee-sets were also made in Europe, for instance at Meissen, and just as in the case of the tea services these coffee-sets influenced the shapes of pieces ordered from China. Again, as in the case of the tea services, silver and pewter coffee-pots were used as models. At first, these were similar in shape to teapots, as is shown by two silver pieces in the Victoria and Albert Museum.[2] The teapot has a conical body and a short spout, whilst the oldest known silver coffee-pot[3] has the same shape with only one difference: the spout is not opposite to the handle but at right angles to it. Both models were copied in Chinese porcelain (fig. 26) from the beginning of the eighteenth century, with Chinese (Plate 194) or western decoration (Plate 128),[4] in blue-and-white as well as in polychrome. The most popular shape was the covered bulging pot with lip and spout of Plate 138.

In contrast with the coffee-pot made in Europe, which occurs in the various 'Louis' shapes, the pot made to order in China, and painted either with Chinese or western decoration, is always sober in shape by comparison. In the demands[5] of the Dutch Company for the year 1767, the following information is given about coffee-pots: 'The coffee-pots, the like of which have never been seen, to wit, they are not beautiful. We believe that they have been in stock for about 50 years, and that they will stay there for another 100 years without being sold. After in England a factory has been invented of

[1] From 1696 coffee had been cultivated in Java. In 1759, 3,480,536 pounds of coffee were shipped to Holland; 26 years later, the amount was 13 million pounds.

[2] *Charles II Domestic Silver* (Victoria and Albert Museum, London) pl. 7.

[3] Ibid., ill. 13.

[4] In the Rijksmuseum at Amsterdam there is a coffee-pot of Delft ware, which might have been the example for the Chinese one, though the latter is octagonal and the Delft one has vertical ribs. M. A. Heukensfeldt Jansen, *Delfts Aardewerk* (Rijksmuseum, Amsterdam, 1960) ill. 13.

[5] J. G. A. N. de Vries, *Porselein*, p. 25.

fine English earthenware the which is frequently sent over here and is sold because of its beautiful shapes; because one usually gets bad shapes from China such a factory grows even more strongly and to put a stop to this together with this there goe some samples of shapes.' It is evident there was strong competition from Wedgwood and Leeds. In the Day Registers at Batavia coffee-cups are mentioned frequently. In 1640, for instance, they were sent to Mocha on the south-east coast of Arabia.

Originally there was no difference between tea- and coffee-cups. In the twenties and thirties of the eighteenth century, however, the cup like the one of Plate 145, which was first made about 1715 at Meissen, came into use for coffee and was very probably also used for chocolate.[1] The ship *Sloten,* which arrived home in 1758, had in her cargo 2073 coffee-cups and saucers, and these were probably of the type of Plate 145. Besides this there were 2520 cups without saucers, 11,933 pairs (cup-and-saucer) of Dutch big double coffee-cups, and 24,958 pairs of Dutch tea- or single coffee-cups. As in 1730 the *Coxhoorn* had in her cargo 17,040 coffee-cups and saucers, the freight of the *Sloten* points to a gradual increase of the drinking of coffee in the course of the eighteenth century.

CHOCOLATE

In the first half of the sixteenth century the Spaniards imported the first cacao beans into their country from Mexico. At first the drink was used only as a medicine, just as tea had been, but by about 1600 it had reached Italy and the Netherlands from Spain, and by the end of seventeenth century, chocolate was being served at the court in The Hague. It is said that chocolate with milk was first drunk about 1700, and it seems that chocolate came into general use only in 1750. In his letter of 1722 Père d'Entrecolles says that at Ching-tê Chên chocolate-cups were made. Sales catalogues provide evidence of chocolate sets which consisted, for instance, of a chocolate-pot, milk-jug, slop basin and twelve chocolate-cups and saucers. The Day Registers also refer to chocolate-cups and pots. In 1730 the *Coxhoorn* carried 9457 chocolate-cups and saucers, and in 1758 the *Sloten* 1574 chocolate-cups with handles and without saucers. The European factories also supplied chocolate-cups,[2] but the chocolate-pot, invented in Europe and used in silver in the eighties of the seventeenth century at the Court of France, occurs only sporadically in Chinese porcelain. The museum at Kampen in the Netherlands has one decorated in *grisaille* with the arms of the town and the date 1767 (fig. 27). Unlike the chocolate-pots made in Europe this one has no opening in the lid. A little rod with a thickened end was inserted through this opening and used to whisk the chocolate into a foam. About 1725 a similar pot without an opening in the lid was made

[1] L. Schnorr von Carolsfeld, op. cit., ill. 13.

[2] Chocolate-cups with two ears, Vienna 1719. L. Schnorr von Carolsfeld, op. cit., ill. 92; chocolate-jug, op. cit., ill. 95.

27. Chocolate-pot painted in *grisaille*, with arms of town of Kampen, dated 1767. Ht. 18.7 cm., D. 10.5 cm. *Museum De Broederpoort, Kampen*

in Vienna. The *trembleuse*, a tall cup with two handles, and saucer with a circular rim in which to place the cup, was also copied in China, as an example in the Willet-Holthuysen Museum in Amsterdam shows. The cups made in Germany and France in the second quarter of the eighteenth century also served as models.

14 · Dinner services

EUROPE

Dinner services in pottery or porcelain consist of plates, saucers, dishes, tureens and sauce-boats, to which sometimes are added a breakfast- or a tea-set, all the pieces matching in shape and decoration. When and where were they first made?

Before the end of the seventeenth century the common man ate and drank—and this is shown by contemporary paintings and prints—from pewter and pottery plates, dishes and drinking vessels. Till the end of the sixteenth century, and in some cases even later, wooden dishes, bowls and cups[1] were used. Princes, noblemen and rich commoners sometimes owned eating- and drinking-things made of precious metals, which in an emergency were sold or melted down.

From time immemorial man has used pottery, at first simply fired, later usually glazed as well. From the sixteenth century Dutch potters glazed their earthenware with a tin glaze, and also with the age-old lead glaze. One of the oldest tin-glazed earthenware sets is the one ordered by the Duke Albrecht V of Bavaria, at Faenza in 1573. It consisted of plates, dishes, salt-cellars, a canteen, candlesticks and a cooler,[2] but it is a moot question whether the dinner service as we know it now, with uniformity of shape and decoration, existed before 1700. Though it is known that Jan Arentsz van Rheenen made a silver service for the Count of Oldenburg in 1665, there are unfortunately no details of its components.[3] It probably included posset-pots and ewers, and almost certainly candlesticks, such as those with a matching toilet-set, which are in the Municipal Museum at The Hague. They were made sometime after the middle of the seven-

---

[1] Among the relics of the overwintering on Nova Zembla by Barendz and Heemskerck in 1597 are also wooden dishes and plates. Rijksmuseum, Amsterdam.

[2] L. Hager, 'Ein Majolica Tafelgeschirr aus Faenza, im Residenzmuseum München', in *Pantheon*, 1939, pp. 135–9.

[3] H. E. van Gelder, *Haagsche Goud- en Zilversmeden*, etc., p. 101.

teenth century for Veronica van Aerssen van Sommelsdyck.[1] It is a matter of common knowledge that Louis XIV and many of his contemporaries were owners of silver dinner services. Owing to the misfortunes of war, these and other sets were sent to the mint in 1689 and in 1699 to be melted down. Several parts of the silver dinner service, such as the tureen, the sauce-boat and the salt-cellar, later influenced the shape of their Chinese porcelain counterparts. In the first quarter of the eighteenth century the silver sets were enlarged with tea, coffee and chocolate pots and cups, and so on. As the financial difficulties in France increased, a decree of 1709 ordered every citizen to give in his silver at the mint. St. Simon (1675-1755) relates in his memoirs that people in 'high society' had ordered dinner sets in pottery both from Rouen and Delft. The desire to own complete dinner services, which were made from about 1700,[2] was in part a consequence of the better table manners that developed at this time: guests were seated at a well-ordered table, and each had his own place setting.[3]

At the beginning of the eighteenth century, Alexander Louis, Count of Toulouse (1638-1737), and George I, King of England since 1714, ordered Delft services with polychrome decoration. From this it appears that Delft earthenware enjoyed fame beyond the Dutch frontier. The best-known service[4] is the one belonging to Frederick the Great of Prussia, who died in 1713. The Boymans van Beuningen Museum possesses a dish and two wall candlesticks, all painted with the arms of Prussia and Brandenburg in blue, red, green, purple, black and gold. It is a pity that we do not know whether this service also contained tureens and sauce-boats. In the seventeenth and eighteenth centuries, candelabra were often made to match plates and later services.

Chinese porcelain dinner services were also known, for Louis XIV ordered one in China consisting of 1058 pieces, though unhappily there is no record of the types of pieces demanded. A Dancourt[5] comedy of 1688 shows that the difference between Chinese porcelain and Delft ware was fully appreciated at that time, for Dancourt had a lady smash '*toutes ces porcelaines d'Hollande*' in the house of a friend, as people wanted nothing '*que de fines*': that is, Chinese porcelain.

Porcelain services were commissioned from Meissen by Augustus the Strong of Saxony. This ruler's great love of porcelain from the Far East led him to demand services embellished with patterns taken from China and Japan. The oldest is the 'yellow lion' service of about 1730-33, decorated with the well-known Japanese Kakiemon motif of a tiger twining itself round a bamboo; a few years later came the one with red dragons. The most famous perhaps is the service made for the Minister Count Heinrich Brühl between 1737 and 1741, the 'Swan Service'. The latter, originally numbering

---

[1] B. Jansen, Catalogue of the exhibition of silver from The Hague through five centuries. Municipal Museum, The Hague, 1967, ill. 38a–c.

[2] Herbert Brunner, *Altes Tafelsilber* (Munich, 1964) p. 62.

[3] C. J. Hudig, *Zilver*, p. 62.

[4] See note 1, page 119. [5] A. Lane, *French Faience*, p. 16, footnote 1.

2200 pieces, still numbered about 1400 pieces in 1939. In addition to these luxury services, simpler ones were made at Meissen from 1712[1] for the bourgeois, and these included tureens and sauce-boats as well as plates. From 1720 until the fifties of that century, the Meissen factory influenced all other porcelain made in Europe, and it is clear that the various porcelain factories set up in the course of the eighteenth century also started to make services. The public on the Continent and in England began to order from China pieces made in European styles, and the resultant services show western influence in composition as well as shape. It is often difficult to date them, because a particular shape of a tureen or a sauce-boat remained in fashion for a long time.[2] This is not to say that the successive styles of the French kings, which are well represented in European porcelain, were not followed in China: the Chinese potters, however, did not attempt to copy any complicated European pieces, but confined themselves to the more sober styles. As a result, the shapes of Chinese dinner wares are, with few exceptions, simpler than their European counterparts. It is therefore impossible in many cases to be sure whether certain pieces in Chinese services, such as a tureen or a sauce-boat, are copied from European originals or not. This uncertainty is understandable since, until now, no special study has ever been made, either in China or in the West, of those parts of dinner services made in China which are based on western models. Had this been done, a European original might have been found not only for the tureen of Plate 154 but also for other parts of services made to order.

The Dutch East India Company ordered not only these European-type pieces, but also typically Chinese shapes like rice-bowls, though it cannot be ascertained whether they were used by the Dutch repatriated from the Indies for eating rice, or for other purposes. Parts of a set[3] ordered in China about 1765 by the Dutch governor-general at Batavia, P. A. van der Parra (1761–75), were listed as special small dishes for the components of the 'rice-table'.

CHINESE DINNER SERVICES

Before dealing with dinner services ordered in China in the course of the eighteenth century, we must first discuss the dinner services made there till about 1700. The first references to dinner services, painted with a uniform decoration in one or more colours, occur during the Ming dynasty. In the Chia Ching reign (1522–66) the dinner service had become indispensable at the Imperial court. A list[4] of 1544 mentioned 1340 dinner-sets totalling 30,000 pieces ordered from Ching-tê Chên by the Emperor. Services

[1] Gustav Weiss, *Ullstein Porzellanbuch* (Berlin, 1964), p. 124.

[2] Margaret Jourdain and R. Soame Jenyns, *Chinese Export Art in the Eighteenth Century* (London, 1950) p. 45, note 5.

[3] V. I van de Wall, 'Een Historisch Servies', *Nederlandsch Indië Oud en Nieuw* (Amsterdam, 1923/4) p. 290.

[4] R. L. Hobson, *The Wares of the Ming Dynasty*, p. 93.

F. Plate, ruby back, decorated in *famille rose*. Yung Chêng marks and period

ordered in 1554 consisted of the following 27 pieces: 5 fruit-dishes, 5 plates, 5 dishes for vegetables and 5 bowls, together with 3 teacups, one wine-cup, one wine-saucer, one slop basin and one pickle-stand; but no tureen or sauce-boat, which became component parts of every later western set. Similar services were probably imported into Europe by the Portuguese during the sixteenth century. Loys Guyon[1] informs us that at the end of the sixteenth century porcelain was used to serve '*salades de grand prix, fruits et confitures*' at the tables of popes, emperors, kings, dukes and the marquesses of Italy. A French traveller who visited the hospital at Goa at the beginning of the sixteenth century found that they were using Chinese porcelain.[2] At the beginning of the seventeenth century, the French King Henri IV bought a Chinese dinner service in Holland, and when Maria de' Medici visited Amsterdam in 1638 she was presented with a Chinese dinner service. It is, alas, not known of how many pieces these services consisted or how they were made up.

DINNER SERVICES MADE TO ORDER FOR THE WEST
Composition of services

The Batavia Day Registers give us some idea of the composition of the dinner services shipped to the Netherlands between 1610 and 1657. There are references to plates and bowls of various sizes, dishes, fruit-dishes, dishes for vegetables and for pastry, salt-cellars, mustard-pots and oil-and-vinegar sets.

The shipping-lists make it clear, on the one hand that tureens and sauce-boats were not used, the latter being unknown in China at that time, and, on the other hand, that the Chinese made to order various objects of daily use from western models such as salt-cellars (see page 122) and mustard-pots. At this time there is still little resemblance to the uniform dinner service that came into use in the course of the eighteenth century. Several wares mentioned in those shipping-lists are still made today.

At the time in the eighteenth century when the tureen and the sauce-boat were added to the dinner service it was not unusual to find that plates and dishes were of better, finer quality than the tureens and sauce-boats, which were often made of thicker, rather coarse, pitted porcelain. In general, these services were not of uniform quality, because the various pieces were not all made in one place but in different factories at Ching-tê Chên. This made it difficult for the purchasers at Canton to buy sets the component parts of which were of a consistent standard. Another reason for the diversity of character often found within one service was that many people who ordered porcelain wanted their sets to be different from those of their friends, both in shape and in decoration. One also comes across services where the sauce-boat is of a shape twenty years older than that of the tureen, for instance, and these, therefore,

[1] Hugh Honour, *Chinoiserie, the Vision of Cathay* (London, 1961) p. 37.
[2] J. A. Lloyd Hyde, *Chinese Porcelain*, p. 52.

stylistically speaking do not belong together. It is, moreover, evident that a shape once established was made again and again, and that new models were not created every time for every order. A shape that occurs over a long period is the oblong tureen with chamfered corners and handles in the form of boars' heads, which was made about 1765 and is a part of the 'Feith' set in the Groninger museum.[1] Decorated in blue or polychrome (Plate 163) and with slight variations in shape, these tureens are fairly common in the Netherlands. The prototype was probably the example which formed part of the service made to the order of Duke Leopold II of Anhalt Dessau, of which parts are now in the Helena Woolworth McCann Collection in America. It was ordered and made until the eighties of the seventeenth century.

Whereas the decoration of these services in underglaze blue, *famille verte* or Imari was painted at Ching-tê Chên, the *famille rose* decoration was usually added at Canton, on undecorated glazed porcelain carried there from Ching-tê Chên. Thus, though stylistically inconsistent, the service was given a superficial appearance of uniformity by similar polychrome decoration on all the pieces. Sometimes too, parts of a set were painted with a suitable later decoration to make a whole out of dinner, tea and coffee services, which originally did not belong together. This, moreover, would have been one way in which the merchants could have overcome the difficulties, already described in Chapter 7, of getting a complete dinner service from Ching-tê Chên to Canton and, in addition, getting it there at the right time.

Only a few bills for services made to order for the Dutch are still in existence.[2] But there is a copy of one dated 9th May 1751 (in the collection of Mr. J. A. C. Swellengrebel in Hilversum), for a set ordered by Hendrik Swellengrebel, Governor of the Cape of Good Hope (1739–51). The lack of bills makes it difficult to ascertain the exact composition and extent of the *chine de commande* services exported to the Netherlands in the course of the eighteenth century, for they were dispersed by divisions of personal estates, much diminished by breakages, or even wholly lost. Catalogues of the auctions of the Dutch East India Company might have given some indication, if they had been published, but even then the auctioneer would in many cases have made up odd lots to be sold as services which to our eyes would not have been uniform at all.

Fortunately there have remained several catalogues of estates sold at auction in the last thirty years of the eighteenth century. These include dinner and dessert services decorated in underglaze blue as well as in polychrome. They consist of flat plates and soup plates, round and oval tureens, ragout-tureens, platters and dishes for meat and fish, fruit dishes, some with openwork bodies, sauce-boats with their stands, salad-bowls, ice-boxes, salt-cellars, pickle-stands and ewers. On the basis of this information, and

[1] M. A. de Visser, 'Een eetservies van Chinees porselein met het wapen van de familie Feith', *Vrienden van de Nederlandse Ceramiek, Mededelingeblad*, no. 35, 1964, p. 44.
[2] Catalogue *Wonen in de Wijde Wereld*, Tropenmuseum, Amsterdam, 1963–4, no. 228.

also because some large sets are still extant in the Netherlands, it is possible to build up a reasonably accurate picture of the composition of these porcelain services ordered in China. These are to be found in many Dutch museums, as for instance the Fries Museum at Leeuwarden, the Groninger Museum, the Bisdom van Vliet Museum at Haastrecht, and in private collections such as the one in the Noordeinde Palace at The Hague, the Castles Hardenbroek and Zuilen, and in institutes like the Fundatie van Renswoude at Utrecht. Though such services are not quite complete, they none the less give a clear impression of the size and the great variety of wares. The most remarkable pieces are the fruit-stands of Plate 157 copied from a Meissen prototype.[1] They consist of a gnarled tree-trunk, on which two half-clothed youths are climbing. On the trunk is an oval *à jour* plate with a wavy rim. The tree trunks are painted in brown and the rest in green, rose and blue, heightened with gold.

Similar stands form part of the 'Feith' collection and of a service decorated in blue in the Bisdom van Vliet Museum.[2] The 'Feith' service, from about 1770–82, in the Groninger Museum now consists of 168 pieces, 2 rectangular covered tureens, 2 shallow bowls with scalloped rims, 6 salt-cellars, 4 round covered butter-dishes, 4 sauce-boats, 5 small oval boxes with handles of two distinct shapes, 1 tray, a deep saucer or fish-dish, 2 deep oblong dishes, 64 plates, 11 salvers of four different kinds, 8 shallow dishes, 4 small oval boxes without handles, 22 meat-dishes in four sizes, and a fruit-dish.

In addition to services with polychrome decoration we find, in the second half of the century, more and more services decorated in blue-and-white. They are painted with a Chinese landscape (Plate 165), the 'willow pattern' (Plate 177), plants and flowers (Plates 163 and 166), and Chinese ladies in a garden (Plate 179). The dish of Plate 178 has the well-known motif called 'the bird and sunflower' (actually a peony), the drawing of which becomes stylized in the course of the eighteenth century and eventually, towards the end of it, very stiff and dull. The Fries Museum at Leeuwarden owns a service to which belong fish-platters, small ice and cream-dishes, plates, dishes, and saucers with notched rims. Another set in the same museum includes mustard and jam pots. Covered butter dishes such as one from the service in the Fundatie van Renswoude (Plate 174) form part of the service.

The dating of services

Though services ordered for the Netherlands will be chiefly discussed, to give a more complete idea of the development of these wares, some sets made in China for customers from other countries will now be dealt with.

[1] B. L. Grandjean, *Dansk Ostindinsk Porcelain importen fra Kanton, c. 1700–1820,* fig. 55.

[2] Dr. C. H. de Jonge, 'Ceramiek in het Museum der Stichting Bisdom van Vliet te Haastrecht' in *Vrienden van de Nederlandse Ceramiek, Mededelingenblad,* nr. 31, ill. 45. In the museum at Winterthur (U.S.A.) there is a nearly identical fruit-stand with the monogram of Major Samuel Shaw of Boston, J. G. Phillips, *China Trade Porcelain,* p. 30, fig. 18, p. 197, pl. 96. B. L. Grandjean, op. cit., fig. 56.

Dinner services

The service ordered by James Brydges,[1] first Duke of Chandos, about 1715, is among the earliest. An oval basin, and a helmet-shaped ewer, are in the Helena Woolworth McCann collection in the Metropolitan Museum in New York, and in the Museum of Fine Arts in Boston. Both were made after European models and painted with floral decoration in polychrome. Another early service is the one ordered by G. Peers in 1731.[2] It consisted of 500 pieces and cost 228 *tael* or £76, an average of 2 shillings a piece. This is known from the bill which is in the British Museum, as also are some of the plates. There were dishes of five sizes, 312 plates and soup plates, 56 dishes, 5 sauce-boats, salt-cellars, beakers, ewers, etc., all decorated in underglaze blue and polychrome.

It has not yet been possible to find in the Netherlands a *chine de commande* service dating from the first thirty years of the eighteenth century. One of the oldest known is the polychrome dinner and tea service, probably made to the order of a one time Chief Justice at Batavia, Th. van Reverhorst (1708–58), in memory of his parents. Pieces still extant include ragout-tureens (Plate 173), plates (Plate 274), a sugar bowl with lid (Plate 148), cups and saucers and a tea-caddy. The arms of the van Reverhorst family, surrounded by those of related families, are painted on the centre of some of the plates, and on the covers of the sugar bowl and tureens. They are also decorated with a motif frequently found on *chine de commande* of tendrils and shells in gold, which came into use between 1735 and 1740. Of a later date is the service in the Fundatie van Renswoude (Plates 154, 155, 157, 169, 171, 174) painted in *famille rose* and gold with a decoration of flowers, and with the arms of Frederik van Reede (1658–1738). It consists of more than 300 pieces. The tureen of Plate 154, belonging to it, shows so great a similarity with a specimen made by Ignatz Hess at Höchst[3] between 1747 and 1751 that the latter must undoubtedly have served as the model. The clumsy shape and the heavy ornament make its German origin quite acceptable. A tureen made at Delft[4] and now in the Rijksmuseum at Amsterdam is very similar, and indeed it is difficult to decide whether the Höchst or the Delft piece was used as a model for the Chinese one. The shape must have been fashionable for, apart from the examples just mentioned and some at the Castle Hardenbroek, similar tureens were also made for the Danes,[5] Germans and Portuguese.[6] The Central Museum at Utrecht owns one, too, with a Dutch *accollé* coat-of-arms, one of the Temminck family. It would seem that the tureen of the Van Reede set must have been made between 1751 and 1754, but,

[1] J. G. Phillips, op. cit., pl. 17. The prototype of the oval box is in the Boymans-van Beuningen Museum at Rotterdam, Cf. Dr. C. H. de Jonge, op. cit., p. 289, and M. Beurdeley, op. cit., cat. 49a, b.

[2] M. Jourdain and R. Soame Jenyns, *Chinese Export Art in the Eighteenth Century*, p. 109.

[3] J. G. Phillips, op. cit., fig. 41. A nearly identical piece made at Strasburg is shown in G. Fontaine, *La Céramique Française* (Paris, 1964) pl. XXVI.

[4] M. Beurdeley, op. cit., p. 53, fig. 24.

[5] J. G. Phillips, op. cit., pl. 40. M. Beurdeley, op. cit., fig. 23. B. L. Grandjean, op. cit., fig. 88.

[6] M. Beurdeley, op. cit., fig. 19.

on the other hand, a later date is accepted for two similar tureens made for the Danish market. One of them is in the Helena Woolworth-McCann collection and is given a date between 1760 and 1770, and the other one a date of about 1785. It is perhaps therefore more reasonable to suggest that the Van Reede service was ordered between 1760 and 1770, in which case it was presumably commissioned by the Trustees of the Fundatie. However, it is then difficult to understand why the arms appearing on the service are not those of the foundress, Maria Duyst van Vourhout, who married Frederik van Reede in 1683 and died sixteen years after her husband, in 1754. Judging by the decoration of blue, green and rose-red flowerets adorning all the pieces, it is wholly probable that the service was made as a complete set for an arranged date. The same service includes some oblong little boxes with wavy rims, and these also appear as part of the 'Feith' service mentioned earlier which has 1765 for a date.

Reference must be made to the polychrome services made in the last quarter of the century. First comes one in the possession of Queen Juliana of the Netherlands in the Noordeinde palace at The Hague (Plates 160–162). The *accollé* arms of Prince William V (1748–1806) and his wife the Princess Wilhelmina of Prussia (1751–1820), who were married in 1767, are painted on every piece in this service, in red and blue on a purple ground. Apart from a few insignificant details, these coats of arms are identical to those on a print (Plate 161) by R. Vinkeles (1741–1816) after a painting by P. C. Haag (1737–1812), portraying the Princess on horseback. As its counterpart, portraying the Prince, is dated 1779, the former must have been made in the same year. On this basis it is quite probable that the service was made after 1779, but before 1795 when the Stadt-holder and his Household had to take refuge in England, and so a date between 1780 and 1790 seems obvious.

A set (Plates 182–186) dating from the end of the century which was originally made for the British or American markets is in the Fries Museum. It is painted with a classical decoration of festoons, a cat, and the letters J.G.(?) in red and gold. This service still includes 738 pieces and so is a very large one; and it gives us some idea of the great variety of components still in use at the end of the century. It includes small cream-plates, openwork fruit-baskets (Plate 186), ice-pails (Plate 184), shallow covered dishes (Plate 182), custard-cups with intertwined handles, and 45 round and 5 oval hot water plates (Plate 185). A breakfast set once formed part of the service, as various cups, saucers, egg cups and breakfast plates show. It is very similar to a service of between 1800 and 1810 in the Bissell collection at Wilmington (U.S.A.),[1] ordered by Henri Chanopin Belin when he was governor of Guadeloupe. A so-called Mandarin set, in the possession of Queen Juliana of the Netherlands, kept at the Lange Voorhout palace at The Hague, was made between 1820 and 1830. It consists of large and small tureens, fish-platters with their trivets, large and small plates, small oval openwork covered dishes on their trays, and fruit-dishes (Plate 181). The decoration is of Chinese ladies

[1] Jean McClure Mudge, *Chinese Export Porcelain for the American Trade, 1785–1835*, fig. 128a, b.

and gentlemen either in an interior, or on the veranda, or in front of a house, and occasionally men on horseback are depicted. The enamel colours are purple, blue, brown-yellow and red.

PRICES

In the East India Company demands for 1767, prices for services were also given. So the price of 250 *tael*—the *tael* at the time reckoned of around 3.50 Dutch florins or 6s. 8d. in English money—was found to be too high for a blue porcelain service. Blue-and-white table services of 29 pieces each cost 2 *tael* and 8 *maes* 'and should at landing the prices be higher, such white with gold must no more be sent'.

TUREENS

Rectangular, round and oval tureens, made for Europeans, are important features in services.

Rectangular tureens

The oldest kind is of the shape shown in colour plate C. This beautiful specimen, owned by the abbey of Berne in North Brabant, is painted with floral decoration in *famille verte*. The covered tureen on its stand is a true copy of the one made in the Guillebaud factory at Rouen of about 1728. The shape is transitional between the Louis XIV and rococo styles. It is one of the few Chinese tureens the European original of which is known, and copied in China so accurately in shape as well as in decoration. Since the original was French the copy was almost certainly ordered by a Frenchman, and was in all probability made not later than 1735, because otherwise shape and decoration would have been out of fashion. As far as can be ascertained this is the oldest tureen still extant.[1] The Chinese floral decoration on the Rouen piece[2] was adopted by the Chinese painter with only very small alterations in shape and colour, and he will probably not have realized that he was copying the decorative work of one of his predecessors. The enamel colours used were among others blue, yellow, green and red.

A widespread type is the tureen with a deep splayed foot, sloping sides and dog's-head or boar's-head handles. The cover is generally slightly domed and has a knob in the shape of a fruit (Plate 155). One of the older types is the tureen of the service made for the Duke Leopold II of Anhalt Dessau about 1750, parts of which are in the Helena Woolworth-McCann collection, in New York. In later specimens like that in the

[1] M. Beurdeley, op. cit., cat. 106.

[2] This tureen in the Musée des Beaux Arts at Rouen was part of a set the town presented to the Duke of Montmorancy-Luxembourg when he was appointed governor of Normandy in 1728. W. B. Honey, *European Ceramic Art*, etc., ill. 88.

'Feith' service, the angles of the body are no longer sharply defined, but more rounded and flowing, and the rims on the tureen cover too have changed from angular to curved. This shape also appears in the tureen belonging to a set[1] once intended as a present for King Frederick the Great of Prussia (1740–86). The tureen in question, a few plates, dishes and two *jardinières*[2] (Plate 156) are in Huis Doorn. As on the tureen of von Anhalt Dessau the arms are painted in polychrome enamels on one of the long sides and run over on to the lid. On either side of the forty-quartered arms, which are placed on an ermine cloak, stands a primitive man with a banner. It is noticeable that the wreath of eight circles enclosing the monogram F.R. (Fredericus Rex), alternating with the Prussian and Brandenburg eagles, is nearly identical with that on the Delft plates,[3] marked P.A.K., ordered by the Prussian King Frederick I who died in 1713. Because of the close resemblance one is tempted to suppose that the designer of the service for Frederick the Great had taken the Delft monogram as his pattern. It is, however, more probable that both monograms were taken from the same coat of arms. It is possible to date this service accurately because the ship that carried it to Emden was wrecked on the German coast in 1755. It is known that the service was ordered in Canton by the Königliche Preuzische Asiatische Compagnie zu Embden auf Canton in China, 'founded in 1751 and intended as a gift for the king', but never presented to him as part of the set was lost in the shipwreck. When the Compagnie was discontinued in 1757 the surviving part of the service was sold at auction. Bearing in mind these dates, it is therefore certain that the service was ordered at Canton about 1753 or 1754. The tureen in the Fundatie van Renswoude in Utrecht, probably made between 1750 and 1760, has *famille rose* decoration of flowers and red hares' heads for handles (colour plate D). Later tureens like the one in the Bisdom van Vliet Museum[4] are deeper than the Frederick one of Plate 156, but with a foot shallower, for instance, than the tureen of Plate 165. The latter is adorned with a 'water-and-mountains' landscape in underglaze blue, with a pagoda and a gate in the foreground. This rather roughly-painted decoration lacks the attraction of the work belonging to the first half of the century. Judging from the style of painting and the hard blue, this tureen and the other parts of the service were made in the last quarter of the century. Though attempts to find a tureen made in Europe either in silver or pottery which could have been used as a model for the Chinese one have been in vain, the West must have supplied the original. Tureens strikingly similar in shape were made in porcelain at Vienna[5] around 1735–40,

[1] J. Gutschmidt, 'Das chinesische Tafelservice mit den groszen Königlich Preuszischen Staatswappen', *Zeitschrift des Vereins für die Geschichte Berlins*, 52 Jahrg., 4de part 1935. A. Westers, 'Een wapenschotel van Chine de Commande' (An armorial plate in *chine de commande*), *Bulletin Museum Boymans-van Beuningen*, 1959, p. 39.

[2] M. Beurdeley, op. cit., cat. 60, jardinière with the arms of O'Brien, made between 1746 and 1757.

[3] Dr. C. H. de Jonge, op. cit., ill. 250 and 263.

[4] M. Beurdeley, op. cit., cat. 80.

[5] W. B. Honey, *German porcelain*, pl. 17a.

and in earthenware at Rouen, 1720–30, and at Delft[1] and Sinceny[2] between 1750 and 1770.

Although rectangular tureens are common, octagonal ones, such as that of illustration 164, are rather rare. To judge from the style of the blue-and-white decoration of flowers and leaves, this tureen dates from the end of the eighteenth century.

Round and oval tureens

The round pottery tureen for soup was used in Europe long before 1700, and by the beginning of the eighteenth century, it formed an important part of dinner services. In *chine de commande* services there are several variations on this shape. One of the oldest made in China is the round tureen with vertical ribs belonging to the 'Feith' set. It has small holes in the top of the cover to let the steam escape. The knob on the cover consists of a bundle of stalks. An identical specimen may be found in the service in the Castle Hardenbroek, and in that which the Swedish author Count Carl Gustavus Tessin (1695–1770) had ordered in China about 1750. It is in the Gothenburg Museum. Because of this we know that this tureen was made between 1745 and 1750. Another kind of round tureen is in the Museum Bisdom van Vliet (Plate 166). This one has a globular body, pierced loop handles, and on the double-domed cover a fruit for a knob. The floral decoration is in blue. The oval tureen first appears in the thirties of the eighteenth century. One of the earliest is probably the one of Plate 175 belonging to a 'Parasol' set (see Chapter 15). A fine specimen with lobed body on a splay foot (Plate 159) is part of a set in the Bisdom van Vliet Museum.[3] It is painted with a floral decoration in *famille rose* and a 'spearhead' motif round the rim. In the same museum there is an oval tureen with rounded sides (Plate 163) decorated in blue with roughly painted flowering stalks and a 'Fitzhugh' rim. Quite a different character is shown in the tureen of Plate 183. Originally made for the English or American market, the elegant body in a late eighteenth-century shape has two twined handles, and the cover is crowned by a knob in Wedgwood style. A similar tureen in the Helena Woolworth-McCann collection was made between 1790 and 1800.[4] The shape was probably borrowed from a Wedgwood specimen of 1774. A much rarer shape is the oval tureen of Plate 160 with its slightly lobed body. It belongs to the William V set at The Hague.

Sometimes one comes across an oval tureen with handles formed from small winged heads (Plate 167), copied from a Meissen tureen[5] of about 1732.

[1] W. G. Fourest, *Les Faïences de Delft,* pl. XXXI, no. 1.   [2] A. Lane, op. cit., pl. 30 B, 31.

[3] Dr. de Jonge has reproduced this service in her article on the Bisdom van Vliet Museum in *Mededelingenblad* of the *Vereniging van Vrienden de Nederlandse Ceramiek,* no. 31, 1963, ill. 20 and 23, but she has mistakenly attributed it to 'Lowestoft'.

[4] J. G. Phillips, op. cit., p. 82 and 181. A similar one is in the Bissell Collection. Cf. J. McClure Mudge, op. cit., fig. 128a. See also B. L. Grandjean, op. cit., fig. 99.

[5] H. Rakebrand, *Meissener Tafelgeschirr des 18 Jahrhunderts* (Darmstadt 1918) pl. 2.

Dinner services

Quite different is the ragout-tureen of Plate 173, with handles at the front and back, which belongs to the Van Reverhorst service already mentioned. Very probably a silver covered dish served as a model here. In the second half, or towards the end of the century the covered vegetable-dish came into use. Both the shallow dish and the shaped cover are lobed at the corners, and the lid had a short-necked knob. The one shown here (Plate 182) was made between 1790 and 1800.

SAUCE-BOATS

An important piece in all dinner services was the sauce-boat. There were three common shapes used in the eighteenth century, all of which can still be found in silver. The oldest type[1] on a low foot has a pouring lip at both ends and two handles, one in the middle of each side. The silver model of about 1735 was imitated in pewter, pottery, and until the end of the eighteenth century, or even later, in Chinese porcelain (Plate 162).

The second model, which is found in silver from the forties of the century, has a boat-shaped body[2] ending in a pouring-lip at one end and in a handle at the other. In contrast with the silver prototype, which stands on small feet, the ceramic sauce-boat has a narrow or a splay-foot. As part of a dinner service made in China to the order of the West, this latter type (Plate 158, fig. 28) occurs in many variations. Sometimes the rim is wavy, sometimes straight. They are decorated in polychrome as well as in blue (the latter till well into the nineteenth century). Frequently they stand on a leaf-shaped tray.

A helmet-shaped sauce-boat, the third model, like the one in the Fries Museum (fig. 29) was probably also borrowed from an English silver original of about 1737.[3] The style of blue decoration indicates a date towards the end of the eighteenth century.

Sauce-boats were several times mentioned in the 'demands', the orders placed in China by the Dutch Company. At one time they were 'no good at all, are very narrow

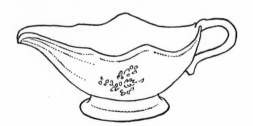

28. Sauce-boat with *famille rose* decoration of coat of arms and flowers. Mid eighteenth century. Ht. 7 cm., D. 22.5 cm. *Fundatie van Renswoude, Utrecht*

[1] H. M. Gans and Th. M. Duyvene de Wit-Klinkhamer, *Dutch Silver*, pl. 72.
[2] Ibid., pl. 99. B. Watney, *English Blue and White Porcelain of the Eighteenth Century*, London, 1963, pl. 30B, 18B.
[3] Judith Banister, *English Silver* (London, 1969), pl. 45. Ashmolean Museum, Oxford.

29. Helmet-shaped sauce-boat with blue-and-white decoration of flowers and fence. Late eighteenth century. Ht. 15 cm. *Fries Museum, Leeuwarden*

and shallow, hardly any liquid can be put in them'. In the demands for 1767 we read about them, 'The finer the stone the better; otherwise they are like Delft'.

DISHES

The plates and dishes which occur in various sizes are of course among the most important parts of the dinner services. The usual shapes for dinner-plates are the round flat one (Plate 179), or the round deep ones with broad rims, generally flat but sometimes wavy. Octagonal plates also occur. Oblong dishes with cut-off corners were placed under the tureens, against spilling, and were also used as serving dishes (Plates 165, 177), as also were large (Plates 158, 159) and small round and oval specimens (Plate 166). For their decoration the reader is referred to Chapters 9 and 15.

SALT-CELLARS

The salt-cellar was an important part of the dinner service too. In Europe it was made of silver, pewter and pottery and, from the end of the seventeenth century, also of Chinese porcelain. Several salt-cellars made in China were clearly copied from western ones (fig. 30). During the eighteenth century the most frequently occurring shape is the

30. Salt-cellar with decoration in blue-and-white of Chinese ladies, alternating with flowers in gadroon-like panels. Late seventeenth century. Ht. 6 cm. *Groninger Museum*

oval one (Plates 162 and 171), and the oblong one with cut off corners (Plate 172). The latter, which also exist in Delft ware, is decorated, for instance, with a floral ornament in *famille rose,* or with a coat of arms as seen on a specimen of the 'Feith' set. The small oval dish, usually on feet, with pierced outer wall and decorated in *famille rose* (Plate 159) came into being. Although it clearly suggests a silver salt-cellar, the origin of this shape must be sought in pottery shapes. An identical shape can be seen in a Delft salt-cellar,[1] decorated in blue, in the Centraal Museum at Utrecht. Like the Chinese specimen it has a small inner liner which can be taken out. On stylistic grounds it may be taken that this shape was first made between 1775 and 1785, and that it was still in use at the beginning of the nineteenth century is shown by pieces in the Bissell collection at Wilmington. The early eighteenth century hexagonal salt-cellar of Plate 176 is western in shape with its hollowed top and small feet, but the honeycomb openwork decoration of the walls and the blue-and-white floral motif are wholly Chinese.

MISCELLANEOUS ARTICLES

A square salad-bowl with tucked-in corners, adorned with a Chinese landscape (Plate 165), is undoubtedly borrowed from a Delft bowl of a shape that came into use between 1740 and 1750.[2] A specimen in the Bissell collection provides evidence that the type was still in use in the beginning of the nineteenth century. It is not possible to state with certainty whether this is the kind described in the 'demands' as 'The salad-basin fashioned like accompanying Delft sample with pattern of flower-work and without figures'.[3]

A round colander (Plate 159), with or without undulating rim, decorated in polychrome or blue, usually formed part of a dinner service from the second half of the eighteenth century. One may also come across small oval tureen-shaped covered dishes (Plates 168 and 170) probably used for butter, small oval basins with wavy rims (Plates 162 and 169), and oblong round or oval fish-platters with their strainer (Plate 180). The 'demands' mention 'Round fish-dishes with cut-through Plates; in the middle of the plate must be a hole wherein a finger can fit to lift it up.'[4] Basket-shaped oval fruit-dishes in openwork on an oval tray, with or without a wavy rim, and decorated in blue or in *famille rose,* usually formed part of late eighteenth century dinner services. In one type, the crossed bands of the openwork were often decorated with a floweret in relief on each crossing (Plate 158). Similar work is found in a Derby basket or basin,[5] dated between 1756 and 1760. The classical shape of the baskets made in China indicate a date after 1770.

[1] A table-piece made at Leeds about 1775 in the Fitzwilliam Museum at Cambridge has the same kind of small openwork dish. See D. C. Towner, *English Cream-coloured Earthenware,* p. 49.

[2] Dr. C. H. de Jonge, op. cit., ill. 272.

[3] J. G. A. N. de Vries, *Porselein,* p. 24. J. M. McClure, op. cit., fig. 128a.

[4] J. G. A. N. de Vries, op. cit., pp. 24-5.   [5] B. Watney, op. cit., pl. 64c.

The second kind (Plate 186) belongs to the dinner-set with the cat in the Fries Museum. The openwork walls of the basket are reminiscent of bamboo-stems.[1] This model is found in services made in China until the first thirty years of the nineteenth century or later. The custard-cup (Plate 173) is an occasional feature of services made for the Dutch market, like the Van Reverhorst set. One may also find ice-pails (Plate 184) and hot-water plates (Plate 185). The ice-pail has a shallow loose tray to put the ice on. The shape is perhaps borrowed from a Derby set.[2] The hot-water round or oval plates are about an inch in depth, have a nearly flat rim and two hollowed handles, one to pour the water in and the other to let the steam escape. As early as the sixteenth century double-walled bowls of 'Swatow' type were used in China. The hot water was poured in through an opening in the bottom.[3] A specimen of a hot-water plate may also be seen in the Helena Woolworth-McCann collection. It has the same shape as the one of Plate 185.

Chestnut-vases with openwork walls[4] were probably made for the British market. Sometimes they also form part of *chine de commande* sets ordered for the Netherlands.

Finally there is the punch-bowl ladle (Plate 188), without doubt an English invention. The specimen reproduced here consists of a lobed oval bowl with a porcelain projection to fit the handle. It is decorated in *famille rose* in the Lowestoft manner.

TUREEN IN THE SHAPE OF AN ANIMAL

In the second half of the eighteenth century tureens were also made in the shape of an animal, a duck, a goose, or a fish. The question is whether they were made to order for the West. But there is no doubt that this was the case, for the European public of that time was much interested in this kind of ware. Tureens made in the shape of an animal were also made at Delft, Chelsea, Strasburg, Höchst, Bayreuth, Marseilles and elsewhere,[5] in the second half of the century. They were used not for soup, but for pie: those sold at the sale of the Martha Raap estate in 1778, were described as 'Extrafine, coloured pie-tureen represented as a goose'. Such pieces are generally decorated in naturalistic style, the duck of Plate 191, for instance, being painted in iron-red, brown,

---

[1] J. McClure Mudge, op. cit., fig. 64, c. 1800–12. J. G. Phillips, op. cit., pl. 48–50. A similar openwork rim also appears on a dish decorated in *famille rose* in W. Gulland, *Chinese Porcelain*, 2nd ed., vol. II, ill. 680, 681 and 693.

[2] W. E. Cox, *The Book of Pottery and Porcelain*, pp. 756–7. They were also made at Fürstenburg, see E. Hannover, *Pottery and Porcelain* (London, 1925) vol. III, fig. 289. An ice-bucket decorated in blue is in the museum at Winterthur, U.S.A., see J. McClure Mudge, op. cit., figs. 76 and 128a.

[3] B. Gyllensvärd, *Chinese Ceramics in the Carl Kempe Collection* (Stockholm, 1965) ill. 837

[4] J. G. Phillips, op. cit., p. 129, pl. 50.

[5] J. G. Phillips, op. cit., p. 174, pl. 72, 73. M. Beurdeley, op. cit., cat. 97, 103, 181. Dr. C. H. de Jonge, op. cit., p. 325. J. L. Dixon, *English Porcelain of the Eighteenth Century* (London, 1952) pl. 19. W. Cox, op. cit., p. 755, fig. 1077 and Arthur Lane, *French Faience*, pl. 67B.

green, blue, and a little gold. The fact that tureens in the shape of birds, such as white geese, were presented as late as 1803 to the India Marine Society at Salem, U.S.A., proves how much they were to the public taste.[1] The tureen in the shape of a fish (Plate 190) was also made to order of the West, as is proved by a specimen in the Gothenburg Historical Museum.[2]

[1] J. McClure Mudge, op. cit., p. 74.
[2] Stig Roth, *Chinese Porcelain imported by the Swedish East India Company in the Gothenburg Historical Museum*, p. 15, fig. 36.

15 · Eighteenth-century Chinese porcelain decorated with European subjects

In Chapter 12 K'ang Hsi porcelain decorated in underglaze blue was discussed. Here blue and polychrome decorations used after 1720 will be dealt with. During the reign of K'ang Hsi European subjects were only sporadically copied, but from the second quarter of the eighteenth century the Chinese porcelain painters copied prints, drawings and perhaps even paintings, sent to Canton.

Plates and saucers in particular were decorated with scenes and figure subjects and coats of arms, since the flat planes of those pieces were eminently suitable to such portrayals. Nonetheless punch-bowls, beakers, jugs, tea-things, tureens, and pilgrim flasks have been decorated from time to time with similar representations.

A study of Chinese porcelain painted with subjects taken from European pictures, drawings and prints, reveals that it is exceptional to find one and the same composition painted on European and on Chinese wares. However the seamstress of Plate 211, whose portrait appears on Chinese porcelain, is also represented on a Delft brush-back in the Rijksmuseum at Amsterdam.

It strikes one that though scenes borrowed from Watteau and Boucher were frequently used in the decoration of both Chinese and European porcelain, they are never the same scenes. On the other hand, the same subject has figured on Italian majolica as well as on Chinese porcelain—but here it goes back to different originals. The Judgement of Paris (Plate 225), for example, which frequently appears on Chinese porcelain, is wholly different from the same composition on Italian majolica. The same is as true of subjects such as Perseus and Andromeda or Europa and the Bull as for a Crucifixion or a harbour-view.

The copying of European subjects was a difficult task for the Chinese porcelain painters, because these originals were manifestations of a culture which was in all respects different from their own. Even though the Chinese followed the examples given them as accurately as possible, elements may be detected which are not western

Eighteenth-century Chinese porcelain with European decoration

elements. When a painting was executed by a poor copyist, the Chinese character comes to the fore more clearly than when a skilful painter did the job. In this connection contemporary opinions may be valuable and Père du Halde points out that the Cantonese were very clever when it came to making exact copies of European drawings. According to Samuel Shaw,[1] who in 1784 was supercargo of the American ship *Empress of China,* and from 1785 till 1790 American consul in Canton, many painters were quite good at copying, but were lacking in original talent. When one compares how a European and a Chinese artist have painted a genre piece the different conceptions are striking. The former knows how to portray such scenes with charm in an attractive way, and in a manner characteristic of the eighteenth century. These qualities are, in general, lacking in Chinese copies. In a similar way the Chinese painters had no notion of armorial bearings. Sometimes they made errors in orthography, because they did not know the meaning of what they saw. In this way they painted under a representation *in encre de chine* of *Les Trois Maries* (The Three Marias), *Les Trois Marins* (The Three Sailors). On another piece a lily in an escutcheon was changed into a cross (family Moens), or they copied an explanatory statement like, 'These are the arms of myself and my wife', or 'Stink and Stank' was painted instead of 'Think and Thank'. As yet another time the instructions 'red', 'green' and 'blue' were copied with the subject, with the extra mistake that under the red enamel the word 'blue' appeared.

Notwithstanding the instruction in perspective given them by Italian and French artists, the Chinese were in great difficulties when it came to a three-dimensional representation with shading, and they were barely successful when applying western perspective.

From the reign of Yung Chêng (1723–35) scenes as well as armorial bearings were almost always painted in colours. Just as during the Ming period, plates and saucers were made with or without a rim in Ch'ing times also. From the last quarter of the seventeenth century the export trade kept increasing, and the Chinese porcelain makers began to adapt their porcelain more and more to the taste of their European customers. The latter wanted round, and later also octagonal, plates and dishes with broad, flat rims, sometimes lobed or scalloped like the metal or earthenware ones in use in Europe. The wide, flat rims[2] were originally probably meant to put herbs or seasoning on, and they first appear on plates made for the western market. Those plates are but rarely adorned with braiding or other decoration in relief[3] as was sometimes the case in Europe. Occasionally a *bianco-sopra-bianco* decoration was used (Plate 245), for example a moulded decoration of tendrils with leaves and flowers. Usually the decoration on the centre, the well-border, and the rim of the plates or dishes are quite unrelated, and this type of decoration accentuates the shape of the piece.

[1] J. McClure Mudge, *Chinese Export Porcelain for the American Trade, 1785–1835,* p. 150.
[2] W. B. Honey, *Guide to the Later Chinese Porcelain,* p. 32.
[3] J. G. Phillips, *China Trade Porcelain,* p. 130, pl. 51.

Eighteenth-century Chinese porcelain with European decoration

Accurate dating of porcelain made to order is possible only when there is a dated bill, as in the case of the Peers set (Chapter 14), when a coat of arms is known (Plate 160), or when the porcelain is provided with a date. But sometimes two plates with identical decoration may bear different dates, as in the plate of Chris. Schooneman. The one shown here (Plate 244) is clearly dated 1756, while the example illustrated by Jourdain and Jenyns[1] is dated 1736. This happened because European numerals meant nothing to the Chinese painter; so the decoration as well as the numerals must be taken into account when dating a piece. Even without the correct date, it is in many cases possible to establish the approximate period when a piece was made, on stylistic grounds. Here the decoration of rim or border, subjects, colours used, and in some cases the model that was copied, when it is known, can give an indication. The shape of the foot-rim may also be helpful: in the Yung Chêng period, it becomes V-shaped.

It is not known for certain who actually ordered the porcelain decorated with European subjects, but it seems probable that it was made on demand by the different Companies, individual traders or private persons, either direct or using a local merchant as intermediary. There is no doubt that the Dutch Company in Canton quite often gave instructions for Chinese porcelain painted with specific scenes. In 1779 and 1780, for instance, they ordered thousands of pieces of porcelain with the *Kersenplukker* motif, the 'Cherrypicker, and a rim decoration imitating braided cord' (Plate 213). This name was the one given to the well-known scene of Plate 214.

RIMS

Before the influence of the West in the decoration on the rims of bowls, plates or vases started to penetrate in the second quarter of the eighteenth century, the Chinese had already for centuries decorated them in their own way. The characteristic Wan Li rim was discussed on p. 49. The rims of the K'ang Hsi plates are painted in a variety of styles: sometimes in underglaze blue, or in the colours of the *famille verte,* or with oblong panels against a background of diaperwork strewn with flowerets.

Panels or cartouches, as ornaments on rims of plates and dishes, occurring in China even before Wan Li times, were developed during the Wan Li and Transitional periods, and from the time of K'ang Hsi are much in evidence on *chine de commande.* Although this type of decoration is common in the Netherlands, for instance on silver dishes, from the beginning of the seventeenth century, this is unlikely to have influenced its Chinese counterpart. One of the oldest specimens in the Netherlands is on a silver dish by Adam van Vianen in the Rijksmuseum, made in 1614. Around the same time in Holland, the rims of tin-glazed Delft plates are ornamented with panels, but the decorations in the panels are derived from Chinese Wan Li emblems. Besides those we have rims with panels taken from Italian plates, made in the last quarter of the fifteenth

[1] Margaret Jourdain and R. Soame Jenyns, *Chinese Export Art in the Eighteenth Century,* plate 99.

G. Armorial plate with *famille verte* decoration. First quarter eighteenth century

century.[1] The panels, the short sides of which are marked by a curved line or three short dashes, are painted with plants, flowers, insects, birds or emblems. The spaces between the panels are generally filled in with diaper pattern (see e.g. Plates 231, 264, 265), which is built up from lozenges, hexagons (honeycombs) or circles. Diaperwork had already appeared in the K'ang Hsi period as a decoration of narrow rims, and by the time of Yung Chêng it had become one of the most frequent ornaments. It was used in *famille rose* especially, for instance in the 'seven-bordered' decoration of Plate 85. Panels with freely-drawn (Plate 265) or more formal (Plate 271) nosegays, alternating with a Chinese landscape, appear from the first quarter of the eighteenth century. Sometimes one also finds a decoration in shaped panels against a white background (Plates 266, 271).

Because the earliest appearance of European motifs in rim-decoration is at the beginning of the eighteenth century, sixteenth and seventeenth century western rim decoration had no influence on Chinese porcelain. Louis XIV motifs were the first to be used as rim ornaments on export wares (Plates 241, 270). As a rule, this type of decoration was a free interpretation of ornamental engravings by A. Berain (1678–1726), Daniel Marot (1661–1752) and Claude Gillot (1673–1722). At about this time, that is from the first quarter of the eighteenth century, more and more porcelain with European decoration was being ordered from China.

But, besides a European or quasi-European rim-decoration, Chinese ornamentation remains, often occurring on plates (Plates 233, 266) and dishes which have western subjects in the centre. The influence of the ornamental designs by the French artists already mentioned appears in the rim-decoration, painted in red and blue enamels and gold, of the cup and saucer of Plate 275. This decoration of angular festoons enclosing dancing manikins shows similarity to a rim-decoration which occurs on a series of buffoons in prints after Callot, in a book published at Amsterdam[2] in 1716.

Another Louis XIV type of rim decoration consists of a festoon of tendrils,[3] interspersed with four escutcheons and four swags alternating with acanthus leaves. Painted in red, green and rose-red enamels and gold, it is used on the plate of Plate 272, where it is combined with a well-border of diaperwork and shaped panels. The latter are filled with a quasi-Louis XIV motif. A Louis XIV rim decoration found in many different variations and generally executed in *encre de chine* was used on plates wholly decorated in this technique (Plate 298), as well as in combination with enamel paints

---

[1] See Dr. C. H. de Jonge, *Oud-Nederlandsche Majolica en Delftsch Aardewerk,* ill. 20, 21.

[2] This book *Il calotto resuscitato* has a Dutch subtitle which translated reads 'The world is full of fools' nests, the smallest buffoons are the best'. The small figures painted on the cup and saucer of illustration 275 are perhaps from Callot (1592–1635). W. B. Honey, *Dresden China* (London, 1954) p. 16.

[3] This motif was probably taken from engravings by Daniet Marot, for it is reminiscent of two compositions by him for tiles in vertical wall panels. See A. Lane, 'Delft Tiles from Hampton Court and Daniel Marot', *Bulletin of the Rijksmuseum,* VII, 1959, pp. 12–21.

31. Rim-decoration on plate from Du Paquier porcelain factory Vienna, 1730–40

(Plates 270, 273). It is seen as the well border on the oblong dish with scalloped rim, decorated with the arms of the Falck family (Plate 273). A similar ornamentation (fig. 31), also executed in *encre de chine,* is found in Europe on Vienna porcelain from the factory of Claude du Paquier (1730–44) and it is possible that it reached China via the Netherlands. Vienna porcelain was much in vogue there, as is evident from a paragraph in the *Leidsche Courant* of 1st January 1729, where the *beauté singulière* of this porcelain is described.

Another popular rim decoration found on *chine de commande* is the meander scroll (fig. 60 and Plate 274), used in combination with a shell or a flower. Was the painter inspired here by the Buddhist symbols of the shell and the wheel? The rim of the dish of Plate 273 is decorated with a scroll pattern, divided in the middle of each side by a formal motif framed by leaves.

A cornucopia,[1] a shell, and a rococo trelliswork motif were painted in polychrome enamel on the rim of a plate with the arms of the Snoeck family (fig. 32). The same motifs appear on a set of plates in the Fries Museum, ornamented with scenes showing

32. Plate, blue-and-white, with arms of Snoeck family in gold; rim painted with shell motif and cornucopia. 1760–70. *Helena Woolworth-McCann Collection, New York*

[1] J. G. Phillips, op. cit., p. 71, pl. 5.

aspects of tea cultivation. The elements of this border decoration are for the most part European, especially the cornucopia, the shell which often appears on Rouen earthenware between 1750 and 1760, and on Meissen porcelain between 1745 and 1750, and also the trelliswork. The latter motif features in designs for ornaments by the Frenchmen Pillement (1727–1808) and Jacques de Joue (1687–1761). It is, however, remarkable that this western element of decoration is used here with so typically Chinese a subject as the cultivation of tea. We may therefore conclude that these plates were made for export to Europe.[1]

A decoration which came into use a little earlier than the cornucopia was also taken from Meissen (fig. 33) where it was painted in gold between 1723 and 1735 by J. G. Herold. It was copied on Chinese porcelain (Plate 242) between 1745 and 1760. Altered a little it also appears as a well-border decoration, in combination with a purely Chinese rim-decoration. A recurring motif on *chine de commande,* which probably originated in Canton, is reminiscent of the fleur-de-lis (fig. 54). Phillips[2] has given it the name 'spearhead' motif (Plates 231, 244, 270) and surmises that it is a simplification of the lambrequin motif. It was sometimes used in gold with red outlines on the rim and the well-borders of plates. It also appears on English Bow ware and on a vase, Chinese in shape and decoration, made at Worcester[3] in about 1755. If the Worcester porcelain painter took this motif from China, it must have been known there before 1755, and so it is not impossible that it was used in the forties of the century. It was used on *chine de commande* for the American market until after 1800.

By the end of the eighteenth century two distinct styles of rim-decoration on *chine de commande* had become established; for instance, on dinner and other services. This is particularly apparent from services decorated in underglaze blue. In fulfilling orders placed by western traders, in the years between about 1740–50 and 1785, although the European influence had steadily increased, the Chinese decoration always remained in use to some extent. The Chinese porcelain painters not only copied the style of the French kings and of *L'empire,* but also made use of the decorations on English ceramics, including festoons (Plate 279) sometimes broken by a central flower motif, or short garlands (Plate 280) tied with a flowery bow. Other rim-decorations are the braided

33. Meissen rim-decoration. Similar decoration is common on Chinese porcelain after 2nd quarter of eighteenth century, in gold with red outline. Also found on well-borders

[1] Nanne Ottema, *Chineesche Ceramiek,* pl. 216.
[2] J. G. Phillips, op. cit., p. 58. H. Garner, *Oriental Blue-and-White,* pl. 30c and 75.
[3] J. L. Dixon, *English Porcelain of the Eighteenth Century,* pl. 47 (Bow), pl. 69 (Worcester).

Eighteenth-century Chinese porcelain with European decoration

cord, the Greek key border, the chain (Plate 281), a row of arrow-heads, or a scroll of flowery tendrils (Plate 281) and dotted lines. By comparing these decorations with those on European porcelain, it is often possible to date a piece.

Some museums, among them the Victoria and Albert, have Chinese plates with four rim-decorations, each with a different number.[1] The name of a Chinese trader of Canton, Syngghong (c. 1790), is written on the back of one of these plates. A customer could order the particular border decoration he wanted simply by giving its number to a western merchant; and in the course of time he would receive plates painted with that decoration. The Rijksmuseum at Amsterdam has two of these plates with classical motifs on their rims.

Finally, there is the Fitzhugh rim-decoration (Plate 177). It occurs in pieces for the English and the American markets in the last 30–35 years of the eighteenth century, and the beginning of the nineteenth,[2] and from time to time one comes across it on blue-and-white dinner services exported to the Netherlands. This decoration was probably not applied at Canton but at Ching-tê Chên. The Fitzhugh pattern is usually made up of diaperwork with butterflies and flowers. Sometimes it also includes Greek key or meander borders, of which various diaper patterns form symmetrical parts. It is, however, difficult to trace the origin of this pattern. It is not impossible that it developed from Louis XIV rims, which appear on English and Dutch Delft plates, the latter marked A.P.K.[3] until the sixties, and on Makkum ware (fig. 34) until the eighties

34. Degenerate Louis XIV rim-decoration on Dutch Makkum plate by Jan Eelkes, centre with decoration of Lot and daughters. 1779. *Collection Bodenheim-Rehrman, Amsterdam*

[1] J. G. Phillips, op. cit., p. 36, fig. 22.

[2] According to M. Beurdeley, *Porcelaine de la Compagnie des Indes*, p. 32, a certain Fitzhugh was the first who ordered porcelain with this kind of decoration. J. A. Lloyd Hyde in *Oriental Lowestoft*, pl. VII points out that 'Fitzhugh' stood perhaps for a botched Foochow. For the American market, services with this decoration were also made in orange and green. A butterfly also appears as a rim-decoration in sepia of plates with Juno and the peacock on the central part.

[3] Dr. C. H. de Jonge, op. cit., pl. VIII.

of the eighteenth century. One should also think of the rims of the 'Fan'—or 'peacock's tail' dishes from the third quarter of the eighteenth century.[1] In England, the Fitzhugh pattern was painted, among others, on Derby[2] ware of c. 1770.

Whereas the Fitzhugh pattern is found from time to time on Chinese porcelain in Europe, it seems that pieces with the so-called Canton and Nanking rims,[3] which frequently appear on Chinese porcelain for the American market, were not sent to the Netherlands.

Subjects painted on porcelain in China to the order of the West (those present in the Netherlands will be chiefly discussed), such as genre-paintings, 'gallant', mythological and religious subjects, harbour-views and ships, portraits, political events, and 'armorial ware' will be dealt with in this sequence.

GENRE-SCENES

There are two subjects on *chine de commande,* the 'Ladies with a Parasol', and the 'Doctors', which were probably made from designs by Cornelis Pronk. These are the only plates of which both the designer and the people who ordered the design, the Dutch East India Company, are known.[4] A third design, called 'the Bower', was in all probability also designed by Pronk; also a decoration of an acanthus leaf on a yellow background, shown in fig. 35 (see p. 152).

35. Plate with a design of a violet acanthus leaf on a yellow background, c. 1735 to 1740. *Metropolitan Museum, New York*

[1] Dr. C. H. de Jonge, op. cit., ill. 285.

[2] B. Watney, *English Blue and White Porcelain of the Eighteenth Century,* pl. 58A.

[3] J. McClure Mudge, *Chinese Export Porcelain for the American Trade, 1785–1835,* figs. 75–79. In Canton and Nanking borders there is a different pattern of crossing lines.

[4] J. de Hullu, 'De Porseleinhandel der Oost-Indische Compagnie en Cornelis Pronk als haar teekenaar', *Oud Holland,* 1915. J. G. A. N. de Vries, *Porselein,* pp. 8–9. T. Volker, *The Japanese Porcelain trade after 1683,* pp. 78 ff, ill. 23a, b, 24 and 25.

Eighteenth-century Chinese porcelain with European decoration

Pronk received the commission in August 1734. The agreement says that Cornelis Pronk, painter and drawing-master residing at Amsterdam 'shall make all designs and models' (probably drawn profiles) 'to our satisfaction, of all such porcelains as will be ordered from time to time in The Indies, with all their colours properly put in, blue as well as gilt and other colours, and in various fashions; that he shall have to be occupied at this during the whole course of the year, and for this enjoy a sum of 1200 florins current money each year, beginning with May 1st of this year 1734, and to be paid from this time onwards every half year the true half to the sum of six hundred florins', etc. . . . 'Everything in due time and as long as the Honourable Company will think it necessary to employ him. And as every piece or model which shall be chosen to be sent to the Indies will have to be copied six times, the aforesaid Monsieur Pronk, occupied at making the models shall be allowed to have those models or drawings copied for account of the Company and to have his costs or what he shall have to spend and pay to the copyists, reimbursed to him separately above the aforesaid 1200 florins for the period of three consecutive years.'

We can ascribe to Pronk the drawing of one plate of the 'Ladies with a Parasol' (fig. 36), and a salt-cellar in the Rijksmuseum in Amsterdam. There are several versions, Chinese as well as Japanese. The best-known plates are those with decorated rims, sometimes in underglaze blue, and with the clothing of the ladies painted in iron-red enamel, the short coat of the lady in the foreground being adorned with gold. The closest to the artist's design are the plates with a rim-decoration of four rows of 'honey-combs'. The type in the Municipal Museum at The Hague is perhaps the oldest. It is painted in rose-red, light blue, light green, yellow and brown enamels (Plate 195). Painted less accurately and somewhat more carelessly are the plates which have only three rows of honeycombs, and of these more than one version is known. On the best specimen (Plate 193) in the Groninger Museum, the lady holding the parasol is still a European but with Chinese features. In the versions in the Zeeuws Museum at Middelburg and the Palazzo Venezia in Rome (Plate 175, part of a dinner-service of 300), the ladies are still more oriental and the one in the foreground is, moreover, badly drawn. Other differences, for instance, are in the grasses in the foreground and behind the figures and in the parasol. The rims of the 'Parasol' plates usually have, alternately, an oblong cartouche with a bird, and a narrow panel with a Chinese lady. The shape of these cartouches is different too in the different versions. According to Beurdeley,[1] Pronk took his designs from a small saucer in the Groninger Museum with the same

[1] M. Beurdeley, op. cit., p. 61, ill. 32. M. Feddersen, *Chinese Decorative Art*, p. 97, says that in a private collection at Hamburg there is a plate with this design, but with the mark of the Cozzi factory at Venice. Fr. Stazzi, *Italian Porcelain*, Milan, 1964, fig. 35. Miss De Visser notes that the Company tried to have similar plates made in Japan, but without success. Probably the Japanese version was ordered by private people who were prepared to pay a higher price than the East India Company. T. Volker, *The Japanese Porcelain Trade*, etc., p. 79; R. Soame Jenyns, *Japanese Porcelain*, pp. 70–73, pl. 46a, b.

36. Design for 'Parasol' plate, probably by C. Pronk to the order of the Dutch East India Company. 1734–37. *Rijksmuseum, Amsterdam*

subject (Plate 192); but on this piece the birds are walking in front of the figures instead of towards them, and because of this the result lacks the unity of the Pronk design.

Finally, there is a version in *famille rose*, which has only two rows[1] of honeycombs, without panels on the rim. These plates, the design of which is an accurate copy and properly drawn, are probably of the same date as the plate at The Hague.

The design as such must have been quite the fashion, because it is also found on blue-and-white tea services, be it more or less badly drawn. In the Rijksmuseum at

[1] M. Beurdeley, op. cit., fig. 35, Paris, Musée Guimet.

Amsterdam there is a coffee-pot (Plate 194) in blue-and-white, and on this the design is very close to the best plate version of Plate 195.

The design called 'The Doctors' shows three Chinese seated, and in some versions one more, standing, behind a low table (Plate 197) under a tree. It is painted in rose-red, red and green enamels, and is adorned with gold. The rim is decorated with fishes in oval medallions, with birds between them, and on the outer rim triangles of diaper-work. A design (Plate 198) for this plate, but without the standing man and without the birds and the fishes, is published in reproduction by Van Goidsenhoven.[1] Western influence is visible in the shape of the table on which a large dish is standing. Pronk, if he is the original designer, probably took his subject from a Chinese prototype of which he did not know the meaning. Perhaps the seated Chinese are deities, which is suggested by their large and long ears, or perhaps they were meant to be old gentlemen playing Chinese chess as they are in some versions.[2]

This design was much in vogue too. It is found on plates and dishes of various dimensions, from 6 to 20 inches, on cups and saucers, and on bottle-shaped vases (Plate 201), with the subject painted in enamel colours, and also in blue-and-white on saucers (Plate 199), and on a small jug (Plate 200).

The original design of the 'Bower' subject on plates and dishes painted in polychrome enamels (Plate 202), rightly attributed to Pronk, has alas not yet come to light. In an arbour, which is more like a *berceau* or bower, as found in eighteenth-century gardens, two ladies in quasi-Chinese dress are seated with a boy, and other boys are playing hide-and-seek round the bower. On the diaper-ornamented rim there are cartouches with small nosegays and butterflies. Between the cartouches there are acanthus leaves at the well edge and shells at the outer rim. In contrast with both the former designs, this one is clearly inspired by a European example. On beer-mugs, and other articles of daily use such as dishes, this design also appears in blue-and-white.

The scene of a lady and a gentleman in eighteenth-century dress, promenading a dog in a park (Plate 203) dates from the end of the K'ang Hsi period. The decoration is wholly in underglaze blue, with overglaze red and some gold in the vein of Japanese Imari. Instead of European trees and flowers the Chinese porcelain painter has painted those of his native country. The rim is also decorated with Chinese flowers and symbols. Some people choose to see Louis XIV and Madame de Maintenon in this walking

[1] J. P. van Goidsenhoven, *La Céramique chinoise sous les Ts'ing*, 1644–1851, ill. 264. In Jacquemart and Le Blant, op. cit., a vase with three 'sages' is represented on pl. XI. Cups and saucers also exist with these figures.

[2] I would like to point out that the pseudo-Chinese seated at the right is holding a fish, clearly visible in illustration 201, but also present in the others. This suggests the Parable of the Fishes in pseudo-Chinese shape whilst, regarding this vase especially, the old Chinese trinity in portrayals, Lao Tzǔ, Confucius and Buddha, comes to mind. Whatever the original meaning of the design had been, perhaps no more than three gentlemen with a big fish with in the 'four men version' the fishmonger at the back, such as it is, it is a fine piece of *chinoiserie*. [Translator's note.]

couple, but in fact they must be a Dutch rather than a French pair. This is indicated by their dress, which is not smart and gay enough to warrant such an attribution. In the Netherlands this subject is sometimes called the 'Portrait of a happy Fries couple', and without any good cause was also dubbed the 'Dutch Governor General Diederik Durven (1676–1740) and his lady'. Hence it is in England sometimes called 'Governor Duff'. There are several versions on plates, dishes, trays, etc., with considerable differences in the composition, especially in the figures, which are rather clumsily drawn. It is clear that the Chinese painter was also at a loss when painting the dog, which is generally out of drawing.

A mezzotint of a skating peasant couple by C. Dusart (1660–1704) was copied fairly well on a plate (Plate 204). The figures are drawn against a brown background and for their dress red, purple and light blue are used. This more pictorial treatment of a subject came into use in the Yung Chêng period. The rim of this plate is decorated with exotic fruits alternating with flowers, and is painted in red, yellow, green and blue enamels. This rim-decoration, unique of its kind, reminds one of the chased rims with fruits of seventeenth-century silver dishes. A similar pictorial treatment is used on a plate decorated with two Scots (Plate 205), in the Zeeuws Museum at Middelburg. It is also apparent on the plate with the fishing boy of Plate 206. The former plate was doubtlessly ordered for the British market. One of the men is at the 'stand-easy' position and the other about to walk playing the bagpipes; both men wear a yellow, blue and red checked kilt. The rim is decorated with oblong cartouches, two with finely-drawn Chinese landscapes, the other with a bird on a branch.

The fishing boy of Plate 206 is taken from a Dutch print (Plate 207) by Abr. Bloemaert (1564–1651), and the plate was doubtlessly made for the Dutch market. This plate, which one also finds executed entirely in *encre de chine* (Plate 298), is, for the manner of painting as well as the fine violet-tinted watercolour-like paints, assuredly one of the most beautiful pieces of porcelain made to order. The Dutch landscape in the background of the specimen illustrated here becomes a Chinese mountain landscape on a different version of the subject. On the former, the panels on the rim are painted with Chinese mountain-and-water landscapes, against a background of diaperwork with chrysanthemums in between.

In contrast with the decoration on this plate, which was faithful to its original, is the decoration called 'Spring', after an engraving by Larmessin from a painting by Nicolas Lancret (1690–1743). Here very little is left of the original composition (Plate 208), and the charm which characterizes the print is absent in the porcelain. The print shows a young lady with a basket of fruit and a young man holding a spade, whilst a girl in simpler dress is watering flowers. Apart from the fact that the Chinese painter has replaced the fountain at the left by a tree, he also left out the trees in the background (Plate 210), in this way making it easier for himself to use this subject. Whereas on a plate, and on a boat-shaped small tray (Plate 210), the composition itself was left more or less intact, on the tea-jar of Plate 209, it has been split into two parts and the figures, painted in rose-red, with some black and gold, have become quite deformed.

One of the best-known subjects is that of the 'Cherrypicker' after a print by Nic. Ponce (1746–1831). Painted in green, lilac, red and blue, it occurs over and over again on plates and tea services, and shows a young man standing on a ladder, throwing cherries to a young woman who catches them in her skirt. According to De Vries[1] the French seek to identify the man as Jean Jacques Rousseau and the woman as Madame de Warrens. Here too the Chinese painter has simplified the composition, first by leaving out the donkey present on the print, and secondly by considerably reducing the number of the trees. The woman, who is always shown as a Chinese, is painted, like the trees, in a hard green, and she exists in several versions. In one (Plate 214) the woman is standing like her original in the print; on the other (Plate 213) she is sitting on the ground dressed in a yellow coatee, and the man is wearing a gilt coat. In the first version the lovely girl of the print has been changed into an unattractive woman with sharp features. The first consignment of porcelain decorated with this subject was probably shipped to Europe in the early seventies of the eighteenth century.

The Flehite Museum at Amersfoort owns a set of fluted cups and saucers, decorated with a European (Plate 216) wearing a kimono painted in red and gold, and lying on a Chinese bed, the scene enclosed in a blue border, the background strewn with flowerets. The whole decoration of this set is very painstakingly executed.

It would take too long to describe separately all the genre subjects used on porcelain made to order. Among other popular ones are the scenes known as a 'European riding an Elephant', a 'Hunter with a Dog talking to a Lady seated behind a Tree' (after Moreau le Jeune), 'Don Quixote and Sancho Panza', 'Drinking Peasants round a Table' (after David Teniers), a 'Gentleman and Lady sitting on the Floor looking at a Bird-cage', and a 'Flute-playing Gentleman and Lady with Parrot'. This last is shown on our colour plate E. A remarkable feature of the plate is the rim decorated in *bianco-sopra-bianco,* and panels painted in purple with Chinese landscapes, all against a background of mountains.

As already mentioned, scenes were painted on vases too. This is shown in Plate 215, where the vase is also decorated with both a European ornament round the neck and with a Chinese one of flowers. On the sides of the vase are two scenes: one shows an interior with red-brown walls where a gentleman, wearing a wig and a green coat, and smoking a long clay pipe, is sitting at a table watching his Chinese 'boy' who is in a red-brown kimono pouring out his gin. The other scene shows a young woman wearing a straw hat and holding a basket of fruit, and is a subject taken from a French print. Both these portraits are well painted, and only the harsh green used for the trees betrays that they were executed by a Chinese porcelain painter.

Finally, mention may be made of the very prettily painted seamstress of Plate 211.

[1] J. G. A. N. de Vries, op. cit., p. 16.

Eighteenth-century Chinese porcelain with European decoration

This is one of the rare cases where *encre de chine* is combined with enamel paints. The Chinese painter has succeeded extremely well in this faithful copy of a European original, perhaps a print by B. Picart.

'GALLANT' AND IDYLLIC SCENES

Prints after paintings by artists like Watteau (1684–1721), Lancret, Boucher and Picart (1673–1733), were copied more or less faithfully on Chinese porcelain. One of the most beautiful plates is the well-drawn, charming representation of the fable of La Fontaine, *Les oies du Frère Philippe,* which inspired Lancret's painting (Plate 217). The composition shows a monk, Frère Philippe, holding on to a young man wearing a blue coat and red knee-breeches, who is taken unawares by the appearance of two lovely young ladies under a parasol held high by a young moor. The Middelburg Museum owns a plate decorated with this subject (Plate 218), on which the ladies are dressed in a rose-red and in a yellow skirt, both with blue bodice. A set of similar plates is in the Municipal Museum at The Hague,[1] and on these the dresses are painted in a grey wash with the faces and the legs in flesh-colour. The figures on these plates are excellently copied so that the people look Europeans and not Orientals. The rim is decorated with alternately large and small sprays of rose-red and green flowers.

Beautiful in colour, but less good in the drawing, is the scene on the cup and saucer of Plate 220, showing a gentlemen in a rose-red coat and a lady in a blue and yellow dress. The lady is holding a branch with leaves and a flower, certainly Chinese rather than European in conception. In contrast with other versions of this plate the lady on this specimen is decently dressed.

Prints after Watteau supply yet more subject-matter for decoration, such as *Les Coquettes* or *Le Retour du Bal,* a print by H. S. Thomassin (Plate 219). The scene is painted on the porcelain saucer (Plate 221) in yellow, rose-red and turquoise enamels outlined in *encre de chine,* and so approximates to the character of the print. It shows Italian comedians in fancy dress. The Chinese painter has succeeded rather poorly in his copy of the print in reversed image on the saucer, and he has not really rendered the character of a Watteau painting. Did the Chinese porcelain painter copy his subject from a sample print or did he make use of a stencil? If the latter technique was employed the drawing must have been put face down on the saucer thus producing the scene in reversed image on the porcelain.

A very fine dish is that shown on colour plate F, with a European sitting on the ground and leaning against a large vase which has Chinese decoration. Behind the vase is the head of a boy, and at the right of the scene is a seated Chinese lady. The decoration is painted in delicate colours: light purple, light green, yellow and blue. In view of its

[1] In the Victoria and Albert Museum is a plate decorated in sepia and painted in red and gold. Illustrated in M. Jourdain and R. Soame Jenyns, op. cit., pl. 92.

exceptional quality and of the fact that on the back, in two concentric blue circles, is the reign-mark of Yung Chêng, it may be that this dish was made for the Chinese market.

Of very different character is the remarkable scene of a Chinese interior (Plate 222), in which a bewigged European gentleman dressed in a green kimono[1] stands looking over his shoulder at a short half-naked person, probably a servant functioning as a tribute-bearer, leading a spotted dog on a chain. The Chinese painter, whether purposely or inadvertently, placed the Europeans against a background filled with Chinese symbolism; for he has put peacock's feathers, two branches of coral, and a fungus (ling chih) in the big vase adorned with meander and *ju-i* motifs, which stands at the back of the scene. The feathers are symbolic of high rank, the others both of longevity.

The Boymans-van Beuningen Museum owns a small saucer with a slightly naughty portrait painted in polychrome enamels of 'Perette and the milk-pail'. A young woman carrying a milk-pail on her head is stepping over a stile; the saucer shows her with her petticoats raised.[2]

Pilgrim bottles (see Chapter 9) were also painted with European scenes. The bottle of Plate 223, with dragon-shaped handles on a square neck, shows a love-scene on both sides of the body. The side shown here is of a pair of lovers lying beneath a tree, both dressed in eighteenth-century western attire. The scene is painted in yellow, rose-red, green and light blue enamels, and is enacted against a Chinese mountain landscape. Hovering above the couple on a kind of cloud one sees a trumpet-blowing angel. All the figures, as usual, betray a western influence.

MYTHOLOGICAL SCENES

Mythological scenes were very fashionable in the late eighteenth century; the fact that women in the nude could be portrayed in this way was doubtless their great attraction. In general the Chinese porcelain painter is somewhat at a loss when drawing western nudes. This is quite apparent in the scene 'Neptune and the Nereids' of Plate 224, painted in blue on a large dish and on a tea service. This treatment of the subject brings an involuntary reminder of Dutch blue tiles decorated with mermen, mermaids and dolphins, but, in contrast with the former decoration the latter consists of a few lines only. It is also possible that this scene was taken from similar ones which were painted as a decoration on sea-charts. Or could there be a connection between our scene and the groups of figures adorning a fountain in the gardens of Versailles and elsewhere? The hard blue of the decoration indicates the second half of the eighteenth century, though it is not impossible that this composition was used for the first time in the thirties of the century.

[1] Louise Spruit, 'Een decor in *encre de chine*', *Antiek*, 2, 1967–68, p. 179.
[2] M. Beurdeley, op. cit., p. 64.

Eighteenth-century Chinese porcelain with European decoration

In the 'Judgement of Paris' of Plate 225,[1] the goddesses Juno, Venus and Minerva are placed in a Chinese landscape, in polychrome, and as heavy, inelegant, ludicrous beings. The sitting Paris is holding a shepherd's crook in his right hand and looks like a wrestler rather than a Greek god. Cupid sitting on the ground is the most attractively rendered of the whole group. This scene appears on cups and dishes as well as on plates. The rim of the plates is decorated either with four panels (Plate 226) painted with scenes of Chinese junks on a river, or with a border of shells linked by rococo scrolls (Plate 225). At least one plate is known on which the nudes are covered in part by overpainting[2] (see p. 160).

'Leda and the Swan' is also a dearly beloved subject, painted on porcelain in green, rose-red and blue (Plate 227). Leda and her companions, also in the nude, are painted in flesh-colour and much more elegantly rendered than the goddesses with Paris. This scene, taken from a painting (Plate 228) by Correggio (1489–1534), proves that the Chinese porcelain painter has followed the principal parts of the painting rather well, but the treatment of the figures with their slit-eyes, and especially the trees, shows that the artist was no European. He has taken liberties with the composition by cutting it off at the left and showing only one nude boy next to Leda instead of several figures. Apart from a few trees the forest has been replaced by rocks. The subject on the plate is, incidentally, also a reversed image.

Other subjects frequently found on export wares, usually painted in *famille rose,* are 'Venus and Hermes', or Apollo or Cupid, and also 'Amor and Psyche', 'Neptune and Amphitrite' in a triumphal car (Plate 230), 'Apollo and Diana' (Plate 233), 'Apollo and Daphne', 'Europa and the Bull', 'The Toilet of Venus', 'Perseus and Andromeda' and 'Juno with the Peacock'. A plate showing 'Venus and Hermes' (Plate 233 left) is fairly well drawn and painted in the *famille rose* manner. It has a rim-decoration of flower sprays. In contrast with it, and with most of the others in which the figures form the principal elements, the scene of 'Cephalus killing Procris' (Plate 229) has the forest, Chinese in character, playing the leading part.

The 'Four Elements', from paintings by Francesco Albani (1578–1660, Galleria Sabauda, Turin), were also used on *chine de commande* plates and saucers. The scene illustrating 'Earth' (Plate 232) has—just as in the case of the 'Judgement of Paris'—misshapen nude women. The four figures are shown on a triumphal car surrounded by nude rather unattractive amors, in a landscape with Chinese mountains for a backdrop. The rim of the plate is painted with leafy tendrils, for only about half of its breadth, the rest of it being taken up by part of the scene; a remarkable aberration.

Sometimes different rim-decorations are used on plates with the same main subject, as in the case of the 'Judgement of Paris' (Plates 225 and 226), and sometimes only one

[1] There are some examples of these plates (Milan, Castello Sforzesco) where the decoration is painted in purple. The rim-decoration of these is taken from Claude de Paquier at Vienna (see p. 130).

[2] M. Beurdeley, op. cit., cat. 131.

version is known as in the case of the half-naked couple of Plate 231 sitting under trees. Two specimens of this plate, one in the Historical Museum of Rotterdam, and one in the Stodel collection at Amsterdam, are wholly identical, both having been made between 1745 and 1760.

RELIGIOUS SUBJECTS

Biblical subjects from the New Testament are restricted to 'The Baptism of Christ', 'The Crucifixion' and 'The Ascension'. Porcelain decorated in this way is sometimes called Jesuit porcelain. It was, however, ordered not only by Roman Catholics, clerical, missionary or private, but also by Protestants. If we are to believe Père d'Entrecolles in his letter of 1712, the porcelain with Christ on the Cross[1] between Mary and John, of which a fragment was shown him, was made in 1696 or 1697, and the last of it was exported to Japan, but so far as we know not a single piece with this decoration has survived. It is possible that the subject was taken from prints from the Bible published for Père Nadal by Plantin of Antwerp, at the end of the seventeenth century.[2]

The cups and saucer of Plates 235 and 236 are among the oldest pieces showing this version of the Crucifixion. They were made at Ching-tê Chên, and painted in underglaze blue with rather clumsy line drawing. They date from the beginning of the eighteenth century rather than the end of the seventeenth. It is noteworthy that the letters I.N.R.I. on the cross are so well written. The rim-decoration of the saucer consists of flowers and leaves reminiscent of the seventeenth century; that on the cup is of spirals placed side by side.

The Crucifixion of Plate 238, on a cup and saucer in the Rijksmuseum, is in green, brown and blue enamel. A piece with the same scene in the Groninger Museum has a spearhead decoration in addition and it is therefore quite possible that these pieces were made from the forties of the eighteenth century, when the spearhead rim decoration became popular.

There are several versions of the Ascension, the best known being the one where Christ ascends to Heaven[3] in a nimbus, an angel is sitting on the grave, and some soldiers are sleeping in the foreground (Plate 241). It is executed in purplish red and red enamel with some gold. In the Rijksmuseum there is a specimen painted in blue, yellow, green, red and purple. In the Princessehof Museum there is a small saucer with this subject, where Christ is gazed after by the Apostles (Plate 239). The painting, in underglaze blue and polychrome, is rather pictorial.

[1] On Delft earthenware too there are crucifixions, Mr. S. van Gyn Museum at Dordrecht, illustrated in *Masterworks of Delft,* Princessehof Museum, 2nd June–4th August, 1962, ill. 45. J. G. Phillips, op. cit., pl. 52; this is taken from a print by Merian.

[2] P. Pelliot, *Les Influences européennes sur l'Art chinois du XVIIe et au XVIIIe siècle* (Paris, 1948).

[3] This composition also exists executed in *grisaille,* and includes the three Marys in the right background. J. G. Phillips, op. cit., p. 135, pl. 53.

Very different in character is the Baptism of Christ (Plate 237), badly drawn with a red wash and some gold. The rim is decorated with a bird holding in his beak two tendrils. Two *putti* at the bottom carry a tablet with the caption Matt. 3 : 16.

The earliest scene from the Old Testament is that of Adam and Eve (Plate 234) on a plate of the K'ang Hsi period in underglaze blue. Adam is to the left of the tree and Eve to the right. He is accompanied by a he-goat (?) and she by several similar animals. The rim-decoration of tendrils and flowers reminds one of those found in the second half of the seventeenth century. The piece is marked, but of course incorrectly, Ch'êng Hua (1465–87).

A certain sprightliness characterizes the scene with 'Rebecca at the Well' (Plate 240). Rebecca is shown pouring water into a pitcher, and watched by Abraham's servant. The scene is painted in rose-red, yellow, light green and blue. It is found on saucers, cups and saucers (Amsterdam, Rijksmuseum) and also on plates.

Other scenes from the Old Testament are 'Susanna and the Elders', 'Noah and his daughters' and 'Joseph and Potiphar's Wife'. The last one is taken from a print by Marcantonio Raimondi after Raphael.

HARBOUR-VIEWS AND SHIPS

Between 1730 and 1740 C. F. Herold painted many pieces of Meissen porcelain, such as tea services, with a harbour-view.[1] The interest in harbours resulted in their use on dishes, plates and tureens, often within a Meissen cartouche (Plate 245). Meissen influence can also be detected on a plate showing Table Bay (Plate 242), where the gilt rim-decoration is of a type much used at Meissen between 1730 and 1750. Judging from this it is quite possible that the Chinese plate was made between 1730 and 1750. Table Mountain is in the background, with Capetown in the foreground, in the midst of green trees.

Though the little plate of Plate 249 has no harbour-view, it is discussed here because the *chinoiserie* of the central part was inspired by Meissen examples. On it are portrayed a Chinese lady and gentleman, seated on either side of a pedestal on which a jar with a branch of coral is standing. The colours used are green, rose-red, black and gold. *Chinoiseries* like this are found on Meissen porcelain, between 1725 and 1730, designed by Herold or under his influence. In common with the plate showing Table Bay, other pieces were certainly made for the Dutch market; one with Neptune sitting on a whale, making for a man-of-war flying the Dutch colours, and another with three sailing-ships (1750–70), and the caption *Glucklig Arivement*,[2] 'Happy Arrival'.[3]

---

[1] Harbour-views have been taken from, or been inspired by a set of Italian views of harbours after designs by J. W. Baur, published in 1682 by Melchior Kysell. Other artists, like J. G. Heintze, painted harbour-views.

[2] J. G. Phillips, op. cit., pl. 62.　　　　[3] M. Beurdeley, op. cit., cat. 141.

Another well-known scene is that of the *Nieuwe Stadsherberg*, 'New Town-inn', at the waterfront of Amsterdam,[1] and must have been a popular subject, popular especially with natives of Amsterdam. It was painted on plates and tea services. The building is rendered fairly well, though it appears from the manner of drawing that the work was not done by a Dutch hand (Plate 243). When this scene is used on small plates, two little angels hold a crown above the Inn. The rim of the plate of Plate 243 is decorated with small sprays of flowers.

One of the very well-known representations is that of the ship *Vryburg* (Plate 244), portrayed, all sails set, on the roads of Whampoa. This plate was made to the order of captain Jacob Ryzik whose name appears on the rim at the top. During the eighteenth century it was the custom for a captain to have his ship portrayed. Delft ware of the time frequently includes a ship, and the name of the ship and that of her captain are sometimes mentioned on the plate. By ordering a plate in China captain Ryzik continued this custom. By further mentioning that the ship is *Ter Reede Wanpho in China int Jaar 1756* ('On the Whampoa roads in China in the year 1756') everybody who read this caption would know that the captain traded to Canton. There are also plates ordered by first mates; see for instance, *Chris.t Schooneman opp.r Stuerman op: t' Schip Vrijburg*.[2] When one compares the surviving plates, of many different sizes, it seems that the ship is not always given the same length, and some show it sailing to the right and some to the left. The ship and the rigging are rendered in black, with the rest of the decoration in red enamel, green and gold.

Sometimes, too, the Chinese artists combined western and oriental elements. This is shown by the harbour-view of Plate 245. The houses on the quay and the sampan moored to the bank are Chinese, while the two merchants standing there are European. The Meissen cartouche, framing the composition, shows western influence, as does the *bianco-sopra-bianco* treatment.

The interest in exotic scenes is clearly detectable from a small saucer painted with a Chinese sailing-junk (Plate 246). The arms of the City of Amsterdam nevertheless prove that this piece is a true *chine de commande* specimen. Although no western elements are present in the scene in polychrome enamels, of a Chinese sea-going junk anchored in front of a fortification in the Pearl River near Canton,[3] the cups and saucers decorated with this view were certainly made to supply a western demand (Plate 247).

Scenes showing a sailor bidding farewell to his sweetheart[4] were also much favoured.

[1] D. F. Lunsingh Scheurleer, 'De Nieuwe Stadsherberg in het IJ voor Amsterdam op Chinees porselein', *Antiek*, 2, 1968/69, p. 484.

[2] M. Jourdain and R. Soame Jenyns, op. cit., fig. 99.

[3] Clare le Corbeiller, 'Trade winds from China', *Bulletin of the Metropolitan Museum*, New York, Jan. 1962. This may well show one of the forts on the Pearl River near Canton; they were named Dutch Folly, French Folly, etc.

[4] Bredo L. Grandjean, *Dansk Ostindisk Porcelaen*, pl. 65.

H. Plate with Imari-style decoration. First quarter eighteenth century

Eighteenth-century Chinese porcelain with European decoration

On the plate illustrated (Plate 248) the lovers are shown in the foreground in unnatural attitudes. The girl is dressed in a purple skirt and yellow coatee. The landscape and the rim-decoration are Chinese, but the ship is a European ship.

PORTRAITS AND POLITICAL EVENTS

Compared with figures in general, true portraits are not very common. Most of them, moreover, are not painted in enamels, but in *encre de chine*. Nevertheless there are some. The half-length portraits of the Empress Maria Theresa (1717–80) and her prince-consort Francis of Loraine are found on cups and saucers. They are passably painted (Plate 251). As Maria Theresa was married to her cousin in January 1736, it may be surmised that this porcelain was made on the occasion of their marriage, and so a little before or after that date.

A few full-length portraits are known, such as the one of Petrus de Wolff after a print (Plate 253) by P. Schenk (1660–1718). The Chinese porcelain painter has done his best to copy the portrait accurately. On the plate shown in Plate 252, it is painted in sepia, and the trees are more western than usual. The rim-decoration of yellow on blue flower sprays, however, is Chinese, as are the narrow bands of tendrils flanking the rim. The well-border includes a panel with an inscription reading 'Petrus de Wolff Pettpril'.

A rare historical subject is the 'Triumph of the City of Batavia'. It shows a young woman, flag in hand, symbolizing the Dutch East India Company and receiving tribute from some natives. On her right is the Dutch Lion and the God of Trade. The flowers on the rim are painted in polychrome enamels.[1]

Very well known is the scene of Plate 255, *Des Stiers Wreedheyt* 'the Bull's Cruelty', which was painted on Chinese porcelain in the Netherlands as well as in China (see page 182). The peasant lying on the ground is wearing a blue coat and the woman a blue jacket. The spearhead motif is used to ornament the rim.

Among the best-known *chine de commande* plates are the so-called *Actie-bordjes* 'share-plates'. It is not always realized that they were made in China and commemorate the affair of the South Sea Bubble. The failure of the scheme in 1720 made a deep impression and was the occasion for the appearance of a set of caricatures known under the name of *Het Grote Tafereel der Dwaasheid*, 'The Great Scene of Folly'. These were used on three sets of six small plates.[2] The dancing harlequin portrayed on them was probably taken from the prints, although until now no prints have come to light,

[1] M. Beurdeley, op. cit., cat. 176.

[2] D. F. Lunsingh Scheurleer, 'In China vervaardigde Actie-bordjes', *Antiek*, 2, 1968–69, p. 184. On a plate in the Cinquantenaire Museum in Brussels, there is also a harlequin, with the inscription *waar Synse dan Seg broer* ('where are they then say brother') and a tile-picture also has a dancing harlequin. J. Helbig, *Faïences Hollandaises*, pp. 98, 173. The Rijksmuseum has a plate with a harlequin and the saying *ha ha axsies*. F. Hudig, *Delfter Fayence*, p. 212.

which may have served as inspiration. On either side of the harlequin there is an inscription of two lines painted in black enamel. They say *50 percent op Delft gewonnen* '50 percent profit on Delft' (Plate 254), *Weg Gekke Actionisten,* 'Away [with you] foolish shareholders' (Plate 256) and *De Actiemars op de tang,* 'the Share-march [played] on the Tongs' (Plate 258). The three plates not reproduced here have the mottoes, *Schyt Actiens en windhandel,* 'Shares and swindle', *Pardie al myn Acties kwÿt,* 'By God, lost all my shares', and *Wie op Uytrecht of nieuw Amsterdam,* 'Who wants to speculate on Utrecht or New Amsterdam?' The rim of the plates is painted in underglaze blue and ornamented with green enamel dashes.

The figures are painted in blue and green, with iron-red and gold added in several places. The treatment of the different figures, with their somewhat Chinese features, confirms the Chinese origin of the plates. There is a second, rarer, version of this set (Plates 257, 259), in which the harlequins have become completely oriental, and are shown in attitudes recalling skaters. The tabouret on which one of the harlequins is sitting has become a shell-like stool, the inscriptions have disappeared, and a window or a door added to the background wall. And, finally, the rim-decorations on the two sets are completely different, that on the second set being all in gold. The outer rim is painted with a variation on the diaper-pattern, broken in several places by Chinese petals. Within this is a border of motifs used at Meissen from about 1723 to 1735 (see fig. 33, page 131), and a similar motif is used for the well-border. On the strength of this decoration one may conclude that the plates were made in China between 1723 and 1735. Yet a third version of these plates is known. The figures are painted even more badly than those on the second set, and the rim-decoration is wholly Chinese and consists of honeycombs in polychrome with a bat in between.

ARMORIAL PORCELAIN
Europe

To be able to recognize each other in battle or at tournaments, it was the custom amongst the nobility in Europe, from the middle ages, to use a coat of arms. This was placed on a banner, cuirass, helmet or shield, and because the shield is admirably suited to the purpose, it became in heraldry the bearer of the coat of arms.

Imitating the noble families, the guilds, towns, provinces, states and commoners started to use their own coats of arms, on shield shapes which varied according to the period and prevailing style. A silver drinking horn, of the *Kloveniers gilde* of Amsterdam dated 1547, is one of the oldest objects in the Netherlands showing a coat of arms. From the end of the sixteenth century, Spain and Italy were foremost in their use of heraldic decoration, and coats of arms appeared on ceramic wares. The oldest known arms on ceramic wares in the Netherlands are painted in polychrome on two tiles of majolica (Abbot Reekamp), made also about 1547 at Antwerp. They are now in the Groninger

Eighteenth-century Chinese porcelain with European decoration

Museum. A majolica jug in the Zwolle Museum is somewhat later, about the end of the sixteenth century. The body is painted in polychrome, with the arms of the towns of Kampen, Zwolle and Deventer.

In the course of the seventeenth century, more and more tin-glazed plates were made at Delft and elsewhere with arms painted on the centre. They were objects of daily use, and to a considerable extent replaced the earlier silver and silver-gilt dishes with engraved coats of arms. Understandably, people also wanted Chinese porcelain decorated with them. The Portuguese were probably the first to have their coats of arms painted on Chinese porcelain. In the Princessehof at Leeuwarden is a dish with the coat of arms of King Sebastian I of Portugal (see page 47). So far as now can be ascertained, the Dutch first ordered armorial porcelain in China shortly before or about 1700. But it is in many cases impossible to identify the arms because they were sometimes wrong from a heraldic point of view, or not quite clear, and to make the situation still more confused imaginary coats of arms were also painted on porcelain.

As with other decorative motifs, originals for coats of arms were sent from Europe, and the heraldic devices most often used were the shield, helmet, mantling, supporters and their footholds. The mantling, often in renaissance style, forms an important part of the arms. During the eighteenth century it was sometimes used in such an exaggerated form that it gives little help in dating a piece. The shield may be of more use in this respect when, for instance, it has a characteristically rococo shape. However, it sometimes happened that one mantling—perhaps the porcelain painters in Canton had a sample from which to work—was used to frame different arms. The framing of the arms of Verheull (Plate 271) was also used for an English coat of arms.[1]

In armorial plates two groups are to be distinguished: those in which the arms were depicted in underglaze blue, made at Ching-tê Chên, and the ones decorated at Canton, which were painted in polychrome enamels over the glaze.

Underglaze blue

In comparison with the polychrome group, there are relatively few pieces of armorial porcelain decorated in underglaze blue. The eighteenth-century preference for armorial plates decorated in polychrome enamels, as part of a dinner service, had its origin in the increasing demand for articles of luxury.

Among the oldest armorial plates are those with the arms of the Van der Stel family (Plate 260). The bearings are framed by a baroque cartouche and the rim of the plate is decorated with flowers and fruits on stalks. This plate must have been made between 1715 and 1720: it would have been ordered at the time when members of the family

[1] Mr. A. Staring kindly told the author that Christiaaen Anthonie Verheull, sea-captain, was in the Indies with a special commission in 1784–85, and there ordered the plates. For the same frame with different coats of arms see J. A. Lloyd Hyde, op. cit., no. 25.

held high positions at The Cape, and in the Indies, and because they all died before 1723, the plate was certainly made before that date.

Whereas the Van der Stel coat of arms shows a baroque cartouche, the impaled arms of Van Bleyswyk (1673–1739) and Anna Antonia van Hemert (1689–1762), who were married in 1708, are framed in a mantling resembling curled leaves. It may be assumed that this small plate (Plate 261) was made shortly after the wedding.

Two plates in the De Sypesteyn museum at Loosdrecht, with a rococo escutcheon, prove that armorial plates decorated in underglaze blue were still ordered after 1750–60. The plate reproduced in Plate 262 shows two unidentified impaled arms, one with three stars and the other with a standing bear. The outer rim is decorated with the honeycomb motif. These plates were made between 1750 and 1770.

There are also plates (Plate 263) decorated entirely in underglaze blue, with the exception of the coat of arms of the Chasteleyn family, which was executed in polychrome enamels in the centre. This is probably one of a group of plates made in quantity at Ching-tê Chên, which were then provided with a coat of arms at Canton.

Arms in polychrome

The coats of arms in *famille verte* are among the oldest, and those painted in Imari style, in blue, red and gold were made somewhat later. Armorial porcelain in *famille rose* was first made during the reign of Yung Chêng. To the first category belong the dishes with the rim in relief, the central part decorated with the arms in *famille verte* of, for instance, a country, France, a province or region, Holland, Friesland, Luxemburg and Hainaut, or a city, Amsterdam or Zutphen (colour plate G). These dishes were probably made in the K'ang Hsi period about 1700, though they were still made somewhat later on. The arms are shown on a shield with a crown, above, and below it the name on a scroll. The escutcheon is surrounded by flowering tendrils with two birds. Rim and well-border are decorated with petal-shaped panels reminiscent of the Wan Li tradition. The panels are provided alternatively with a Chinese in a landscape and one of the Hundred Antiquities. The space at their tops along the scalloped edge of the dish is filled in with the honeycomb motif.

The decoration on the different plates of this group, the diameter of which varies between 12 and about 15 inches, is, apart from minor details, mostly the same.

Related to this group is a set of dishes (Plate 264) also decorated in *famille verte,* perhaps made in the K'ang Hsi period though in all probability a little later. It is quite possible that both groups were still made during the first three decades of the century. On these dishes the three parts, rim, well-border and central part, are decorated separately. The shape of the escutcheon is the same, though it is a little smaller in relation to the surrounding space. The flowers and leaves are usually more finely done and instead of two there are now four birds. The difference is greatest in the well-border and the rim.

They are here decorated with the diaper pattern with shaped panels showing variously a Chinese landscape, a seated Chinaman and branches with flying birds. In both groups the decoration, apart from the arms, is wholly Chinese.

There is a third group (Plate 265), less often seen than the others, with a diameter of about 18 to 20 inches and decorated in *famille rose*. The rim-decoration is all but identical with that of the second group. The decoration of the central part, however, is quite distinct. The escutcheon is placed in a kind of architectural stage setting. It is not impossible that certain parts may have been painted in the Netherlands, such as the arch for which a triumphal arch may have been the model. Above the pilasters there is a kind of cornice, flanking a lunette with a winged angel's head crowned by a pediment. Chinese ladies stand between the pilasters on either side of the escutcheon.

Armorial porcelain painted in Imari colours is rather rare. In the De Sypesteyn Museum there is a piece (Plate 266) with accollée arms, the left one of which belongs to the Sautein family. The rim is decorated with a house under trees, four times repeated, separated by panels of conventionalized flowers. This plate was probably made in the first quarter of the century.

Once in a while an armorial piece is dated. This is the case with a tea service of which some cups and saucers and a teapot without its lid remain (Plate 267). This service was without doubt ordered by the Dutch East India Company for the Directors, because in a cartouche appear the emblem of the Company, V.O.C., painted in rose and yellow enamels, the date, 1728, and the motto *Res concordia parvae crescunt*. On a crowned rectangular escutcheon there is a lion rampant holding seven arrows, symbolic of the Seven Provinces. Two lions function as supporters. This decoration was taken from the reverse of a *zilveren ryder,* 'silver rider', a Company dollar struck for the Company in the mint of Hoorn in 1728.[1]

The plates with the arms of the Neufville family in *famille rose* (Plate 268) were made in the Yung Chêng period. At the top of the rim, which is decorated with large and small sprays of flowers, is the family crest. The well-border has diaperwork strewn with flowers.

The plates (Plate 274) made in memory of Professor Doctor Mauritius van Reverhorst (1666–1722) and his wife Emerentia Schrevelius (1679–1746), who were married in 1702, were probably ordered by their son Theodorus (see page 116). In this case nine coats of arms were depicted instead of the customary one. In the middle of the central part of the plate the coat of arms of the Van Reverhorst family is painted in red, blue and green enamels. It is crowned by a crest, with at either side the escutcheons of four related families. The dinner service of which this plate forms part was made between 1735 and 1740.

The rim-decoration of the van Reverhorst plate, shells linked by scrolls, is also used,

[1] T. Volker, 'Early Chine de commande', *Bulletin Museum Boymans-van Beuningen* (Rotterdam, 1958) p. 18.

Eighteenth-century Chinese porcelain with European decoration

albeit more coarsely, on a tray and a cup showing the impaled arms (Plate 276) of Hendrik van Ysselmonde tot Paaslo (1719–74) and Anna Elisabeth van Haersolte van Staverden, who were married in 1764. The escutcheons, rococo in style and painted in polychrome enamels, are surrounded by flowers, eagles and a pedestal with a flower-vase. This tea service was probably made in the middle of the century.

A plate (Plate 269) with a ruby-back *famille rose* decoration comes in quite a different category. It is decorated with more or less conventionalized bat-shaped panels of flowers. The spaces between the panels are filled with the so-called 'Y' diaper pattern,[1] common in the Yung Chêng period and later. The panels at the top of the plate include one with the arms of the City of Amsterdam.

A plate with the arms of Discher (Plate 278), with the spearhead motif round the rim, is of the same date. The escutcheon is painted in *encre de chine* and white enamel, the helmet and mantling in red and gold, and the arms are encircled with the following legend, *Ter gedagtenis van Hermannus Laurents Discher Hooft van Commissarissen en Prauwvoerders op Batavia, A. 1749.* 'In memory of Hermanus Laurents Discher Head of the Stewards and Proa-men at Batavia Anno 1749'.[2]

In the middle of the century the coat of arms generally becomes smaller in relation to the central part of the piece, a development which is continued in later years. The escutcheon itself becomes smaller too. This is visible on the dinner service made to order for Prince William V of Orange (Plate 160). A good example of a decoration in *encre de chine* together with *famille rose*, is shown by the oblong dish with the coat of arms of the Falck family (Plate 273). This combination of two techniques is also found on the magnificent plate, with *bianco-sopra-bianco* background, and the coat of arms of the Herzeele family (Plate 270), painted in red and gold. The inner part of the rim has the spearhead motif.

A plate with the arms of Verhuell (Plate 271) has a rim-decoration of sprays in gold, alternating with Chinese landscapes painted in rose-red, yellow, blue and black, between two narrow bands of the spearhead motif. The coat is placed on a shield from which flags, spears, axes and cannon protrude. Instead of three tournament rings, the Chinese porcelain painter has painted a pair of spectacles on the upper part of the escutcheon. The service to which this plate belongs, painted in *famille rose*, red and gold, was ordered by Christiaaen Anthonie Verhuell (see note 1, page 147).

The design of the plate with the impaled arms of S. Bal and L. Cats (Plate 277), who according to the date on the plate were married in 1779, gives a somewhat child-

[1] R. L. Hobson, *Handbook,* p. 95, fig. 149, shows a cup and saucer with the same decoration by Yang-lin.

[2] From the end of the seventeenth century silver plates and dishes had been made at Batavia with an engraved inscription reading *ter gedach(g)tenis' aan,* 'in memory of—' (name of the deceased). This fashion must have inspired Discher or his heirs to order a similar plate in porcelain from China. W. G. F. C. Rissink, 'Ter Gedagtenisse van', *Bulletin van de Koninklijke Nederlandse Oudheidkundige Bond,* 1965, p. 172 ff.

like impression. The bearings are painted on a double shell in rococo style, and a boy and girl play the part of supporters. The small sprays of flowers round the central decoration are more attractively painted.

In the last quarter of the century, apart from wares with Chinese decoration, porcelain with a purely western decoration was made. This classical ornamentation without Chinese elements must as a general rule have been copied from European porcelain. A cup and saucer, made probably between 1780 and 1790 (Plate 280), has a Louis XVI style of decoration, mostly in red and green, of festoons with a vase in the centre and the motto *Jamais abattu*, 'never disheartened'. Plates 279 and 281 show plates with other types of Louis XVI decoration.

For many years it was believed that Chinese porcelain was decorated in great quantities in a factory at Lowestoft;[1] and it was even supposed that certain Chinese porcelain painted with small flowers had been made there. This is impossible, for one of the most important ingredients of Chinese porcelain, kaolin, did not exist at Lowestoft, where in place of kaolin bone ash was used. The supposition that large services of Chinese porcelain—for example armorial wares—were decorated there was due to a mistake— corrected in later editions—in the early editions of William Chaffers' *Marks and Monograms on Pottery and Porcelain*. The myth was probably born of the fact that the words 'Allen Lowestoft'[2] are inscribed on the base of a Chinese pouring jug[3] in the Victoria and Albert Museum. The religious scenes, which appear on this jug, were painted in China, and the flowerets on the lid (fired in the muffle kiln) were added at Lowestoft. Because of this, any similar decoration of small flowers came to be known as 'Lowestoft', and collectors and traders, especially in England and in the United States, called Chinese export porcelain commissioned from the West 'Oriental Lowestoft', which is a very misleading term.

MISCELLANEOUS SUBJECTS

After the death of K'ang Hsi in 1722, various subjects in underglaze blue and polychrome were painted on porcelain, such as the eight of spades painted in blue on the plate of Plate 282, which judging from the hard blue can probably be dated to sometime between 1760 and 1780.

In the last quarter of the century the so-called 'willow pattern' appears (Plates 177, 180) which, though inspired by Chinese paintings, originated in England at about

---

[1] There was at Lowestoft from 1757 to 1823 a small factory with a biscuit and an enamel kiln where bone china was made.

[2] Robert Allen was a porcelain painter from 1774 to 1825. Lloyd Hyde says that the Lowestoft factory possessed ships, and bought porcelain in Rotterdam, which was decorated at Lowestoft before being sold in London. See J. L. Dixon, *English Porcelain of the Eighteenth Century*, p. 28.

[3] This pouring jug is illustrated in J. A. Lloyd Hyde, *Oriental Lowestoft*, plate IV.

1780,[1] and was frequently used on dinner services. The principal decoration consists of a river-view, with a small bridge and an island with a willow tree, which gave its name to the pattern. It is usually bordered with the 'Fitzhugh' rim-decoration (Plates 177, 180). In China the willow pattern decoration was regarded as genre-painting, and not as the illustration of a Chinese novel or some other text.

Reference should also be made to the decoration ascribed to Cornelis Pronk—a violet acanthus leaf on a yellow ground—occurring on plates and dishes and also on milk-jugs, sugar-basins, cups, etc. Acanthus leaves in a smaller size can be seen on the 'Bower' plate (Plate 202), which was probably also designed by Pronk. Since the acanthus leaf was repeatedly used in decoration (among others by Daniel Marot) we cannot be certain that the decoration shown in fig. 36 was actually designed by Pronk.

[1] F. St. George Spendlove, 'The Willow Pattern: English and Chinese', *Far Eastern Ceramic Bulletin*, 1956.

16 · *Encre de chine* decoration on Chinese export porcelain

Encre de chine is the name that has been given to a type of decoration of Chinese porcelain painted in a deep black, sometimes tending to sepia, to which additions of a little flesh-colour and gold were often made. After 1730 it became very fashionable in Europe. The term is derived from the Chinese term *ts'ai shui mo*, but it is somewhat misleading and has generally been avoided by English writers. The alternative term *en grisaille*, derived from a kind of built-up decoration in European painted enamels is also used, but the decoration in fact has little resemblance to the painted enamel decoration from which it is derived.

Encre de chine decoration has sometimes been looked upon as a mourning ware. Dinner services decorated in pure black without gold with religious subjects, or with Louis XV festoons and other formal patterns, such as we see in polychrome on Meissen porcelain, will certainly have served as mourning ware. But by far the greater part of Chinese porcelain decorated in black was without doubt an article of fashion. The allegorical and mythological subjects, especially those taken from 'gallant' prints, are often in this style, but it is difficult to imagine pieces so decorated being put to daily use by people plunged into mourning. After it was realized how magnificently this technique lent itself to the reproduction of prints and engravings on porcelain, without doubt many a piece with this decoration will have been made for display pure and simple. This is borne out by the fact that most of these pieces show no signs of wear and appear to have been little used.

Encre de chine porcelain has a charm of its own, because of the refined combination of black and gold, with perhaps a little flesh-colour, or because of the fine contrast between a perfectly rendered engraving and the festive red and gold of the cartouche framing it. Further, there are extremely pretty pieces in sepia monochrome, taken from European prints. Sometimes the rim of the piece is purely Chinese and the subject western, sometimes the reverse is the case. The figures of Europeans are frequently out of drawing, and even when the whole subject is a true copy of a western sample, the hand of the Chinese porcelain painter sometimes betrays itself in the rendering of a branch, a rock, a cloud or drapery. Besides a fair quantity of excellent pieces, there are also many more modest ones for people who are attracted to this kind of ware. Moreover, an untold number of pieces decorated in this technique survive, apparently mass-produced assembly-line work, made at the time when decoration in black was all the rage, and the less well-to-do desired a set of this porcelain also. The least attractive of this mass-produced porcelain are those pieces with mythological subjects, in many cases unidentifiable, which nearly always combine the black with flesh-colour.

It is possible to find out, at least approximately, when this porcelain was first made for export. For one thing, we know that it cannot have been before 1722, as it was in that year that Père d'Entrecolles described how attempts had been made at Ching-tê Chên to paint vases in the finest ink, but in vain, as the ink vanished in the firing.

If the invention of decoration in black with a touch of gold may be ascribed to the time when Nien Hsi-yao was in office,[1] from 1726–36, the starting date could be moved from 1722 to 1726. It seems obvious that the new invention of *ts'ai shui mo,* as the monochrome black decoration was called, came into use first of all for the Chinese home market, but very soon afterwards was not only exported to Europe but ordered from Europe as well. In the Ashmolean Museum at Oxford there is a plate decorated in black and gold showing a purely Chinese landscape on the central part, and four panels with small Chinese landscapes on the rim. In the central part right across the Chinese landscape there is an escutcheon in black, and in the panel at the top a helmet and crest (Plate 283). The arms are those of Elwick and the plate forms part of a set made for John Elwick of Cornhill, London, a director of the English East India Company. He died in September 1730. Here, indeed, we have a purely Chinese decoration used for the European who ordered the set. The landscape on the plate is identical with one on a small cup and saucer of very thin porcelain, decorated in sepia and gold, now at the Middelburg Museum (Plate 286). A combination of Chinese and European decorations on one and the same piece—both pieces just mentioned are, moreover, European in shape—is not uncommon. The Groninger Museum has a piece with a wholly Chinese landscape in black, and European mirror monograms on the rim. The importance of the plate at the Ashmolean is that it must have been made before 1730, the year when Elwick died.

It is not only that Chinese porcelain decorated in *t'sai shui mo* found its way to Europe shortly after it was first made. About 1730 the technique must also have been used already on pieces ordered from European examples. A plate in the Rijksmuseum at Amsterdam, decorated in black, flesh-colour and some gold, with a wedding-allegory and the arms of burgomaster Nic. Geelvinck and his first wife Johanna Jacoba Graafland,

[1] R. Soame Jenyns, *Later Chinese Porcelain,* p. 44, plates LVIII and LXXVII (1) pieces decorated in sepia, with Yung Chêng marks.

(Plate 284) is a case in point. They were married in 1729 and Johanna Jacoba died in 1740. It is hardly credible that this plate was intended as a mourning piece, in which case it would have to be dated 1740–41, and so we may take it that the plate was ordered before the wedding in 1729 or shortly afterwards in memory of it. Nevertheless the fact that this decoration is common about 1740 and afterwards, might argue in favour of a later date. It was a representation dearly loved, especially in the Netherlands and in England. In it the allegorical group always remained unchanged, and only the coat of arms on the pillars, and sometimes a motto, gave the piece its personal character. In the Fries Museum there is a similar piece with the motto *'semper amor pro te firmissimus atque fidelis'* 'always my love for you both strong and true', but in the foreground of this plate we find, instead of the customary tritons, the ship *Sloten* in polychrome on a blue sea. Below the whole composition is the motto *Alles heeft eenen bestemden :ydt, ende alle voornemen onder den hemel heeft nen tydt,* 'To everything there is a season, and a time to every purpose under the heaven' (Ecclesiastes 3, vs. 1). Plates showing the ship *Sloten* form part of the Sligenberg collection and of the Nederlandsch Historisch Scheepvaart-museum, both at Amsterdam. In the British Museum there is a plate decorated in sepia, which may be dated about 1750, with the same subject, and a triton to adorn the foreground. And in the Victoria and Albert Museum there is a plaque decorated in sepia and pale red with the same subject, dated 1741.

The Boymans-van Beuningen Museum at Rotterdam owns a similar plate, with the arms of Johan van Bergen van der Gyp and Elisabeth Arnaudina van Beaumont Cornelis, who were married on 18th November 1736. There is also one in the Metropolitan Museum, New York, with the arms of the families Beaumont and Backers of Dordrecht.[1]

The case of the *Sloten* plate is remarkable, because it has not yet been possible to ascertain whether the service, of which these plates form a part, was ordered by the owners or by the captain of a ship built in 1746 and already scrapped in 1768. The coats of arms represented cannot be positively connected with the families concerned.

The wedding commemoration is probably the earliest datable example of decoration in *encre de chine* found in the Netherlands and it raises the question of the source for this subject, a question that crops up repeatedly in connection with European subjects on the export wares. And the frequency with which this particular allegorical wedding commemoration appears on pieces of quite different quality raises a second question: what are the reasons for the variations in quality? There are many excellently painted specimens of a particular decoration in black, but others also which were evidently made on the assembly-line principle or at least very cheaply. There is some

[1] W. B. Honey, *The Ceramic Art of China and The Far East*, p. 158, dates the wedding allegory to about 1730–40. Warren Cox in *The Book of Pottery and Porcelain* suggests that it was taken from the title page of an eighteenth-century book of wedding songs. J. A. Lloyd Hyde, *Oriental Lowestoft*, p. 88, believes it was from a seventeenth-century book.

considerable difference in the style of painting. Sometimes the engraving which served as a sample was imitated most faithfully; at other times the decoration is much more like a freehand painting in monochrome. The material used in the technique is a dry black or brown-black pigment closely related to that which was earlier used for outlines, in, for instance, *famille verte*[1] painting. After the technique had been mastered, it was also used as part of the *famille verte* palette, for instance with gold combs in the coiffure of ladies, and as part of the *famille rose* technique.[2] Although it is probable that the monochrome pieces of *encre de chine* porcelain, which have the Yung Chêng reign mark, were made for the home market, and so would have been manufactured entirely at Ching-tê Chên, soon after the export trade to Europe had been established, the Cantonese porcelain painters took over this new technique. It is commonly said that Peking, and the potters at Ching-tê Chên, had a great contempt for the work of the Cantonese porcelain painters. Canton had of old been a town working for export. Long before Europeans came to place their orders there, the Cantonese had supplied to the demand of buyers from various Asian countries.[3] The enormous artistic demands made of porcelain-painters of Ching-tê Chên, by the experts at the Imperial Court, did not concern the Cantonese. From father to son they were prepared to answer to the strangest, most bizarre demands of foreign customers, and so it was obvious that Canton was the town where, after the fashion for this ware had grown in the West, export porcelain was decorated in black and sepia. The early eggshell pieces decorated in black and gold, which may be regarded as Cantonese work, come from the same town which supplied the coarse, slovenly-finished mass-produced articles from the years between 1750 and 1780, when the rage for designs in black had reached its climax in Europe.[4] All this porcelain, however, was made at Ching-tê Chên and the differences in quality of the porcelain itself originated there. Canton was a town of decorators of porcelain, and of enamel workers, a town of muffle kilns, not of makers of porcelain.

Faultless copies of European prints and engravings were made there, such as those on the famous sepia plates in the British Museum, the 'Submersion of Achilles in the River Styx', and the 'Triumph of Mordecai', the western examples of which the Chinese porcelain painter has copied so perfectly that it is no wonder they have been taken for Chinese plates decorated by European porcelain-painters.[5]

Plates with views of Amsterdam, now in the Municipal Museum of that city, have the same high quality (Plate 290). It is sometimes difficult to realize that these perfect show-pieces originated in the same town as the many incorrectly-drawn, badly-

[1] R. L. Hobson, *Chinese Pottery and Porcelain*, vol. II, p. 214.

[2] J. P. van Goidsenhoven, *La céramique Chinoise sous les Ts'ing 1644–1851*, p. 182. M. Beurdeley, *Porcelaine de la Compagnie des Indes*, p. 35.

[3] J. G. Phillips, *China Trade Porcelain*, p. 38.

[4] R. L. Hobson, op. cit., p. 211.

[5] J. G. A. N. de Vries, *Porselein*, p. 8; reproduced in M. Jourdain and R. Soame Jenyns, *Chinese Export Art in the Eighteenth Century*, p. 117, and in M. Beurdeley, op. cit., p. 63.

understood subjects which flooded the market in the Netherlands, especially after 1750. But then, we should take into account that Canton was a town with hundreds if not thousands of workshops, which must of course have been of varying quality. Frequently it is possible to find a similarity in the style of painting on different pieces, and this is true of some of the finer wares as well as of those of much poorer quality.

In our opinion there is a clear relation between the magnificent plate in black and gold, in the Centraal Museum at Utrecht, datable to about 1735 (Plate 285), and a cup and saucer in the British Museum (Plate 287). And the typical Yung Chêng knot which holds up the flowering sprig over the (Stadtholder's?) couple, shown in Plate 285, is also present in the ornament round the central part of the plate of Plate 288. The latter is a particularly richly decorated, handsome piece in black and gold, depicting Chinese people in Chinese surroundings. It is in the Groninger Museum. Two smaller plates may be found in the Municipal Museums at Amsterdam. In the British Museum too there are some that are similar.[1] Scenes of the kind reproduced on those pieces were frequently inspired by Chinese opera.

We think that there is a relation also in the style of painting between the plates with the views of Amsterdam, already mentioned, and parts of a large dinner-service with European (Dutch?) landscapes. Some of these pieces are in the Rijksmuseum, some in the British Museum (Plate 292), some in the Municipal museums of Amsterdam and, finally, some in private collections. On close inspection one comes to the conclusion that these Amsterdam views and European landscapes were quite probably decorated in the same workshop at Canton.

The originals for the thirty bigger (8 inches) and six smaller (5½ inches) plates of the Views of Amsterdam have not yet been traced so far as we know. It has been suggested that these Views were copied from prints by Cornelis Pronk, who would have made the designs on contract for the Dutch East India Company.[2] It was not Pronk, however, who provided the design for the plate of the *Haringpakkerstoren,* 'Herringpacker's tower', of the set of Views of Amsterdam, but P. Schenk. The print which was copied by the porcelain-painters occurs in his *Atlas,* and appeared about 1710 (Plates 289, 290). The same Schenk also created the view of the *Oude Kerk* at Amsterdam and perhaps himself designed the version for the plate, less richly decorated, in the Princessehof Museum at Leeuwarden. The rim of this plate, decorated in black and gold,[3] shows a close relation to the rim of one of the pieces of a hunting-set in Vienna porcelain by Du Paquier, who worked in Vienna during the reign of Maria Theresa (1740–80). For the rest, the Princessehof plate seems to have originated in a workshop different from

[1] M. Jourdain and R. Soame Jenyns, op. cit., pl. 84.

[2] J. G. A. N. de Vries, op. cit., pp. 7–8, suggests that the Amsterdam plates should be credited to Cornelis Pronk. This point of view is supported by J. A. Lloyd Hyde, op. cit., p. 84.

[3] J. G. Phillips, op. cit., p. 74. See M. Jourdain and R. Soame Jenyns, op. cit., pl. 85 for the rim of the Princessehof plate.

that where the Amsterdam views were decorated. The way the clouds and buildings and especially the figures are painted make it, however, if not absolutely certain, at least extremely probable that the Amsterdam views and the dinner service with the European landscapes came from one and the same Cantonese workshop.

The original examples for the landscapes have till now eluded detection. Perhaps they were free interpretations of drawings by Pronk, copied in prints by H. Spilman, and reproduced in Tirion's *Verheerlykt Nederland,* 'the Netherlands extolled', because some of the reproductions in this publication, taken in reflected image, have some similarity with the landscapes. There is, however, as yet no certainty.

A good instance of the same subject, in a cheap and an expensive 'edition', is shown by Plates 291 and 293. The motif of the fishing couple seems to be a variant of the theme 'Water' from a set 'The four Elements' fairly common in the eighteenth century.[1] But perhaps the predilection for this particular subject, of which there are many examples decorated in polychrome as well as monochrome, has some connection with the Chinese symbolism of the fish.[2] Two fishes symbolize married bliss and the fish also stands for health, happiness and abundance. In the middle of the century Chinese symbols were no longer a closed book to the West, and it is clear that the significance of the fish motif was known in Europe, for it occasionally appears on certain pieces decorated in black—those with the so-called 'Valentine motif'. This decoration, which first appeared on Worcester porcelain[3] about 1760, combines three motifs, the altar with two flaming hearts, the tree with the golden fruit, and the two billing doves on a quiver.[4] The Chinese did not understand the meaning of the hearts, and sometimes left them out altogether (Plate 295). In the Westfries Museum at Hoorn there is a fine polychrome cup with the Valentine motif, but with one heart only. The fish motif appears on a dolls-house dinner service painted in black with the Valentine decoration. Besides the altar with the flaming hearts, the tree as usual out of drawing, and the doves, there is now a fishing net and rod. This provides evidence of the relation between the enormously popular Valentine motif and that of the fishers. If we accept 1760 as the date of the beginning of the Valentine motif, and on the ground of various style characteristics this is quite justified, then it appears that this motif long remained in vogue; for in 1778 we still find it described as 'a burning altar, and two small doves on a quiver with a bow, and accessories' in the catalogue of a sale held in that year at Amsterdam of the stock of the porcelain-shop of Martha Raap (see p. 70). The fishes too are mentioned there. In the same catalogue are a number of pieces with 'European small

[1] J. A. Lloyd Hyde, *Chinese porcelain for the European Market,* pp. 50–51. The 'fisher' motif was, it is said, taken from a cheap French print of the middle of the century, inspired by a painting 'Water' from the set of the four elements by Jacopo Amigoni (1675–1752).

[2] T. Volker, *The Animal in Far Eastern Art,* pp. 71 ff. W. B. Honey, op. cit., p. 210.

[3] J. L. Dixon, *English Porcelain of the Eighteenth Century,* p. 35, pl. 776.

[4] J. G. Phillips, op. cit., p. 152.

landscapes in gold shields' of which we think it permissible to assume, having regard to the size and the quality (which appear from all the prices noted down by a visitor at the sale) that this was the porcelain set with the European landscapes mentioned above.

Naturally there have been attempts by those concerned with this particular porcelain to divide it chronologically. A bold theory[1] has been put forward that in the Yung Chêng period hands and faces of figures were painted in flesh tints, and that the British Museum had made use of this point in dating Yung Chêng pieces. But it is not as simple as all that, alas, for there are many pieces which, on account of the rim-decoration or the subject, must be dated later than 1735, even though the faces and hands are painted in flesh-colour.

A division on the basis of rims[2] and general characteristics of style seems a safer method. It should be noted that, during the period 1770–85, the subject used in decoration was frequently placed spread over the whole surface of the plate, without any rim-decoration.[3]

It is true that every country ordering porcelain in China had its own preferences, but these generally only affected the decoration. Often the same shapes were used for services, and only the painting was different from order to order. A good example is the covered sugar-bowl of Plate 296, part of the very large set called *Het Wapen van Kampen* in the Broederpoort Museum at the town of Kampen. The knob on the lid is rose-red, the rest of the decoration is in black. The service is dated on all its pieces 1767. It is interesting that a similar piece, without the lid but complete with the split handles, the flowery sprig in relief and a coat of arms, has been illustrated by an author who, as far as is known, was not aware of the existence of the Kampen set, and dated it 1760–70. Near the end of the century the bowl changes its shape, becoming taller and less elegant.[4]

Though its European subjects appear early in the history of *encre de chine*, none the less even in the Yung Chêng period the decorations included a special kind of 'Chinese' subject consisting of unconnected figures, each on its own purely Chinese, but in a composition completely lacking the magnificent balance which characterizes a truly Chinese scene. The figures were probably chosen like that by the troublesome western customer who had no idea of their significance. The rims round these portrayals, with their wide Louis XV volutes, are purely western.

Genuine Chinese scenes come to the fore again after 1785, although until the end typically western subjects were used in decoration. Such were 'Charlotte at Werther's Tomb' (Plate 297), on a cup and saucer in the British Museum, and a 'Young man in the Attire of Werther' playing the flute, which appears on the inside bottom of a

[1] J. P. van Goidsenhoven, op. cit., p. 200.

[2] M. Beurdeley, op. cit., p. 160. J. A. Lloyd Hyde, op. cit., p. 155.

[3] J. G. Phillips, op. cit., p. 132.

[4] J. G. Phillips, op. cit., p. 118. J. A. Lloyd Hyde, op. cit., pl. XXX, no. 108. M. Beurdeley, op. cit., p. 168, cat. 65.

punch-bowl in the Dansk Folkemuseum at Copenhagen, dated 1790. The big reversed monograms, and the elaborate crowns over the escutcheons placed between supporters, are mostly typical of pieces decorated for the Danish and Swedish markets. Typically Dutch are such subjects as theologians (Plate 294), reformists, the 'Fisher' after Bloemaert (Plate 298, compare Plate 206), which is also known in polychrome, 'Juno in the Clouds', the 'Cither-player' (Plate 299), the 'Embroiderers', biblical scenes (Plate 300), and of course all kinds of mythological and allegorical portrayals concerned with trade and navigation. A good example of such a subject in two variations, a richer and a simpler one, is shown in Plate 301, two small plates, one with Neptune and Mercury and one with Mercury by himself, the former a very fine, thin porcelain painted in black and gold, the latter of a much coarser clay and decorated in black alone.

It is known that some people took exception to lightly clad figures, like those in the 'Judgement of Paris' of Plates 225 and 226, which occur in black as well as in polychrome. To meet the demands of these customers, this group was sometimes 'dressed', and the extra decoration was added presumably in the Netherlands, and so similar pieces come under the term 'clobbered ware'.[1] But in China, too, specimens in chaste and in unchaste style were made of one and the same subject (Plates 302 and 303). The meaning of the frequently depicted subject is not clear: Minerva (?) with her shield protects a slumbering young man against the arrow which Cupid, sitting on the prow of the triumphal car of Venus, is aiming at him. Is this subject intended as a spur to work for a student? It is striking that the unchaste version is of lesser quality than the chaste one. The same Venus in a garland of clumsy clouds appears, for instance, on a plate in the Kunstindustriemuseum at Copenhagen, where the goddess waylays a loving couple, and the same couple is shown on a plate in the Princessehof Museum, but here the sky is empty and there is no Venus. It is obvious that the customers ordered only those elements which met their pleasure, and had elements left out and combined at will.

It is possible to trace most of the models for the portrait services, as for instance the set with the portrait of Willem van Haren (1710–68), *Grietman op de Bild* head of a Friesian village community. Parts of this service are found in the Fries Museum and in the Princessehof, both at Leeuwarden, and in the museum Mr. Simon van Gyn at Dordrecht. The subject was taken from a copperplate engraving by C. de Putter, after a painting by Berbardus Accama (1697–1756). A cup and saucer with the portrait of Johannes Cocceius, taken from an engraving by A. Blotelingh (1640–90), was after a portrait by Anton Palamedes (1601–73). The prints or engravings, which were serving as samples for several other subjects executed in black, could also be traced to their origins.[2]

'Jesuit China' was a name formerly current for porcelain decorated in black. The

---

[1] M. Beurdeley, op. cit., p. 183, cat. 130–1. J. A. Lloyd Hyde, op. cit., p. 81, pl. 43. Also reproduced in J. P. van Goidsenhoven, op. cit., p. 260.

[2] M. Beurdeley, op. cit., pp. 56ff.

name can easily be explained, when one thinks of the important part played by Jesuits (who were already engaged on missionary work in China in the sixteenth century) at the Imperial Court. It is true that they brought European engravings to China in the first place, to acquaint the emperor with the western way of looking at things,[1] particularly western perspective which was foreign to China. But it remains to be seen whether, as is suggested by the name Jesuit china, they imported all the prints and engravings which served as samples for the decoration of *encre de chine* porcelain: a good many of the subjects were far from religious, not to say scabrous and, moreover, we may take it that various subjects, for instance, portraits of reformists and Protestant ministers well known in the Netherlands, were delivered at Canton by Protestant Dutchmen, or at least in their name.

The only embellishment used besides gold on porcelain decorated in black or sepia, was flesh-colour for hands and faces, though occasionally we find black and sepia on the same piece. Usually it is *ts'ai shui mo,* at the most with some flesh-colour or gold. There is one exception recorded however, to wit, a bowl with the portrait of three Europeans in black with flesh-colour, but also with red for the hair (Plate 304).[2] Elsewhere there is a reproduction of a plate, part of a service, decorated with European figures, also with red hair, which according to the accompanying text was made for the Portuguese market. Because only the Dutch and the English, and not the Portuguese, were called 'red-haired foreigners', the question arises whether this set was indeed meant originally for the Portuguese market.[3]

It has already been mentioned that *encre de chine* was certainly no mourning ware, although a small set in the municipal museum 't Coopmanchus, at Franeker in Friesland, decorated in black only and with the religious subject of the Crucifixion, may have been used as such.

The 'Views of Amsterdam' discussed earlier seem to form a good instance of a set of show-plates, they are so immaculate. On the other hand, the plates with the portraits of King Frederick V and Queen Juliana Maria of Denmark in black, in the Bisdom van Vliet Museum at Haastrecht,[3] appear to be somewhat worn and so, on the contrary, must have been used.

The many lighthearted subjects, the punch-bowls with hunting-scenes, and the allegories, were phenomena of fashion which is confirmed in many cases by their appearance in both black and polychrome versions. *Encre de chine* was 'in' from its very beginning in about 1730, as far as we now know, until about 1790. For in consequence of the French Revolution and the Napoleonic wars, and the strong position of the European, and especially the English porcelain factories, there was no longer any

[1] J. A. Lloyd Hyde, op. cit., pp. 39, 40. About the Jesuits in China, see M. Beurdeley, op. cit., pp. 140 ff. Also P. Pelliot, *Les influences européennes sur l'art Chinois au XVIIIe et au XVIIIe siècle.*

[2] J. A. Lloyd Hyde, op. cit., p. 69.

[3] B. L. Grandjean, *Dansk Ostindisk Porcelaen,* figs. 35 and 36.

money to be made out of importing Chinese porcelain, quite apart from the fact that at that time people in Europe were more or less bored with it.

A good specimen of a late set decorated in black is in the museum at Middelburg. Subjects are the Nieuwe Kerk, the Abdytoren, and the Mint of that town (Plate 305). The model used was a very rare print by Th. Koning, which appeared in the December number of 1777 of the *Chronykalmanak*[1] of Zeeland (Plate 306).

On the good quality pieces of *encre de chine* porcelain the original models were accurately copied, but on the mass-produced pieces there were often misinterpretations of the subject. In this misinterpretation the question of perspective, and the western use of shadow and shading, played their parts, for our own way of painting perspective became known in China only after 1715, via the Jesuit painters. With this in mind it is not so strange that on a plate portraying the Resurrection, in the Groninger Museum, branches grow out of the arms of a soldier fleeing into the bush, and that on a handled cup in the same museum showing the Crucifixion, the dice the Roman soldiers are using at the foot of the Cross have been changed into small roses. On some plates showing the Crucifixion, the Crown of Thorns has been changed into a garland of flowers.[2] It is tempting to assume that the porcelain painter was perhaps a Christian, or at least acquainted with Christian subjects, and that he purposely refused to picture the painful and opprobrious crown, because the Chinese do not like to picture suffering and humiliation. More acceptable, however, seems the theory that the porcelain painter was acquainted with a flowery headdress from other export wares, such as that described a little further on. Dead human beings and animals do not occur in Chinese pictorial art, and nudes are unknown. Sometimes Christ, as on the small set at Franeker, is portrayed as a woman, the painter apparently not knowing what to do with his subject. And so it is not to be wondered at that an incomprehensible crown of thorns was changed into a wreath of flowers, like those used by the painter, when he was drawing female figures.

Interesting too is the representation of a man in a three-cornered hat and knicker-bockers, and a woman in European attire with some golden flowers in her hair, sitting under a tree, with in the background a couple of smaller figures looking on. This subject, which can be dated between 1770 and 1785, is described in a handbook,[3] as 'a man and a woman under a tree, with two little children next to the woman'. In our opinion the subject shows a married couple with a servant girl and her beau. In March 1962 a small tea-set decorated in black was sold at auction in Amsterdam with this subject, described in the catalogue as 'two married couples next to a tree'. Instead of flowers the woman in this case has a gold coronet for a headdress.

In the Middelburg Museum there are six very fine soup plates with a simple rim-

[1] J. G. A. N. de Vries, op. cit., p. 9, and J. P. van Goidsenhoven, op. cit., p. 259, have wrongly attributed the example to Pronk.

[2] Described by J. G. A. N. de Vries, op. cit., p. 5.

[3] Reproduced in J. G. Phillips, op. cit., p. 155, and in M. Beurdeley, op. cit., p. 185, cat. 139.

decoration—two gold bands with a red line in between—painted on the central part with various birds in sepia. Here once again it becomes apparent how difficult it often is to ascertain the origin of a certain decoration. Plate 307 shows one of the finest plates which appears to be copied from an engraving 'Poultry-yard', by Francis Place, after F. Barlow[1] (Plate 308). Another of these six plates pictures a poultry-yard with ostriches, which is taken from an engraving by J. Griffier after Barlow. Now it is known that Jan I. Griffier (1652–1718) etched five large plates showing birds, in a set published by Fr. Place (1647–1728), and so one would be inclined to think that the decoration of the six Middelburg plates would consist of the set 'Barlow by Griffier', five pieces, and 'Barlow by Place', one piece.

Mention may also be made that the same subject was sometimes executed in black and sepia, and even in iron-red and gold, for instance the Baptism of Christ of Plate 237.

In addition to subjects taken from prints, including botanical prints, though these are rather rare (Plate 309), purely Chinese subjects were used during the whole period of *encre de chine* porcelain. The European customer, who ordered the plate in Plate 310, probably did not realize in the least that this plate, together with two others forming a set, portrayed the eighteen Lohans of Buddhism. The plate, made about 1775, is wholly Chinese in subject, but the technique, working in depth by cross-hatching, is quite western. The painter has returned to the technique used before, when working for the western market, but he had also recourse to a Chinese subject, because in the later years hardly any new prints were imported from Europe. Another remarkable instance of this technique is found in a small tea service, decorated in sepia, with one of those standing outline-drawings catalogued in the various exercise-books for Chinese calli-graphic painters as *Chieh-tzŭ yüan hua chüan* (*The Mustard Seed Garden*),[2] apparently also known to the porcelain painters. Because, as mentioned above, after 1770 not many new European prints were imported into China, the porcelain painters were driven to using this kind of subject. And so, the great period of *encre de chine* porcelain terminated as it had begun, with Chinese decoration.

[1] Van Goidsenhoven, op. cit., p. 260, pl. 112 ns. 168–9. The author considers this 'Poultry-yard' as 'Evidently under the influence of Handecoeter'. One is after a design by Pieter Boel (1622–74): Clare Le Corbeiller, 'Trade Winds from China', *Bulletin, The Metropolitan Museum of Art,* January, 1962, p. 196, New York.

[2] See p. 73.

17 · Chinese porcelain with 'Kakiemon', 'Imari' and 'milk and blood' decoration

The 'Kakiemon' and 'Imari' styles of decorating porcelain were imitated in China as well as in Europe. It is not known when this occurred for the first time. Kakiemon porcelain, which was made in Japan earlier than Imari, was probably the first to be copied in China, and it is not impossible that this took place for the first time in the second half or at the end of the seventeenth century.

'KAKIEMON'

The Kakiemon style of porcelain decoration was enamel painting in a delicate manner of simple landscapes, of gnarled pine-trees, bamboo, chrysanthemums, human figures, animals and birds. The colours used were blue, iron-red, yellow, green and sometimes violet-purple. The blue enamel was probably used earlier in Japan than in China.[1] The best known representation is that of the tiger with bamboo and banded hedge (Plate 311). This subject was imitated in China and at Meissen, Chantilly, Chelsea and Bow, which proves this style of decoration to have been much appreciated. Somewhat modified, it was used on Delft ware too. The Groninger Museum owns one oblong and two square trays[2] with the decoration of 'cock and hen' on the central part, surrounded by dragons and flowers on the broad deep rim (Plate 313), made respectively in Japan, China and at Meissen in Germany. Since the last-named is known to have been made at Meissen between 1728 and 1730 it may be concluded that the Japanese prototype was made before that time. Both birds on the Japanese tray are painted more naturalistically and vigorously than on those of its Chinese counterpart.

---

[1] This method of decoration was an invention of the Sakaida family of potters in Japan and especially of one of its members, Kakiemon 1st.

[2] Minke A. de Visser, 'Drie Kakiemon schoteltjes met haan en hen etc.', in *Annual Report* of the Groninger Museum for 1961. See also R. Soame Jenyns, *Japanese Porcelain*, p. 54, pl. 79a.

Porcelain with 'Kakiemon', 'Imari' and 'milk and blood' decoration

'IMARI'

When it became apparent that Japanese Imari porcelain[1] was much in demand in Europe, the Chinese, perhaps encouraged by the Dutch, started to imitate it at Ching-tê Chên. They were successful in selling it to their European customers, because they asked a lower price for their product than the Japanese did for their own version. It has not been possible to ascertain whether the Imari decoration was used in China before the eighteenth century. It is, however, certain that it was made early in that century, which is proved by armorial dinner services, one of which was owned by the first Lord Somers who died in 1716, which makes it certain that this set was made before that year. The second belonged to Sir James Craggs, who died in 1721. Finally, there is a set with the arms of Thomas Pitt, governor of Madras, who left India in 1706 or 1708, which is believed to have been made before his departure. This makes it probable that the first Chinese Imari appeared soon after 1700. There is also some Chinese Imari in the collection of Augustus the Strong and listed in the inventory of 1721. This disproves Volker's theory that Chinese Imari came into being between 1724 and 1734.[2]

The fact that the Yung Chêng list (1732) refers, under the numbers 55 and 56, to porcelain with a gilt design in imitation of Japanese porcelain (probably Imari) is an indication that it was much valued in China at that time.[3]

The colour-scheme of Chinese Imari consists of underglaze blue and overglaze iron-red and gold. The body is thinner, more brittle, and whiter than that of the Japanese kind. The footrim is often unglazed and brownish and, unlike the Japanese dishes, there are no spur-marks on the base (Colour Plate H).

Sometimes it is difficult to see the difference between the two kinds, especially when Japanese decoration, for instance the conventionalized chrysanthemum (*kiku mon*), is imitated, or when the decoration has in it typically Japanese elements. The latter is the case of a plate in the Princessehof Museum (Plate 315), the centre of which is decorated with the conventionalized, here twelve-petalled, chrysanthemum, surrounded by the Eight Precious Things. On the eight panels of the rim one may also see many-petalled conventionalized chrysanthemums, alternating with flower sprays. A plate in the Rijks-museum at Amsterdam (Plate 312), the rim of which has a cloud-pattern, alternating with flowers and a small fence, reminiscent of a Japanese garden, also shows Japanese influence. A plate, once in the Dresden collection of Augustus the Strong (Plate 316),[4]

---

[1] This porcelain got its name from the town of Imari on the island of Kyushu in Japan. Porcelain made in several places of Kyushu was shipped from that sea-port.

[2] R. Soame Jenyns, op. cit., p. 42.   [3] R. Soame Jenyns, op. cit., p. 118, footnote 3.

[4] This plate was bought in June 1723, and is mentioned as Japanese in the catalogue; the inventory number, a cross and 'NZIO' point in the same direction. I have to thank Dr. F. Reichel, director of the Staatliche Kunstsammlungen at Dresden, who gave me this information. The thin white body and the design prove its Chinese origin. In the Franeker museum there are two similar plates. This may indicate that the Dutch E.I.C. at one time bought a lot of these plates at Canton and sold one or more to Augustus.

has a more Chinese style of decoration. The central part is decorated with a flower-vase behind a low fence, and the rim with alternating round and *ju–i* panels with flowers.

One of the earliest Imari pieces is a plate (Plate 317), with a central decoration of a lady and a gentleman in a chariot drawn by two horses. In shape and rim-decoration this is identical with some K'ang Hsi *famille verte* armorial plates (see colour plate G). On the ground of this similarity, this plate will probably have been made between 1720 and 1730.

The barber's bowl of Plate 314, with a magnificent flower decoration in the centre and an intricate cloud-pattern on the rim, dates from the beginning of the eighteenth century. Coats of arms, for instance of towns, were frequently painted on bowls of this kind, just as they were on the Japanese versions.

Imari decoration also appears on teapots, cups and saucers, covered bowls, and on porcelain of western shape.

'MILK AND BLOOD'

'Milk and blood' is the term used to describe a style of decoration painted in iron-red with a little gold and sometimes underglaze blue. It is by some people regarded as a degeneration of the Imari manner. It appears on coarser as well as on eggshell porcelain. The oldest pieces are supposed to date from the twenties of the eighteenth century, a belief that gains support from a plate painted in iron-red (Plate 318), with the same subject as the plate of Plate 317. On the later pieces made in the Yung Chêng period a dull black is sometimes added to the colour scheme. The 'milk and blood' decoration was much in vogue in Europe at that time. The subjects were painted wholly in line in iron red. The central part of the plate, shown in Plate 319, has a ship on a river with mountains in the background. The rim has thinly outlined tulip-shaped panels and flower sprigs. Decoration of this kind is also found on pieces with a central subject of people in front of a house. Other objects besides plates were ornamented in this technique, such as the thin-necked bottles of Plate 320, decorated with chrysanthemums and tassels. Sometimes the palette was added to by the use of *famille rose* enamels, either on the whole piece or on the rim of plates only. Armorial plates were occasionally painted in this technique.

18 · Ceramics made at Yi-hsing and Tehua

The Day Register of the Dutch East India Company at Batavia has entries of, 'From Chang Chou 7 cases of red teapots', in 1679 and in 1680 of '320 figured red teapots' from Macao.[1] In the same year the *Ternate* carried 1635 Chinese teapots to Amsterdam.[2] These were probably teapots of red stoneware made at Yi-Hsing. In the Netherlands they were called East Indian, or Indian, teapots because the Company shipped them during the seventeenth century, and later, to the Netherlands via Batavia. This red stoneware, which is very similar to earthenware made in Middle and Central America, was commonly called 'boccaro' or 'buccaro'. From the beginning of the tea-drinking habit in Europe, roughly in the middle of the seventeeth century, there was an increasing demand for Chinese teapots which, as they were later also made to the order of the West, can be included in the group of export wares.

The red stoneware pots, which retain heat well, are difficult to date because they were for so long made in the same tradition. That they were known in the Netherlands before 1680 is proved by the fact that Lambertus Cleffius in 1672, and Ary de Milde about 1680, knew already how to imitate those pots.[3] In England John Dwight (1684), and the Elers brothers (about 1690), made similar pots. In the Netherlands teapots were rather costly, as had once been the case in China, for in the sixteenth century a high Chinese official paid 500 tael for a teapot. In Holland and also in Germany, the pots were sometimes given a silver or even a gold mounting.

The ware we are now concerned with was made at Yi-hsing in the south of Kiangsu

---

[1] T. Volker, *Porcelain and the Dutch East India Company*, p. 216.

[2] Ibid., p. 167.

[3] Böttger also succeeded extremely well in imitating them and in Germany they were made already between 1709 and 1720. They were sometimes called *terra sigillata*, the clay being so similar to this Roman product. About 1763 Wedgwood also started making them, and this red stoneware was called *rosso antico*.

province, west of Lake T'ai Hu, the clay needed for its manufacture being found in the mountains near by. After firing, the colour of the clay varied from red-brown, dark brown, or buff, to grey-black. These nuances were obtained by the mixing of variously-coloured clays. It is said that the first specimen of this stoneware for the making of tea was made by a Taoist priest living at the beginning of the sixteenth century, a certain Kung Ch'un, who lived in the Chêng Tê period (1506–21), who found out the secret of its composition and started the commercial production of such pots, which soon had a large scale.

Various seventeenth-century potters, the names of many of whom are known to us, started to make other objects in this red stoneware. Chû Chung-mei, who had before this worked at Ching-tê Chên, made flower-vases, scent-boxes, paper-weights and tea-caddies. And later on statuettes, for instance, of Kuan Yin, and even sets for cupboards and cabinets, and other things were made in this clay.

In the first decades of the seventeenth century, the teapot (Plate 322) was first made in the shape which is still in general use. In the Groninger Museum there are two of these pots with 'tax paid' and reign-marks.[1] One (Plate 321, right) has the mark of the T'ien Ch'i period (1621–27), the other (Plate 321 left) that of the first Ch'ing emperor Chun Chih (1644–61). If these marks can be trusted, these pots give a good impression of the teapots of the Dutch 'Golden Age'. They can be observed in the paintings of van Roestraten (1630–98), in both the round and the square models. The ideal teapot was a small, round, somewhat flattened pot, with a handle and a straight spout, and in Japan these are still dearly loved for use at the tea-ceremony. And yet, the Yi-hsing potters also gave their pots the most fantastic shapes, such as that of a pear, an olive, a gourd, a melon, a flower, a bird, or even bamboo-stems. The pots were not infrequently decorated with twigs of the plum tree in relief, as is shown in the still-life by van Roestraten of Plate 146. Sometimes the surface was polished to a shining gloss.

At the end of the eighteenth century, the red stoneware was enamelled with opaque blue, white, rose-red, and other colours of the *famille rose* palette. Similar objects are mentioned in the catalogue of the Martha Raap sale of 24th August 1778.

TÊHUA WARE

Têhua was the chief centre of porcelain-making in the province of Fukien. It is situated about seventy miles north of Amoy. Among the products made there, the white ware *blanc de chine* became famous. The white clay, *pai tz'ŭ*, so the K'ang Hsi encyclopaedia has it, was found at Yung-hing for example.[2] There is no other kind of porcelain where

---

[1] After the potters had paid the tax due on their product it was stamped with a tax-paid mark, with the name of the collector's office, and with the mark of the reigning emperor.

[2] There are different kiln-sites in China where a white ware was made. P. J. Donnelly, *Blanc de Chine*, p. 21.

glaze and body are fused together as well as in the Têhua ware, so that on a shard one cannot see where the clay stops and the glaze begins. It contains more feldspar and relatively less kaolin than other kinds of porcelain.[1] The body is creamy white, vitreous, translucent, and the glaze shows many variations of white from yellowish through ivory to bluish, and sometimes even a pinkish tint. It can easily be understood that it was much appreciated. Besides bowls and dishes in the shape of ceremonial or ritual bronzes, incense-burners were made, brushpots, cups with (Plate 328) or without sprigs of the plum tree and other decorations in relief, and little objects for the writing-table. The vessels are often decorated with flowers, tendrils and sometimes animals in relief.

The clay is also eminently suitable for modelling and was used for making statuettes, small and large—some even more than a yard high—portraying Buddha, Ta Mô (Bodhidharma), Taoist Immortals, Kuan Yin, and other deities, human beings, animals, the 'Chinese lion' (Plate 324), serpents and birds. The heads and hands of the figures are sometimes moulded separately (Plate 327). In the eighteenth century in Europe (the Netherlands and Germany) various statuettes and other objects, such as cups, were painted, and the same happened in China, where red, green, brown and yellow enamel were used. All this quite apart of course from the Têhua white porcelain, the 'first quality Fukien' of the seventeenth century and later. Cold-painted figures which have never been in the muffle kiln are also known.[3]

European merchants succeeded in creating a good demand for Têhua porcelain. From the K'ang Hsi period onwards right up to the present, it has been shipped to Europe in considerable quantities. After the middle of the seventeenth century porcelain was made at Têhua which shows European influence, for instance, the mug of figure 37, with the protruding rings round the body, and the bulging mug of figure 38, the bowl with two horizontal handles and the albarello.

At first *blanc de chine* was shipped to the West from Ch'üan Chou and then, in the course of the seventeenth century, via Amoy. The porcelain arriving in Europe varied considerably in quality and colour. Some statuettes are coarsely made; others on the other hand are extremely finely and accurately moulded, details like the fingers or the head being sometimes overfine in execution.

In the West there was also a considerable interest in statuettes portraying Buddha or Kuan Yin,[4] as is proved by figures of these deities in the Johanneum at Dresden. The collection there also has female dancers, horsemen, children playing and laughing, and

[1] The large proportion of quartz gives this porcelain its translucence. In this it bears a similarity with the European *pâte tendre*. See also W. Bondy, *Kang Hsi*, p. 70 ff.

[2] T. Volker, op. cit., pp. 54 and 66. Also R. Soame Jenyns, *Later Chinese Porcelain*, p. 83.

[3] W. Bondy, op. cit., pl. 190 shows a standing female figure, 32 inches high, enriched with 'cold-painting'.

[4] W. Bondy, op. cit., pl. 193, Kuan Yin seated. The first Jesuits saw an outward similarity between Kuan Yin with a child and Mary with Jesus. In a few Japanese museums some figures of this deity are kept as relics of the first Christians in Japan.

37. Têhua mug, probably after European model, eighteenth century. Ht. 6 cm. *British Museum, London*

38. Têhua mug, also European in shape. eighteenth century. Ht. 6 cm. *British Museum, London*

animals, lions, elephants, tigers. These figures, made in the K'ang Hsi period, were supplied to Augustus the Strong through the intermediary of the Dutch East India Company. Some of the objects, as for instance a bowl, have metal mounts. In the Netherlands, too, many a piece of *blanc de chine* was sold to which the 1637 inventory of the Amsterdam painter Jan Basse bears witness; it includes references to a Kuan Yin and altar lions. The fact that Delft imitated statuettes of Kuan Yin, also shows that they were much appreciated. On a painting by van Roestraten (Plate 137) a hexagonal teapot is portrayed with sunk panels decorated with figures in relief.

Blanc de chine was imitated in other European countries much more than in the Netherlands. The *pâte tendre* of St. Cloud is sometimes so similar to Fukien porcelain that it may be difficult to distinguish between them. At Meissen,[1] St. Cloud, Chantilly and Mennecy,[2] Bow and Chelsea[3] statuettes as well as service ware was imitated. Sometimes the Chinese *blanc de chine* was even mistaken for Meissen, or ascribed to Dwight of Fulham.[4]

Statuettes or figure-groups of Europeans are quite well known. It is possible that they were made for the Chinese home market, for people who wanted to have a representation of the foreigners from the West. And, just as in the case of the pictures of Europeans on other export wares, so the Europeans depicted in *blanc de chine* are often ludicrous beings with Chinese features, and to our eyes look like caricatures. The statue of a seated Dutchman, made at the end of the seventeenth or the beginning of the eighteenth centuries (Plate 323), has a decoration in relief on the tabouret, and this, a bird on a branch, is wholly Chinese, but the expression on the man's face is remarkably European. Some-

[1] W. B. Honey, *Dresden China*, pl. 1. VII.
[2] W. B. Honey, *French Porcelain*, pl. 8, 14, 29, 34b, c and d.
[3] G. Savage, *Eighteenth Century English Porcelain* (London, 1964) pl. 41b, c.
[4] R. L. Hobson, *Handbook*, p. 117.

times a European was portrayed sitting on a *ch'i-lin* (Plate 329). Statuettes of a Dutch-man and two Chinese women were exported to the West, and also groups like that of Plate 325. The woman in this has a seventeenth-century headdress and the men wear three-cornered hats, but instead of European furniture the potter has used Chinese—probably the only kind he knew. The statuettes of Europeans with whistles attached (Plates 326, 329) and usually not higher than 1½ inches, were probably also made to the order of the West.

Because some of the figures were moulded again and again in the same old moulds, the seams are often visible,[1] and because the same kind of clay was used for ages it is frequently impossible to date this porcelain. In general it does not bear any mark or date. None the less in several collections there are marked and dated pieces like those in the British Museum, a statue of the God of Power, and a mortar, dated respectively 1610 and 1511.

Finally, porcelain with the colour of creamy milk was also made at Ching-tê Chên, with a thin-walled body and a less thick glaze than that of the Têhua *blanc de chine*. Père d'Entrecolles believed that figures of Kuan Yin were also made there.

---

[1] Where the statuettes are open at the bottom the pedestals often have fire cracks.

19 · Porcelain figures

As early as the Han dynasty, the Chinese were masters in the making of small figures in various materials—stone, bronze, wood or clay—and in the Ming period many glazed, but even more unglazed, biscuit, figures were made. The unglazed porcelain was painted with green, brown, violet-blue, aubergine, yellow and turquoise enamels. The heads often remained unglazed and unpainted.

Biscuit and glazed figures were also made during the Ch'ing period, the former painted with green, blue, aubergine and yellow enamels. As in the case of the Têhua figures the hands were sometimes moulded separately and luted to the arms. There are figures decorated in underglaze blue (Plate 333), with or without overglaze polychrome painting, and the colour-schemes of the *famille verte* and *famille rose* were also used. Subjects included gods and other deities, immortals, fellow countrymen, and animals, and Europeans were also portrayed. It is not impossible that the latter were made, as in the case of the imitations of *blanc de chine* statuettes, at Ching-tê Chên, to the orders of the Chinese themselves.

Even though the statuettes of Europeans were generally fairly true to nature, it is nevertheless quite clear that they were not moulded by western hands, as can easily be seen from the figures of Louis XIV and Madame de Montespan (Plate 334). It is known that both these figures were made at the end of the seventeenth or the beginning of the eighteenth centuries, and shipped to Europe at that time, because similar ones also form part of the collection of Augustus the Strong. Both figures have open mouths—a fairly common characteristic in Chinese figures but unusual in European statuettes. They are 18 cm. high, are dressed in European attire, wear painted wigs and dress, and have arms and hands separately moulded. There are different specimens of these figures which were painted in other colours: sometimes the man is dressed in a white coat strewn with flowers; in another copy the coat is painted in green and yellow and decorated with Chinese characters. In the case of the Madame de Montespan, Chinese motifs like the *fêng-huang* are painted on the skirt, the Chinese artist having apparently forgotten that he was portraying Europeans and not Chinese. There are also differences in moulding, for instance with regard to the dress.[1] Besides these figures there are others like the one of a young girl dressed in a coatee which is done up with a sash; she has a strangely shaped hat for a headdress.[2] Further, there are the figures of a man and woman wearing a seventeenth-century costume.[3] All these biscuit figures are decorated with polychrome enamels. If there could possibly be any doubt whether these figures were made to order from Europe, there can be no doubt at all in the case of a candlestick in the shape of a woman dressed in western attire of the first half of the eighteenth century,[4] and in the case of a candlestick with two dogs,[5] or a dancing couple.[6] A Meissen group of a dancing couple made by J. J. Kändler[7] about 1740 was imitated in China (Plate 331).

The many imitations made at Delft and elsewhere clearly prove that the Ching-tê Chên statuettes of Kuan Yin, for instance, and of the begging monk Pu-t'ai Ho-shang, were exported to the Netherlands.

ANIMALS

It is difficult to realize that the polychrome parrots made at Delft have their prototype in similar birds modelled in China in polychrome porcelain. Like their Dutch imitations these birds are sitting up, and as it were grown into one with, a rock. A second piece of evidence that these birds were shipped to Europe in the eighteenth century, is produced by those of their kind which with the aid of gilt-bronze have been transformed into candelabra. The water-colour portrait of Mr. Mauritius by C. Troost in the Rijksmuseum, dated 1741, shows a cock standing on a table, proving that these birds too were exported. Probably polychrome cows, true copies of Delft cows, were also made in porcelain in China to the order of the Dutch.

From the beginning of the eighteenth century little porcelain dogs[8] were made in China, in imitation of European and sometimes also of Chinese examples. They are usually shown sitting on their hindlegs with open mouths showing their teeth. Most attractive are the kind represented by Plate 330, sturdy, yellow-glazed on the biscuit,

---

[1] M. Beurdeley, *Porcelain de la Compagnie des Indes*, pl. IV.

[2] M. Jourdain and R. Soame Jenyns, *Chinese Export Art in the Eighteenth Century*, pl. 75.

[3] M. Beurdeley, op. cit., pl. XVIII.

[4] G. Wills, 'Chinese Lowestoft and export porcelain' in *The Concise Encyclopaedia of Antiques*, II, 1960.

[5] G. Wills, op. cit., pl. 56c.

[6] Anthony du Boulay, *Chinese Porcelain*, pl. 122.

[7] Reproduced in H. Gröger, *Johann Joachim Kändler der Meister des Porzellans* (Hanau, 1956), pl. 26. Imitated at Bow about 1758. See J. L. Dixon, *English Porcelain of the Eighteenth Century*, pl. 58. Imitated at Chelsea about 1754.

[8] M. Beurdeley, op. cit., pl. IX. D. F. Lunsingh Scheurleer, 'Enige weinig voorkomende Chinese porseleine', *Antiek*, 2, 1967–68, p. 351 ff.

and with a green collar.[1] Much less likeable are the dogs with pointed jaws (Plate 332), painted in iron-red, which have something repellent and venomous about them. They were probably made between 1750 and 1770. Similar dogs modelled at Delft or elsewhere in the Netherlands may have served as samples.

The pugs,[2] sitting or lying down, made by Kändler about 1735, were imitated in Chinese porcelain,[3] and it is possible that dogs modelled at Chelsea, Bow[4] and Longton Hall, about the middle of the century, inspired by Meissen, were used also as models for the Chinese ones.

[1] M. Beurdeley, op. cit., cat. 103, 104. J. G. Phillips, *China Trade Porcelain*, pl. 73.
[2] E. Zimmermann, *Meissener Porzellan* (Leipzig, 1926) pl. 30. W. B. Honey, *Dresden China* (London, 1954) p. 121.
[3] M. Beurdeley, op. cit., cat. 196.
[4] G. Savage, *English Porcelain*, pl. 89a, Chelsea; pl. 89b, Derby.

20 · Brown-glazed and Mandarin porcelain

Brown-glazed export porcelain is sometimes called Batavian ware after the place from where much of it was shipped to Europe. The brown glaze occurs in several variations, from light brown or Nanking-yellow, also called buff or egg-yellow, to dark brown or capuchin-brown, after a capuchin friar's cassock. In France it is commonly called *café au lait* or *feuille morte*. This brown, ferruginous glaze was fixed on the porcelain body in the high temperature of the porcelain kiln. It was first used in Ming times, and afterwards in the period of K'ang Hsi and his successors. The decoration was usually painted on reserved panels, often shaped like a fan or a leaf. The painting of flowering branches, and frequently a peony, was done in the *famille verte* palette (Plate 187), and from the Ch'ien Lung period onwards in the *famille rose* colour-scheme (Plate 189). Underglaze blue by itself, as well as in combination with overglaze red and gold was also used.

Plates or saucers (Plate 187), cups and bowls, brown-glazed on the outside, while the inside has decoration in underglaze blue or overglaze enamels, are fairly common. Covered bowls (Plate 189), garnitures, and particularly tea wares were decorated in this fashion. Sometimes the brown was painted with silver, which in many cases has become black due to oxidation. Père d'Entrecolles mentions particularly a silver decoration on a brown glaze; and on account of the beautiful glaze magnificent effects were obtained.

MANDARIN PORCELAIN

This kind of export porcelain is named after a Chinese official, the mandarin,[1] who frequently plays the principal part in the scenes depicted on the porcelain. He is shown

[1] The word mandarin comes from the Portuguese word *mandar*, meaning to command. By this name Europeans in China meant a government official.

dressed in Manchu attire, a long coat and trousers, boots with thick felted soles and, when in winter dress, a fur-coat. There are many specimens of this ware where the mandarin is absent, but which otherwise have the same characteristics (Plates 335–339).

During the second half of the eighteenth century, Mandarin porcelain was much in fashion, and was exported to the Netherlands in large quantities. Even in the nineteenth century it was still in considerable demand there.

It is easily recognizable by its colour-schemes, which distinguish it from other enamelled porcelains. Sometimes a rather strong underglaze blue was used, in combination with iron-red, and more especially green and purple overglaze colours. And from time to time black was also used. The iron-red, and perhaps also the black, were painted on the porcelain without a flux and fired in the muffle kiln.[1] Common as well as egg-shell porcelain was painted with this kind of decoration. Sometimes the body surface is of the 'orange-peel' variety. The enamel colours were not always sufficiently well fused with the glaze, and when this happened, if the piece were much used the colours sometimes wore down or on occasion even came off. Gold was often added in a further firing.

Vases, cups and saucers, and plates generally have their decorations applied in large or small irregularly-shaped panels within a simple contour line, or bordered by scrolls or tendrils. On some pieces the shaped border panels were filled with diaperwork painted with flowerets, for example in rose-red, or with vine tendrils; on others they are decorated with birds perched on branches. The large panels on vases, or on the centres of the plates were ornamented with scenes, vividly painted in blue and *famille rose*—such as a house and a terrace (Plates 335–337), where a Chinese lady is sitting at a table surrounded by other figures, often including a mandarin. The background may be filled by a mountain-and-water landscape, or by a river-mouth with lobster-fishers. Air and water are frequently suggested by the white of the porcelain body (Plate 338). In general this porcelain gives rather a motley impression because of the contrasting colours. In the early pieces they were rather soft-hued, but in the later ones the colours were hard and unattractive.

The scenes are generally accurately painted with much attention to detail. In addition to the rococo rims, already described, the swastika, cloud-pattern and garlands were also used. The shape of polygonal vases was often weak, and the angles are sometimes ribbed in relief (Plate 339). The demand was for extravagant and colourful wares, which led to the application of flowering branches, human figures, and rodents in polychrome relief, and this blurred the original shapes.

In the province of Groningen in the Netherlands, where this porcelain was in great demand, a distinction was made between 'gentleman's' and 'peasant's' Mandarin porcelain. The former was richly and variegatedly decorated with gold added, but this was absent on the latter kind. Western influence is visible in the rococo tendrils and

[1] J. P. van Goidsenhoven, *La Céramique Chinoise sous les Ts'ing*, pl. 98.

sometimes in the way the Chinese ladies are portrayed. On a plate in the collection of the Princessehof Museum, decorated in green, rose-red and red, a lady sitting at a table has her legs crossed. This is a western and certainly not a Chinese way of sitting. Similarly, the coiffure of the ladies is not always high-looped as in China, but sometimes laid flat on the head.[1]

[1] Minke A. de Visser, *Explanatory description of the Collection of Chinese and European Porcelain. Chinese and European Stoneware and Earthenware in the Groningen Museum*, p. 35.

21 · Chinese porcelain redecorated in Europe

During the eighteenth, and perhaps as early as the end of the seventeenth century, Chinese and Japanese porcelain, white, blue-and-white and even engraved, was re-decorated in Europe. It was done in the Netherlands, Germany (Meissen), England (Chelsea, Bow and London), and Italy (Venice and Florence). In England the redecorated porcelain came to be called 'clobbered ware'; in the Netherlands it was given the name 'Amsterdam's *bont*' (motley) (Plates 347, 350–353). Formerly it was also called 'Holland porcelain'.[1] Although this redecorated Chinese porcelain has lost its purely native character, which in any case is true of most export wares, it is discussed here if only for the reason that it was and still is taken for porcelain painted in China. And this is easily understood, for in some cases such as the 'Van Leeuwenhoek' plates (Plates 341–344), and with subjects like the *Wonder van Zaandam* (Plate 358), it is indeed difficult to be sure whether the decoration was actually applied in Europe or in China.

In general the Chinese porcelain thus maltreated, and the redecoration painted on it, had but little quality, to say the least. On the other hand we must not forget that there are specimens which have a certain rustic charm of their own.

The name 'Amsterdam's motley' would seem to indicate that town as the place where the export wares were redecorated, but decoration must also have been applied at Delft, where during the eighteenth century most of the Dutch potteries were situated. A communication that a certain Gerrit van de Kaade had, in 1705, opened a shop at Delft,[2] where only 'Oriental porcelain' decorated in Holland was sold, supports this theory. Painting on an already baked and glazed ware, with colours fit for use only in the muffle kiln, was nothing out of the common or new. It was done at Delft and elsewhere on tin-glazed earthenware, with the difference only that the painting was

[1] W. J. Rust, *Nederlands Porselein* (Amsterdam, 1952), p. 157.

[2] H. Havard, *La Céramique Hollandaise* (Amsterdam, 1909) vol. I, p. 144. W. B. Honey, *Dresden China*, p. 160.

done on a tin glaze and not on porcelain. Dominie Mol, the maker of the well-known Dutch porcelain of that name, had a couple of East Indian white tea services redecorated for use in his own house, in 1771.[1]

The Chinese porcelain decorated in the Netherlands was known elsewhere in Europe too. This appears from the inventory of the collection of the Duke of Bourbon, made after his death in 1740: *Deux pots à tabao de porcelaine de la Chine repeinte en Hollande.* The sale catalogue of the Fonspertuis collection, compiled by Edmé Gersaint in 1747, mentions two square bottles of Oriental porcelain, painted with human figures and animals, which were probably added in the Netherlands.

The redecorations added in the Netherlands are of moderate quality, with occasional exceptions like the 'Deurhoff portrait' (Plate 340). In some cases the new decoration, which might consist for instance of iron-red, blue, green, yellow, brown and black enamels, and sometimes gold, were fitted to the original underglaze blue which is still visible. But more often the redecoration was painted over the underglaze blue in a purely arbitrary fashion. On bowls the Chinese rim-decoration in underglaze blue was in many cases left untouched so that the redecoration painted on the wall of the bowl was as it were framed with blue. In the case of engraved decorations, on the other hand, no notice was taken of the original decoration at all. In some cases with an original blue decoration the underglaze blue was blotted out by the glaze.

Identical scenes were painted over and over again on bowls, dishes, vases and bottles, and this may indicate that only a few factories carried out this work, which was probably done with the aid of a stencilling technique. It is quite possible[2] that the re-decoration of Oriental porcelain in the Netherlands was done by the same artists who decorated the Delft wares. The variety of decoration was limited, historical events, daily life, flora and fauna being used.

DATING

There is very little to help in dating Chinese porcelain redecorated in Europe. One of the pieces, which can be dated, is a plate in the British Museum, which at one time was owned by Augustus the Strong, and is decorated with a Chinese lady and a deer.[3] Its inventory number indicates a date before or shortly after 1721. The Rijksmuseum has a plate portraying the ship *Zeeland*, with the date 1700 on the stern of the ship, and this may refer either to the year the plate was made or the ship was launched (Plate 355). In the latter case the plate would have been made after 1700. The ship is shown with

[1] W. J. Rust, op. cit., p. 80, footnote 2.

[2] Dr. H. E. van Gelder, 'De Kunstenaars van ons oud–delfts aardewerk' in *Vrienden van de Nederlandse Ceramiek, Mededelingenblad*, nr. 12, July, 1958, p. 1. See also R. Soame Jenyns, *Japanese Porcelain*, p. 155.

[3] M. Jourdain and R. Soame Jenyns, *Chinese Export Art in the Eighteenth Century*, pl. 100.

the Dutch tricolor at the mast, and the sea is enlivened by two sailing-boats and a row-boat. There are several versions of this subject, identical but for a few small details. The specimen reproduced by Beurdeley[1] has a rim-decoration different from that on the Rijksmuseum plate.

One may of course take it that historical scenes were painted shortly after they had taken place, as otherwise the plates would have seemed out of date and there would have been no demand for them. This would have been the case, for instance, in the portraits of the Princes William IV and William V (Plate 348), and for the decoration depicting scenes from 'The Great Scene of Folly'.

The first porcelain redecorated in the Netherlands, can probably be dated at about 1700. It is also probable that the fashion of thus embellishing Chinese porcelain in the West petered out at the end of the century.

HISTORICAL EVENTS

There are a few well-painted attractive portraits all done on plain white porcelain. In quality they greatly surpass some of the portraits of the Princes William IV and William V. The oldest is probably the portrait (Plate 340) of Willem Deurhoff (1650–1717). The portrait itself, in black, was taken from a print after Bernard Picart (1673–1733), as well as the rim-decoration of the Last Judgement and the Resurrection, and it shows great virtuosity. It is quite possible that this plate was made after Deurhoff's death to the order of his admirers in memory of him. The half-length portrait of Prince William IV in the Boymans-van Beuningen Museum (Plate 250), which until recently had been regarded as entirely Chinese, was almost certainly decorated in the Netherlands. Both the inscription, in perfect Dutch script (cf. Plate 244), and also the manner of painting suggest a Dutch production. The portrait was taken from the reversed image of a mezzotint by J. Faber.[2] It is in polychrome on a background in black. A third beautiful portrait is the one depicting Daniel Raap.[3] According to an inscription on the back of this plate, 'Amsterdam 2 jan. 1750 Pleun Pira fec.', it was made four years before Raap's death. The subject is dressed in a blue coat, with some yellow, sitting at a table with a green table-cloth, and there is a stanza of four lines below.

The three Leeuwenhoek (1632–1723) plates in the Prinsenhof at Delft are equally

[1] M. Beurdeley, op. cit., cat. 244.

[2] Which in turn was taken from a portrait painted by Philips van Dyk (1680–1753). The Prince is also depicted on a Delft plate in the Musée du Cinquantenaire, at Brussels, and on one in the Rijksmuseum at Amsterdam (J. Helbig, *Faïences Hollandaises,* II, p. 49), but these are not in reversed image.

[3] No print is known of Raap, a follower of Deurhoff. The portrait is reproduced by Nanne Ottema, *Chineesche Ceramiek, Handbook,* p. 220, who believed it Chinese. Raap was the leader of the democratic troubles occurring at Amsterdam in 1747–48. After his death his pottery and porcelain shop at the Vijgedam in Amsterdam was looted (Cf. page 70, footnote 4).

well known and handsome. They are a portrait of the scholar (Plate 341) after a mezzo-tint[1] of 1686 by J. Verkolje (Plate 342), his coat of arms (Plate 344), and the sepulchral obelisk in the Oude Kerk at Delft (Plate 343). These three plates have identical rim-decoration, a kind of fleur-de-lis alternating with a different flower in rose-red enamel. The same decoration in the Rijksmuseum is found on a plate showing Herengracht Bay, which is at Amsterdam. The well is bordered by a twisted rope decoration, inspired by similar ones on silver plates, in the colours blue, green and gold, with rose-red festoons. The outer rim-decoration, however, occurs, as far as is known, nowhere but on these four plates. The rope well-border is also found on a plate with Van Leeuwen-hoek's portrait, taken from the same print, dated 1774 on the back, which is in the Musée du Cinquantenaire at Brussels. On the plate of Plate 341, the famous scholar is dressed in a rose-red coat and a white neck-cloth, under which a light-green under-garment is visible. The globe on the print is replaced on the plate by a blue drapery. The tower of the Oude Kerk in the background was probably added at the request of the people who ordered the portrait. The inscription says *Lit van de Koninglijke Societeyt te Londen geboren tot Delft 1632,* 'member of the Royal Society of London born at Delft 1632'. The scholar wearing a full-bottomed wig is shown with a much more lively expression on this and on the Brussels plate, than he has on the original print. The portrait shows no Chinese influence, and the inscriptions are painted in good eighteenth-century Dutch script. On the porcelain decorated in China, on the other hand, Chinese elements are always discernible. As the colours of the enamels are nearer to those used at Delft than to Chinese enamels, it seems certain that the Leeuwenhoek plates were decorated in the Netherlands. This portrait, and the one at Brussels, were in all proba-bility by the hand of the same painter, or painted in the same studio.

It may be supposed that the portrait in the Prinsenhof at Delft was decorated in or about 1774. As both the other plates are identical in execution, one may assume that all three were made at the same time.

The escutcheon of Plate 344 shows a lion rampant on an asymmetric field in gold and with a golden crown. It is painted in green, brown, blue and gold and sits on a shell-like motif with a cornucopia. On the obelisk of Plate 343, there is an inscription in gold, *P. H. Antoni Leeuwenhoek (Reg Anglo) societ.* The portrait on the obelisk and on the vase on top of it are painted in black.

A set of plates in the Fries Museum at Leeuwarden are of far lesser quality. They refer to the great swindle of 1720 (cf. page 145, portraits and political prints). On the central part of one of these plates a town-erier dressed in rose and yellow is

[1] Dr. W. H. van Seters, 'Leeuwenhoek Ceramiek' in *Nederlandsche Tijdschrift voor Genesskunde,* April 1935. The plate at Brussels is reproduced by J. Helbig, op. cit., II, p. 39, fig. 27. Specimens of the plates are in the Museum de Sypesteyn at Loosdrecht and in the Metropolitan at New York. The latter are also reproduced in Warren Cox, *The Book of Pottery and Porcelain,* fig. 896, pl. 169. The author refers to them as Chinese painted.

depicted with a paper in his left hand, with the number '1000', below it are the words *hondert-duisent gulden met armoet,* 'one hundred thousand guilders with poverty' (Plate 354).

In 1747, perhaps in memory of the fact that a hundred years earlier a tragedy had occurred at Zaandam in the Netherlands, which was afterwards called 'The Wonder of Zaandam' or 'The Bull's Cruelty' (cf. page 145, portraits and political prints), plates and services depicting this event were made in 1747. The story is that a farmer and his pregnant wife were walking in a meadow when a bull, frightened by a boy flying a kite, took the woman on its horns and threw her into the air. As a result her child was born prematurely, both the woman and her husband, also mauled and gored by the bull, died, and the child lived for only a year. On the plate of Plate 358, the farmer is seen lying on the ground being mauled by the bull. Above him in the air is the woman, who besides her child has lost a shoe, and to the right a boy is flying his kite. Between the boy and the bull there is a windmill in the distance.[1] Although the polychrome painting is not very good, the painter has copied the subject, probably taken from a popular print, fairly accurately. On the bottom there is the inscription *1647 den 20 Augustus.*

The question of whether a certain piece of Chinese porcelain was decorated in Europe or in China also arises in the case of dishes painted with the 'Peace of Aix la Chapelle', in the Metropolitan Museum of New York and in the collection Völcker van Soelen at Zoelen in the Netherlands. According to publications on this subject it is presumed that the decorating was done in China.[2] It may be accepted, however, that this scene too was painted in Europe, for the enamel colours, iron-red, blue, green, etc., are similar to those already mentioned used at Delft, and this is confirmed by the painting technique. The decoration, probably taken from a print as yet undiscovered, shows a room with a tiled floor and five gentlemen sitting at an oblong table.

In the seventeenth, and particularly about the middle of the eighteenth centuries, the family of the Dutch Stadtholder was frequently portrayed on prints and on pottery and porcelain. Prince William IV was made Stadtholder in 1747, and subjects connected with this occasion were painted on Chinese bowls and plates. On one side of a bowl decorated in underglaze blue there are half-length portraits, on either side of two orange trees. They are taken from paintings dated 1734, by Philips van Dyk (1680–1753), and show Princess Anna[3] on the left, and Prince William IV on the right. The inscription reads *pr W. C. H. F.* or William Carel Hendrik Friso (1711–51). The painting is in green and red enamel. The back of the bowl (Plate 347) has a Gallic cock, to the left

---

[1] M. Beurdeley, op. cit., fig. 66. The author believes the painting was done in China. In the Boymans-van Beuningen Museum at Rotterdam there is a plate on which the mill is to the left, and the flat rim is decorated with sprays. Reproduced in *Bulletin Museum Boymans van Beuningen,* 1957, no. 2.

[2] M. Beurdeley, op. cit., p. 72, fig. 45. W. E. Cox, op. cit., p. 599.

[3] Daughter of King George II of England, married to William in 1734.

of an orange tree,[1] being chased by a Dutch lion. The cock is perhaps Chinese-inspired. There are several variations on this theme. Sometimes there is one orange-tree and the motto *Vivat/Oranje* with the portrait of the prince only, or in a cartouche the letters *W.C.H.F. Verkoore tot Stadhouder in 1747*, 'elected Stadtholder in 1747'. The inside of the bowls is usually decorated with tendrils, flowers and garlands.

One of the best-known decorations on plates is the one painted in red, green, yellow and lilac, with the prince and the princess in a landscape and two trumpet-blowing little angels above them, each with a branch in one hand holding between them a crown. This composition too may be found with various inscriptions like *Nooijt ver Enigt altijd versteenigt*, 'never united always turned to stone' (Plate 345), or, *Altijd bevreest voor het schijde meest,* 'always most afraid of separation', or, *Had ik mij beter gewend—ik had beter gekend,* 'had I tried harder I had known better'. The rim is decorated with panels having birds and coarse diaper work in iron-red. Occasionally Princess Anna is portrayed by herself, with the inscription *gij moet niet haaste of gij Raak aan het laatste,* 'You shall not make haste or you will not last'. As Prince Willem IV is not included, this portrait was probably painted after his death in 1751 (Plate 346).

The number of subjects showing the princely pair increased in the second half of the century, when the position of the Orange family became more unstable, and include the Orange-tree with likenesses of Princess Wilhelmina (1751–1820) and Prince William V (1748–1806) (Plate 348). It has not so far been possible to discover a print which could have been the source for these portraits on porcelain; there is, however, a similarity between this subject and that showing the prince and his princess on plates made at Delft and elsewhere.[2]

One of the late pieces of Chinese porcelain, redecorated in the Netherlands, is a tea service with the inscription 'Doggers bank' (1781). The decoration painted in red, blue, and black enamels is of a merman holding the Dutch tricolor with the name 'Zoutman' and, on the right, two ships (Plate 152, tea-caddy).

SCENES TAKEN FROM DAILY LIFE

One of the most interesting subjects taken from daily life is on a plate (Plate 356) showing the *Walvisvangst,* whaling.[3] This scene, vividly painted in green, yellow, red and blue, with black for the waves, is taken from two prints by Van der Laan (about 1690–1742), drawn and engraved by S. van der Meulen, who is known to have worked from 1700 till his death in 1730.

[1] Dr. P. H. Pott, *Jaarverslag Rijksmuseum voor Volkenkunde* (Leiden 1960) p. 16.

[2] Cf. Catalogue of exhibition *Oranje Boove* in museum Willet Holthuysen at Amsterdam, July–October 1959, in *Vrienden van de Nederlandse Ceramiek Mededelingenblad* and J. de Kleyn, 'Stadhouder Willem V op Engels porselein' in *Antiek*, I, pp. 27ff.

[3] M. Beurdeley, op. cit. (fig. 67), believes this porcelain to be decorated in China.

Chinese porcelain redecorated in Europe

When we see the many versions of the 'cherry- or apple-picker' (cf. Plates 212–214) we may conclude that this subject was at one time much in vogue. The scene shows a man standing on a ladder picking fruit, and is often combined with a pair of lovers sitting beneath the tree. It occurs on tea services and plates. The specimen of Plate 349 was painted on blank Chinese porcelain in red, blue, green and purple. In the background there is a mountain landscape with a church and houses which is also painted on the inside of the cups and bowls.

The same subject in green, yellow, iron-red and some gold appears on the rim of the dish of Plate 357, alternating with a deer-hunting scene. The centre is painted with the popular subject, the 'Music Lesson', a young lady seated and singing, accompanied by a gentleman playing the bass and a lady playing a cither (?). The same scene, but without the cither-player, is on a Delft cuspidor dated 1747 in the Victoria and Albert Museum.[1] Other subjects are the 'bird-fancier',[2] a couple dancing, a 'woman spinning'[3] (for instance on a coffee-pot in the Victoria and Albert Museum, dated between 1740 and 1750), and finally, the subject so often found in the Netherlands, Chinese houses in a mountain-landscape, or a Chinese lady (Plate 351) in a landscape, with a fawn and a little horse. The flower-basket, that old standby of the Chinese porcelain-painter, was also depicted in the Netherlands (Plate 353), and always in the same manner on the outside and the inside of bowls and on teapots. It is worth noting that this flower-basket is of a shape different from that which was painted on Delft ware, as is shown by a plate in the Rijksmuseum.[4] The so-called 'sentry-box' houses also appear (Plate 352).

FLORA AND FAUNA

Birds, among them parrots, were painted in an attractive manner in red, blue, green and yellow on plates and bowls (Plate 350). These birds remind one of those on Delft ware. The Japanese Kakiemon pattern (see page 164) was also used by the redecorators, and so were the cocks and hens that feature on purely Chinese *chine de commande*.

JAPAN

It is not known when Japanese porcelain was decorated in Europe for the first time, although the first examples were probably painted at the end of the seventeenth century. Pieces made in the island of Kyushu, especially bottle-shaped vases and square bottles, were decorated in the Netherlands mostly in brown-red and light turquoise blue. It is notable that in contrast with the 'redecorated Chinese porcelain' the Japanese porcelain

[1] W. W. Winkworth, 'The Delft Enamellers', *Burlington Magazine*, 1928, pl. III.

[2] This subject is borrowed from a print by Schenk Jr. A. L. den Blauwen, 'Ceramiek met chinoiserien naar prenten van P. Schenk Jr.' in *Bulletin of the Rijksmuseum* (Amsterdam, 1964) pp. 35 ff, pl. 7, 9 nr. 20.

[3] W. B. Honey, *Dresden China*, pl. 28a.   [4] F. Hudig, *Delfter Fayence*, p. 139.

decorated in Europe always came blank and unadorned. Such an undecorated bottle-shaped vase is in the Rijksmuseum voor Volkenkunde at Leiden.[1] Some bottles were decorated with parrots, plants, flowers and sometimes figures, in Kakiemon style (see page 164). Historical events, though, were also shown such as the opening of the ship-canal[2] between Haarlem and Leiden (Plate 359), the construction of which was begun in 1656, the canal being thrown open to navigation on 26th September of that year. Two years afterwards a medal was struck in memory of this joyful event. A century later, perhaps in memory of the same event, the ship-canal was depicted on a blank Japanese porcelain bottle. The painting in red, green, blue and turquoise shows the canal with a barge, and in the air a couple of trumpet-blowing angels hold the escutcheons of the cities of Haarlem and Leiden. On another bottle there is the half-length portrait of Stadtholder William IV.[3]

An interesting subject to be found from time to time (Plate 360) is that of a man in knickerbockers who holds a paper in his hand with the inscription *Hoornse Wortelen* 'Hoorn carrots', painted on a square bottle (Plate 361). On the back of the bottle there is a sitting monkey firing a mortar. The subject is connected with a famous swindle of the time. The man is taken from the print *Uytslag der Wind Negotie*, 'result of the stock-jobbery'.[4] An example with an identical monkey has not yet been found, though a monkey sometimes appears on prints depicting the great swindle.

39. Apothecary's pot painted in enamel colours in the Netherlands with Chinese court of justice, after print from Dapper, 1st half eighteenth century. Ht. 22.5 cm. *Groninger Museum*

[1] T. Volker, *Porcelain and the Dutch East India Company*, pl. 39a. These bottles made in Arita during the second half of the seventeenth century occur repeatedly with decoration in underglaze blue, mostly flowers. F. Soame Jenyns, *Japanese Porcelain*, pl. 10a, b. Glass bottles similar to one in the Victoria and Albert Museum with engraved inscription by W. van Heemskerck (1650–80) may have served as models for the porcelain ones. Both kinds have the characteristic 'bobbin' round the neck.

[2] E. Pelinck, 'Een Japanse Fles beschilderd met de Leidse Trekvaart', *Jaarverslag* of Museum de Lakenhal, Leiden, 1952, p. 16.

[3] M. Beurdeley, op. cit., fig. 100, now in the Municipal Museum of Arnhem.

[4] The print belongs to a set called *Het Grote Tafereel der Dwaasheid*, 'the Great Scene of Folly' (see p. 145).

Chinese porcelain redecorated in Europe

In the Groninger Museum there are two very fine apothecary's pots. The decoration on one of them (fig. 39), showing a Chinese court of law, is taken from O. Dapper's *magnum opus*.[1] The decoration on the other, a Chinese gentleman on a horse with two servants, is from a print by P. Schenk, Jr.[2] The scenes on both these pots are fluently and vividly painted in the colour-scheme of the *famille rose*.

[1] O. Dapper, *Gedenkwaerdig Bedrijf der Nederlandsche Oost-Indische Maetschappye op de kuste en in het Keizerrijk van Tai-sing of Sina,* etc., Amsterdam, 1670.

[2] Minke A. de Visser, *Explanatory Description of the Chinese and European Porcelain,* etc., p. 53, pl. 45. A. L. den Blauwen, op. cit., pl. 6 and 9, no. 20.

22 · Marks

Marks do occasionally occur on Chinese porcelain such as the *nien hao* (reign marks: figs. 40, 41), the cyclical date mark, the 'hall' or the marks of commendations and dedication. Porcelain commissioned for western delivery seldom bears the mark of the reign in which it was made, except, for example, bowls such as that shown in Plate 62.

1. The *nien hao* is the name the emperor assumed on succeeding to the throne, which he kept for the duration of his reign or for as long as he wished. Thus Sheng-tsu, when he became emperor in 1662, called himself K'ang Hsi (the joy of peace). At first it was thought that it was only in the royal factories that commissioned porcelain was manufactured, but later this was proved to be incorrect. Usually the *nien hao* appears on the base of the piece in two concentric circles, painted in underglaze blue. Before the reign of Hsüan Tê (1426–35) the mark was rarely used. The royal mark consists of six (or four) characters, which are placed under each other in two columns of three or in three of two. The characters are read from right to left and from top to bottom. Sometimes too they are placed in one horizontal or vertical line. In the first named group of marks the top character in the right-hand column is *ta*, meaning 'great' and the second character of the right-hand column gives the dynasty (Ming or Ch'ing); the third and the top-left reveals the name of the emperor. The middle one means the period (*nien*) and the third 'made by' (*chih*). When there are four characters instead of six the top and the second characters of the right-hand column have been omitted. Of the four remaining, the order is so arranged that the bottom character of the right-hand column is moved up, and the top character of the left-hand column is put below-right.

In fig 41 the brush-down characters (the most common) are on the left and the seal characters on the right.

40. Marks of the Ming Dynasty, 1366–1644

洪武年製 Hung Wu 1368–98	永樂年製 Yung Lo 1403–24	永樂年製 Yung Lo 1403–24
大明宣德年製 Hsüan Tê 1426–35	大明成化年製 Chêng Hua 1465–87	大明弘治年製 Hung Chih 1488–1505
大明正德年製 Chêng Tê 1506–21	大明嘉靖年製 Chia Ching 1522–66	大明隆慶年製 Lung Ch'ing 1567–72
大明萬曆年製 Wan Li 1573–1619	大明天啟年製 T'ien Ch'i 1621–27	崇禎年製 Ch'ung Chêng 1628–43

41. Marks of the Ch'ing Dynasty, 1644–1912

Shun-chih 1644-61

K'ang-hsi 1662-1722

Yung-chêng 1723-35

Ch'ien-lung 1736-95

Chia-ch'ing 1796-1820

Tao-kuang 1821-50

Hsien-fêng 1851-61

T'ung-chih 1862-73

K'uang-hsü 1874-1908

Hsüan-t'ung
1909-12

Hung-hsien 1916
(Yüan shih-k'ai)

Marks

Because the Chinese had such great reverence for the past, the porcelain artists of around the seventeenth, eighteenth and nineteenth centuries used to put marks of illustrious emperors of the Ming dynasty on porcelain which was not manufactured at that time (see Plate 132). On nineteenth-century porcelain, for instance, marks appear of K'ang Hsi and Ch'ien Lung. Japanese artists also put Chinese marks on their porcelain.

2. *Date.* From time to time dates based on a cycle of 60 years are used on porcelain, each date being defined by two characters. The first cycle began in the year 2637 B.C. Regarding the period with which this book is concerned, the 36th year of the 71st cycle falls in 1600, the following begins in 1624, and the 73rd in 1684 and so forth. To find out under which emperor the piece was made, it is possible with the help of a table to calculate the given date in our reckoning. It is dangerous to give a definite date to Chinese porcelain with the help of the *nien hao*, as has already been explained. The form, colour and thickness of the porcelain, as well as the colours of the enamels used, must all be taken into account.

3. *Hall marks.* In these marks—which were already used from time to time during the Ming dynasty—the words *t'ang* (room or pavilion) or *chai* (studio) or *t'ing* (summerhouse) or *hsien* (pavilion or balcony) occur. Since the time of the Emperor Yung Chêng (1723-35) it was customary to place a hall mark on porcelain destined for the royal palace. In fact it was also used on porcelain ordered for the private houses of high dignitaries and merchants. Sometimes it was used to draw attention to the fact that a piece was made, for example, in the Hall of Brilliant Colours.

4. *Names of the potter.* These appear very seldom indeed on porcelain that was made in the royal factories, but on the contrary they do appear on that made by civil concerns. On a Canton-painted cup and saucer in the British Museum we read the name of the painter of Yang-lin. There also exist so-called house-marks, which give the place of work or the pseudonym of the painter.

5. *Marks of recommendation, good wishes, etc.* These are not so rare: *pao shêng*, unique value; *ka chên*, old gem. On a basin in the Groningen Museum is a legend meaning: a jewel among costly vases of rare jade. Among the most common congratulations are: *fu* (luck, fig. 42); *lu* (honour); *shou* (long life); *kuei* (wealth); and again *fu kuei chia ch'i*, a perfect manifestation of the might and honesty; or *wan fu t'ung*, that unending good luck may pertain to all your transactions. Symbols such as the stork, rabbit, hare (fig. 43), peach, *ling chih* (the sacred fungus, fig. 44), swastika (fig. 45) are common on porcelain.

42. *fu*, one of the Twelve Ornaments

43. *t'u*, the hare

44. *ling chih*, the sacred fungus

45. Swastika

46. *yü*, jade

47. *lien hua*, lotus blossom

48. The artemisia leaf

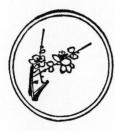

49. *mei hua*, a spray of plum-blossom

50. *ting*, incense-burner

51.a, b Shop-Marks. These are indecipherable

6. *Various marks*. The capital letter G is probably a trademark of a foreign importer. This appears among others on a teapot with *famille verte* decoration in the Museum at Groningen. There also exist marks of quality such as *yü* (jade; and fig. 46), which somewhat resembles a printed capital F. The mark *ta* means 'selected', and this porcelain was destined for sale. Various marks are based on plants, for example *lien hua,* the lotus (fig. 47), plum, artemisia leaf (fig. 48), fruit-blossom (fig. 49).

The incense-burner (*ting,* fig. 50) is also often used as a mark, and other unidentifiable shapes such as those shown in fig. 51a, b. A number of designs, which were used as marks, also appear as patterns.

The *T'ao-lu* informs us that in 1677 the district commissioner, Chang Ch'i-chung, forbade the porcelain makers of Ching-tê Chên to put the reigning-name of the

Emperor K'ang Hsi on their porcelain. This decree was probably brought into force because the emperor did not wish his *nien hao* to be sullied by imitation if the porcelain were broken.

It is not known when this ban was lifted, because at various times we do come across porcelain with the *nien hao* of K'ang-Hsi. And porcelain of the same period is known marked with a double concentric circle in blue. Enclosed in it, also in blue, are Chinese symbols such as the artemisia leaf (fig. 48), lotus (fig. 47), fish, incense-burner (fig. 50), and hare (fig. 43).

23 · Regularly recurring decoration. Iconography

The types of decoration discussed in this chapter are not limited to one particular period but include, for instance, motifs inspired by Buddhism, Taoism and Confucianism. In addition to these, there are the decorations which were in constant use from Ming times such as the *ju-i* and the cloud motifs. Whether the latter had the former for its origin need not be discussed here, but it is a fact that these decorations show so great a similarity that it is sometimes difficult to distinguish between them. In general, the heart-shaped *ju-i* motif consists of two lobes, whereas the cloud motif has more than two.

JU-I

The *ju-i* motif is derived from the upper end of a ceremonial sceptre,[1] and its outline is more or less heart-shaped. It occurs in combination with other decoration, and also as part of a frieze (fig. 52). From time to time a decoration was used composed of elements resembling the fleur-de-lis. This motif, which may also be called *ju-i* (fig. 53) is seen on a small vase made in the period of Hsüan Tê (1426–35), and since at that time there was no question of European influence, it cannot possibly have been derived from the French fleur-de-lis. When Ming porcelain was copied in the Yung Chêng

52. Frieze, *ju-i* motifs on lid of box with Chêng Tê mark. *Royal Ontario Museum, Ontario*

[1] S. Howard Hansford, *A Glossary of Chinese Art and Archaeology* (London, 1961) p. 26. M. Medley, *A Handbook of Chinese Art* (London, 1964) p. 99. Sir Harry Garner, *Chinese and Japanese Cloisonné Enamels* (London, 1962) pp. 83 ff. C. A. S. Williams, *Encyclopaedia of Chinese Symbolism and Art Motives* (New York, 1960) pp. 236 ff. Stanley Charles Nott, *Chinese Jade throughout the Ages* (Tokyo, 1962) p. 63.

53. Frieze, *ju-i*-like motifs resembling fleur-
de-lis decoration on bowl with Yung Chêng
mark. *Riesco collection, London*

54. Frieze, lily-like motifs on shoulder of
Hsüan Tê vase. *Riesco collection, London*

period (1723–35) this motif was used once again. It is not impossible that out of a combination of the *ju-i* and the fleur-de-lis the so-called spearhead motif was born (see
p. 131, fig. 54 and Plates 270, 290).

CLOUD MOTIFS

During the second half of the eighteenth century the *ju-i* motif also occurs in combination with elements borrowed from the West, such as the cornucopia, a rosette sprouting
four spearheads, and the little frieze below a zigzag motif (fig. 55). From early Ming
times the cloud motif was frequently used as a decoration on the shoulder of vases or
as a well-border on dishes. Often the motif is repeated to form a frieze (fig. 56) and is
filled with tendrils, flowers and animals, or a combination of them. It is also quite
common to find border decorations made up from cloud motifs, all similar in shape but
alternately large and small. In the period of K'ang Hsi the cloud motifs used as borders
are generally all of the same size but different in shape, one a somewhat simplified
version of the Ming, alternating with another much flatter and broader, with the sides
extended into short curved points. Both these motifs, like the Ming one, terminate in a
point. Sometimes, even when a border is made from a repetition of one shape only, the

55. Cloud motif built up out of three *ju-i*, in central part of rosette of
four fleurs-de-lis, right, cloud motif and cornucopia taken from
eighteenth-century bowl in *Rijksmuseum voor Volkenkunde, Leiden*

56. Cloud motif, blue-and-white, filled in with tendrils and flowers. By putting these motifs side by side one gets a frieze. 2nd half fourteenth century. *Hobart collection*

motif has become much more complicated. In the course of the eighteenth century the number of variations increases, but the rhythm of the same two elements alternating is maintained, forming a series of mushroom-like motifs (fig. 57). In some cases the Ming prototype is still clearly detectable, but in others, round the bottom of vases for instance, it has degenerated into a series of bracket-shaped curves.

57. Degenerate cloud motif on shoulder of early eighteenth-century vase. Ht. 45.7 cm. *Metropolitan Museum of Art, New York*

The rim-decoration of plates painted in the *famille rose* manner sometimes consists of one motif resembling the *ju-i* rather than the cloud motif, alternating with one which at the inside is closed by a wavy line. The mushroom motif, which is probably a degenerate form of the *ju-i* or cloud, sometimes occurs in combination with a key-fret motif (fig. 58). This also forms part of the Fitzhugh rim (Plates 177, 180 and see page 132), and the decoration was doubtless influenced by the West.

58. Variation on cloud motif frequently used as rim-decoration on *famille rose* porcelain. 2nd half eighteenth century

59. 'French point', probably going back to cloud motif, taken from covered pot sold at auction. *De Roos, Amsterdam, 14th April 1912*

'FRENCH POINT'

The decoration occurring particularly on K'ang Hsi blue-and-white known as 'French point'[1] (fig. 59) must either have developed from the cloud motif or be a degeneration of it, being narrower and more slender. The pottery painters of Delft and elsewhere in Europe frequently used this pattern.

CONVENTIONALIZED LOTUS PANEL

This shaped panel,[2] originally based on the lotus petal of the Buddhist throne, is frequently used as a border motif round the base or shoulder of jugs, etc. (see Plates 39, 42). It is sometimes mistakenly called the *false gadroon,* from its resemblance to the relief decoration found on seventeenth-century European silver.

LAMBREQUIN OR SWAG

This motif,[3] which appears in the engraving of Daniel Marot (1661-1752), was developed from the lambrequin of an escutcheon, or from pendent draperies. It has certainly influenced the rim-decoration of export wares (see Plate 272).

TEXTILES

A decoration which occurs frequently and in numberless variations, and is, according to the *T'ao-shuo,* derived from embroidery, is the diaper pattern (Plates 231, 264,

[1] Dr. C. H. de Jonge, *Oud Nederlandsche-Majolica en Delfts Aardewerk,* fig. 240: a garniture of three vases and two beakers, 1st half eighteenth century.

[2] M. Medley, op. cit., p. 99.

[3] On the other hand, it is possible that the K'ang Hsi cloud motif has influenced the shape of the lambrequin, and the *style rayonnant* connected with it, which was painted on Rouen pottery in blue, or red and blue, at the beginning of the eighteenth century. A. Lane, *French Faience,* p. 21. Jean Berain (1678-1726) also used the decoration.

60. Various scrolls and tendrils

265). It is also known as the brocade pattern or, in the Netherlands, as the 'Marseilles' pattern.

SCROLLS

The scroll decoration (fig. 60 and see p. 130) was already much used in the fourteenth, fifteenth and early sixteenth centuries. It consists of an undulating line with, at frequent intervals, short tendrils which end in a curl of leaf.[1] After this it appears but rarely until it occurs again on the copies of Ming porcelain made in the Yung Chêng and Ch'ien Lung periods. From the beginning of the second quarter of the eighteenth century, however, it was frequently used by the porcelain painters of Ching-tê Chên and Canton.

VARIOUS OTHER DECORATIONS

Amongst other decorations are the swastika (used as a symbol for *wan,* a myriad) both right- and left-hooked, and within a square- or diamond-shaped panel (fig. 45). These, when placed in a row, make a frieze; or in several rows form a diaper-like pattern (Plate 27). There is also the Chinese meander or key-fret pattern in various forms (Plates 17, 60, 63); and finally there is the *lei-wên,* 'cloud and thunder', derived from Shang bronzes (1523–1027 B.C.).[2]

ICONOGRAPHY

The oldest Chinese symbols are the *yin-yang* and the *pa kua.* The former is met with most often in the shape of a capital S within a circle, one half of which is dark and the other light. It symbolizes the dualism of the world, *yang* expressing the male, active,

[1] H. Garner, *Oriental Blue and White,* pls. 1, 4, 17, 21.
[2] W. Watson, *Ancient Chinese Bronzes* (London, 1962) pp. 44 ff., pl. 13a (meander), pl. 4a, 4b (*lei-wên*).

principle standing for heaven, sun, noon, fire, light and warmth, *yin* giving expression to the female, passive principle standing for earth, moon, the North, water, darkness and cold. These symbols are not antagonistic but complement one another.

The *pa kua,* eight trigrams, consist of eight groups of three lines each. The signs are formed by different combinations of unbroken and broken lines and are symbols of the celestial and terrestrial elements. According to tradition the legendary emperor Fu Hsi saw the *pa kua* on the back of a *lung ma,* dragon horse, emerging from the waters of the Yangtse. A less romantic tradition has it that he derived them from the design on the back of a tortoise. However this may be, using them as a basis he conceived a system by which he explained all the phenomena of nature.

Of the three principal religions of Buddhism, Taoism and Confucianism, the last named has supplied the fewest subjects for the decoration of porcelain.

CONFUCIANISM

Confucius, who lived in the sixth century before Christ, is occasionally shown seated, bearded and dressed in official robes and a cap with a tassel. Sometimes he is also depicted in company with Buddha and Lao Tzŭ. These three are symbolized in the shape of a pine-tree, bamboo and a plum-tree, the 'Three Friends'. A dearly-beloved hero was Kuan Yü who lived between 220 and 265. He was canonized by Wan Li (1573–1619) and later created official god of war, Kuan Ti. He is portrayed long-bearded, hefty, fierce, usually in armour and with a halberd, and either standing or on horseback. Sometimes he is confused with K'uei Hsing, the god of literature, who is mostly depicted with budding horns on his head, standing on one leg on the head of a fish-dragon, an emblem of literary ability. On this monster, he ascended to heaven after he had thrown himself into the Yangtse, because, though he had passed his examination successfully, he was not called to office. K'uei Hsing sometimes replaces Wên Ch'ang, the chief god of literature.[1]

TAOISM

Taoist Immortals, symbols (fig. 61), and legends connected with the doctrine, formed an important source of inspiration for the decorators of porcelain. They were used repeatedly, especially during the Chia Ching period (1522–66). The founder of this religion, the philosopher Lao Tzŭ, is one of the personages most frequently depicted. According to legend he had lived for eighty years in his mother's womb and in consequence of this he was born long-haired and thus got his name, Lao Tzŭ, old man-child. He is sometimes identified with Shou Lao, the god of longevity, and portrayed smiling,

[1] This deity rides a mule and is accompanied by flag-bearers. He may be confused with Tung-fang So, who is holding in his hand the peach of longevity.

61. The eight Taoist symbols

with old man's features, high forehead and long beard, riding a water-buffalo or leaning on a knotty staff. The long coat he is wearing is frequently decorated with the character *shou*, longevity (Plate 27). In his hand he has the *ju-i* sceptre ending in a *ling-chih,* the sacred fungus of longevity (fig. 44). Other attributes of his are the scholar's scroll and the peach (Plate 43). He may be shown sitting on a flat rock, sometimes accompanied by a white crane, a spotted deer or a tortoise. Lao Tzŭ is often surrounded by the *Pa hsien,* the Eight Taoist Immortals, demi-gods or genies who wander through the world reforming mankind. They are represented alone or in pairs standing or sitting on a cloud, journeying to the Islands of the Blessed,[1] where the *ling-chih,* the sacred fungus of longevity which protected man from death was said to grow.

Each one of the Immortals (Plates 27–28) is recognizable by his emblem or attribute, Chung-li Ch'üan by his fan and sword, Lu Tung-pin (Plate 333) by his sword. Li T'ieh-kuai is portrayed as a beggar, with an iron crutch and a gourd. Ts'ao Kuo-ch'iu is to be recognized by his castanets, for he is the patron of actors. Lan Ts'ai-ho is rendered in male or female form with a hoe and a flower-basket. Chang kuo-lao is shown riding a white mule and holding the *yuku,* a musical instrument consisting of a bamboo tube and two little sticks. Han Hsing tzŭ, the deity of music, is represented as a young man with a flute. Ho Hsien-ku, the deity of housewives, has the lotus for her attribute. Their emblems or attributes, too, are frequently found on porcelain.

Besides the Islands of the Blessed, Taoism has its paradise, the gardens of Hsi Wang Mu,[2] the 'Royal Mother of the West', situated in the K'un Lun mountains. Here the peach-tree grew with fruits ripening once every three years, and here she lives with her servant-girls, in a beautiful palace, a spotted deer keeping her company. Hsi Wang Mu, the goddess of eternal youth, is sometimes depicted as a princess with a basket,

[1] In the first centuries B.C., the ten ruling Chinese princes sent out expeditions to discover these islands, which were reputed to be somewhere along the coast of the province of Kiangsu.

[2] The first Jesuits in China have sometimes confused her with the Queen of Sheba.

under a peach-tree in flower, or sitting on a flying phoenix or floating on a leaf. Blue-winged birds are her heralds and messengers. Riding an ox she is portrayed on porcelain with five servant-girls, one of them holding a basket with peaches. This was on the occasion when she was visited by the Han Emperor Wu-ti (140–87 B.C.). The story of King Mu Wang of Chou (reigned 1001–946 or 827–781 B.C.) who visited the Royal Mother of the West was also very well known. The eight horses of King Mu, famous for their speed and staying power, became subjects in favour with the porcelain-painters. Popular too were the twin boys, laughing and playing genies, *ho ho êrh hsien,* the Two Immortals of Mirth and Harmony. Sometimes one of the pair is carrying a broom and the other a box with blessings. Pictured in this way they are easily confused with the figures of Ch'an Buddhism, Han-shan and Shih-tê.

BUDDHISM

Buddhist personages and symbols were represented on porcelain as frequently as Taoist. The Buddha himself was portrayed in several manifestations, standing or sitting on a lotus (Plate 94), sitting in the position of teaching, or in Nirvana. Much more frequently than the Buddha, the Bodhisattva, Kuan Yin, is depicted on porcelain. This supernatural being, neither male nor female, was first represented as male, but from the Sung onwards as a female deity. In this shape she became Goddess of Mercy and Giver of Children. She is usually rendered as a sweet young woman, a lotus in one hand, standing or sitting on a lotus-throne, with Buddhist emblems, or sitting on a rock above the sea, with, for attributes, a bird and a vase. Sometimes she carries a baby in her arms. She is also portrayed in several other positions. A white horse (*pai ma*) that supposedly brought the Buddhist legends, the holy script, from India to China, is also used.

Occasionally, pieces are decorated with one of the *lohan* (Sanskrit, *Arhat*), Buddha's disciples who when ready for Nirvana stayed on earth to help mankind. One of the best known Buddhist figures is the mendicant friar Pu-tai ho-shang, who is said to be an incarnation of Amida Buddha. He is mostly portrayed in the shape of a half-nude, pot-bellied, bald-headed fellow, sitting or less frequently standing, with a fly-whisk in his hand, or with a bundle of books, or leaning against a big money-bag, or with children swarming over him.

The eight Buddhist symbols (*pa-chi-hsiang*) (fig. 62) are frequently depicted on porcelain. They are, the wheel, the shell, the parasol, the canopy, the lotus, the vase, the two fishes, and the knot without end. From time to time Bodhidharma, P'u-t'i-ta-mo, or simply Ta Mo, the patriarch of Ch'an Buddhism, is portrayed. He is often represented holding one of his shoes in his hand, while crossing the Yangtse on his return journey to India. He is recognizable by his shoulder-length curly hair and his monk's robe.

62. The eight Buddhist symbols

Besides being one of the eight emblems of Buddhism, the lotus is also a symbol of summer, of fecundity and fertility, and of purity, because it rises immaculate from muddy waters. Other symbols more generally Chinese than Buddhist are the peach, the pomegranate and the Buddha's-Hand citron, symbolical of longevity, many sons, and happiness.

OTHER SYMBOLS

Besides the above-mentioned emblems there are others which have served as decoration on porcelain, such are the *po ku,* hundred antiquities (Plates 67, 78), among them the Four Talents, music (lute), play (chess-board), calligraphy (books), and painting (two scrolls). Further there are the *pa pao,* the Eight Precious Things (fig. 63): the jewel, the cash, the lozenge, a pair of books, the music-stone, the painting, the rhinoceros-horns, and the artemisia leaf (fig. 48). Finally, the *shih êrh chang,* the twelve ornaments, the sun-disk with the sun-bird in the clouds, the moon-hare (fig. 43) pounding the elixir of life, the three stars connected by lines, the dragon with five claws on each foot (also symbolic for the emperor), the pheasant or phoenix (also symbolic for the empress), fire, light, the sacred mountain, and an aquatic plant, temple-vases showing a monkey and a tiger, a bat and an axe.

63. The eight Precious Things

Regularly recurring decoration. Iconography

Several emblems of longevity have already been mentioned, and the Chinese have hundreds of them. The character *shou*, old age, long life, is written, conventionalized and drawn in a great number of versions; a circular form, which includes the swastika, resembles a meander. This symbol, *wan shou*, means 10,000 long lives. The spotted deer, mentioned above, often carries the *ling chih* in its mouth. The egret, the tortoise, the gourd, the pine-tree and the bamboo, belong to the group. The pine-tree because it is a knotty evergreen, the bamboo because it is an evergreen too and, moreover, bends in the wind without breaking. The swastika is a mystic emblem of Buddhism, Buddha's heart, but as it is sometimes used instead of the character *wan*, it is also a longevity symbol.

MYTHS, LEGENDS AND TALES

Many episodes from myth, legend and folklore, from novels and plays, were reproduced at one time or another on porcelain. The wood-cutter Wang-chih one day entering a cave in the woods witnessed two old men, star deities, playing chess. One of them gave him a peach stone to put in his mouth. He did so and watched them playing so long that when they told him to go home he found that the handle of his axe had turned to dust, and when he arrived at his house all his relations had long since passed away. The story of the nine old men of Hsiang-shan is repeatedly depicted on porcelain. The old statesman and poet Po Ch'ü-i, who lived in T'ang times (618–906), had taken leave of the cares of office and, together with his friends, had retired to his country house. There they gathered in a park to enjoy the four talents.

One or more of the Twenty-four Paragons of Filial Piety are represented on porcelain. One of them is Ming Tsung (third century A.D.), whose sick mother wanted bamboo shoot-soup in midwinter. Ming Tsung went looking for bamboo shoots in the snow-covered groves, and his tears so moistened and softened the frozen earth that bamboo shoots started to sprout all around him.[1]

Very popular was the tale of the two star deities, symbolized in the cowherd Ch'ien Niu, who lived separated from his beloved Chih Nü, the spinning-girl, by the Milky Way, and was allowed to meet her only once every year. Well-known too were the stories of Chiang Tzŭ-ya fishing without a hook on the bank of a river, and of Chu Mai-chên who became a minister of the Court and is depicted reading with a faggot on his back, or the meeting of Ming Huang and the beautiful Kuei-fei. Also portrayed

[1] The decoration of Plate 311 was, via Japan, derived from the story of another of the 24 Paragons Yang Hsiang, who one day went with his father to their millet field. The father was attacked by a tiger. Though only fourteen years old, Yang Hsiang hurled himself at the animal, thus saving his father by being killed himself. [Translator's note.]

were the seven sages of the bamboo-grove in a mountainous landscape in the shade of the bamboo. They were retired scholars, statesmen and officials of the third century A.D. and gathered to discuss literature and sometimes got a little merry doing so. The biography of one of the most famous poets of China, Li T'ai-po (701–62), has also supplied some subjects for the porcelain–painter. He is portrayed looking at the water-falls in Szechuan, lying drunk in the shadow of a cask of wine, and he was drowned one night when boating and leaning over the side to embrace the reflection of the moon on the water.

Another popular story is that of Ssŭ-ma Kuang, a Chinese statesman of the eleventh century. As a boy, when he was playing, one of his friends fell into a huge fish-bowl. Ssŭ-ma Kuang saved the boy from drowning by breaking the bowl with a big stone.[1] It is impossible to relate the many tales used as subjects by the porcelain painters, and so a selection has to be made. In the period of K'ang Hsi, semi-legendary heroes of the Han dynasty, episodes from the life of Chang Ch'ien (who in 138 B.C. marched to the north-west where he was taken prisoner), and from the *san kuo chih*, the story of the three kingdoms (A.D. 220–280), wherein Kuan Yü played an important part, were repre-sented on porcelain. So, too, were episodes, scenes and fights, taken from the *shui hu ch'uan*, tales from the water-side.[2]

ANIMALS[3]

In China the four points of the compass have animals for their symbols, the green dragon for the east, the red bird for the south, the white tiger for the west, and the black tortoise for the north. There are, moreover, the four supernatural beings, *lung,* the dragon, *fêng-huang,* the bisexual bird, *fêng* being the male and *huang* the female manifestation. It is often identified with the phoenix (Plate 79). The third is the *ch'i-lin,* also a bisexual being, identified with the unicorn, and the fourth one *kuei,* the tortoise or the turtle.

The dragon, said to be derived from a prehistoric alligator, appears in very many shapes.[4] The classic shape is that of a composite animal having the head of a camel, the antlers of a deer, the scaly body of a serpent, the eyes of a hare, the ears of a cow, and four-clawed legs. In the Ming and Ch'ing dynasties the dragon with five claws on each foot was the symbol of imperial power. It is also a symbol of spring and rain-bringing clouds. It is often represented hovering in the air over the Taoist Island of the Blessed or surrounded by clouds and flames. The phoenix is the emblem of the empress.

[1] In Japanese lore he is known as Shiba Onka. The scene is known in England as 'Hob in the well'.

[2] Partly, but interestingly, translated into English by Pearl Buck under the titles *All Men are Brothers.* [Translator's note.]

[3] P. J. Donnelly, *The Animal in Chinese Art.* Loan exhibition, the Arts Council Gallery, London, 19th June to 19th July 1968.

[4] Cf. T. Volker, *The Animal,* etc.: Dragon.

It has the head of a pheasant and the tail of a peacock or of a pheasant, or, in other words, it keeps a happy mean between pheasant, peacock, and bird of paradise. The birds pay homage to it as their queen. The turtle is a symbol of longevity, strength and endurance. The *ch'i-lin* is depicted with the head of a dragon, the body and legs of a deer, hoofs of a horse and a bushy tail. The body is covered with dragon-scales. It has one horn, but sometimes two which are bent backwards, and flames sprout from its armpits. The tiger, king of the beasts, is often portrayed with the character *wang,* king, on its forehead. According to old traditions it was considered a protector against evil spirits.[1]

The lion was not native to China. It was and still is portrayed more like a Pekinese dog than a real lion. It is the protector of Buddha's law, emblem of peace, matrimonial happiness, courage and tranquillity. Two lions in effigy were used as protectors each on one side of a Buddhist temple entrance. In this shape they are frequently found in *blanc de chine.* The male (Plate 324) is often represented playing with a brocade ball with ribbons (a reminder of the flaming jewel of omnipotence), and the female playing with her cubs.

The bat, *fu,* is an emblem of good luck because *fu* can also mean happiness, good fortune. Five bats stand for the five blessings, virtue, progeny, riches, peace and a long life. The wings of the bat are sometimes represented in the shape of a *ju-i,* sceptre's head. According to some, the *ju-i* is a symbol of Buddha and his doctrine, and the head then represents the lotus. Others believe that its shape is that of the *ling-chih,* the sacred fungus of longevity. A pun on the words *ju-i* gives this expression the meaning, 'as you wish' or 'as you like it'.

The butterfly is a symbol of wedded bliss. A pair of mandarin ducks, often with a lotus, symbolize conjugal bliss and fidelity. The ox is a symbol of spring and agriculture. Spring returning is symbolized by three rams. Endurance is indicated by the carp which has the strength and staying power to swim upstream, take the rapids of *lung mên,* dragon's gate, then and there to be changed into a dragon. A similar dragonfish is an emblem of an examination, successfully passed. The crab is the emblem of a first-class doctor's degree. A pair of fish may stand for wedded bliss.

Various birds have an intimate connection with certain flowers, e.g. the crane with the lotus, and several have also a symbolic meaning. The magpie is the omen of a happy meeting, the quail[2] is a symbol of poverty, the pheasant may be a symbol of beauty. The cricket stands for eternal youth and happiness. The cock is a symbol of the sun, light, and virtue. They were used as offerings to the gods and spirits.

FLOWERS

Flowers play an important part in Chinese lore. The bamboo, orchid, plum-tree in bloom, and chrysanthemum, are called the four gentlemen. Summer was symbolized

---

[1] Ibid., Tiger. [2] The quail appear not only in Chinese, but also on Japanese Imari porcelain.

by the lotus, autumn by the chrysanthemum, winter by the plum-tree, and spring by the peony. The peony is also an emblem of good fortune and womanly beauty. Three peonies mean triple good luck. The water-lily heralds abundance. The iris keeps away malevolent spirits and was therefore placed at the entrance of houses. The willow-tree is a sign of good augury, and is also on guard against evil spirits. The cassia is an emblem of literary honours.

Not only the seasons were symbolized by flowers; the same was also true for the months, and so January has its plum-blossom, February that of the peach, the peony stands for March, and the cherry for April. May goes with magnolia and June with the pomegranate. The lotus goes with July, August is paired with the quince. September has its mallow, October the chrysanthemum. The gardenia symbolizes November and the flower for December is the poppy.

The combining of three fruits: peach, pomegranate and finger citron, symbolizes the Three Abundances of years, sons and happiness.

Notes on the colour plates

A. Plate with deep powder-blue ground (originally embellished with gold) and one central and four border panels in reserve, painted in blue, iron-red, green and pale aubergine enamels, with decorations of plants and flowers growing from rocks, and with bird on central panel. Mark on back of the open lozenge within a double blue circle. 1st quarter 18th century. D. 27 cm. *Collection Bal, Zeeuws Museum, Middelburg.*

B. Wash set consisting of cistern, lid and wall-basin. The water-jar decorated with shaped panels against a Y-pattern gold ground, the centre panel edged with green, the side panels with blue. Each panel has a painting of an openwork flower basket filled with pink and white flowers. Basin and lid of water-jar are similar in decoration; on the lid a red-painted Chinese lion as knob. 2nd quarter 18th century. Cistern, Ht. 47.5 cm., B. 28.5 cm.; lid, Ht. 17 cm.; basin, Ht. 19 cm., B. 23.5 cm. *Huis ten Bosch Palace, The Hague.*

C. Oval tureen and stand with scalloped edges, decorated in *famille verte* with large branches of peony flowers and leaves, a phoenix, butterflies and insects. The lid, tureen and stand edged with broad bands of green trellis diaperwork and half-flowers between panels painted with flower sprays and tendrils; the lid with a handle in green in he form of a snake or eel. *c.* 1730 to 1735. Ht. with lid 16 cm., L. 32.2 cm., B. 23.5 cm. *Heeswijk Abbey, Berne.*

D. Oblong oval tureen and cover, the tureen with red boar's head handles, the lid with a knob in the form of a bursting pomegranate in green and red. Lid and tureen decorated with cocks in blue enamel, iron-red, gold and black, and sprays of flowers in green, pink and purple enamels, iron-red and gold; both edged with a frieze of spearheads in gold outlined in red. *c.* 1750 to 1760. Ht. with lid 18 cm., B. 24 cm., L. 28 cm. *Fundatie van Renswoude, Utrecht.*

E. Plate painted in *famille rose* with decoration of a cartouche enclosing a seated lady and gentleman playing the flute, both in European dress, and between them a golden hoop with a parrot. The rim decorated in *bianco-sopra-bianco* and four scroll-edged panels of Chinese mountain scenes in purple. 3rd quarter 18th century. D. 22.7 cm. *Collection Bal, Zeeuws Museum, Middelburg.*

F. Plate, ruby back, painted in *famille rose* with decoration of a man in European dress sitting on the ground leaning against a big vase, with two (gin?) bottles, a glass and jug at his feet; behind him a Chinese youth and on his left a seated Chinese woman holding a peach. Beyond her two large pots, a fruit-stand and, between the man and the woman, a vase with peony spray. On back, Yung Chêng marks and period. D. 21 cm. *J. M. Morpurgo, Amsterdam.*

G. Plate with scalloped edge decorated in underglaze blue and *famille verte*. In the centre a blue lion on a golden shield surmounted by a coronet and with the name ZUTPHEN below, flanked by birds and sprays of leaves and flowers. The rim, with lotus-petal shaped panels painted alternately with vases of flowers and Chinese figures in landscapes, is edged with spandrels of cell-diaperwork. 1st quarter 18th century. *Huis ten Bosch Palace, The Hague.*

H. Plate, painted in Imari style, with decoration, in underglaze blue, red and gold, of flowers growing behind a fence, the well-border with diaperwork and panels of flowers, and the rim with sprays of blossom. Last quarter 18th century. *Tetar van Elven Museum, Delft.*

The monochrome plates

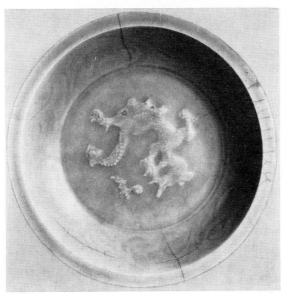

5 | 6
7

12
13 | 14

15 | 16
17 | 18
19 | 20

21 | 22
23 | 24
    | 25

33
34

35
36
37

42
43   44

50 | 51
52 | 53

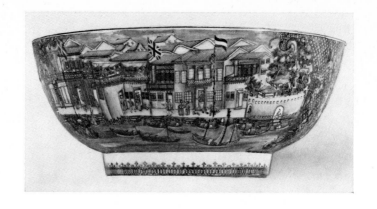

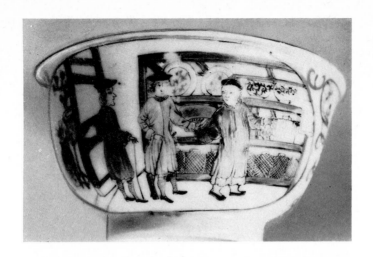

57
58
59

60 | 61
62 | 63
64 | 65

66 | 67
68

69 | 70
71 | 72

73 | 74
75 | 76

77

78	79
80	82
81	

83 | 84
85 | 86

87 | 88
89 | 90

92 | 93
94

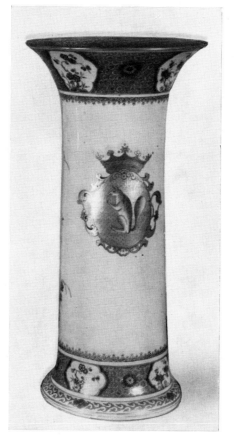

103 | 104
105 | 106

107 | 108
109 | 111
110

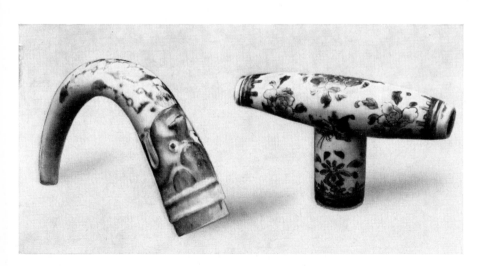

112
113
114

115 | 116
117 | 118

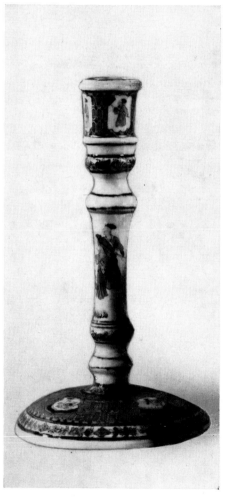

131

133 | 132
134

135 | 136
137 | 138
139 | 140

141 | 142
143 | 144
145

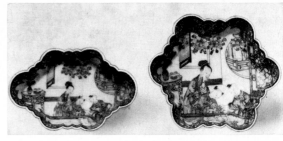

160
161
162

163 164
  165
166 167

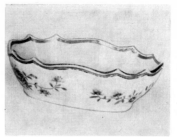

192 | 193
194 | 195
    | 196

197 | 198
199 |
200 | 201

206 | 207
209 | 208
210

211 | 212
      213
      214
215 | 216

223 | 224
225 | 226

227 | 228
229 | 230
231 |
232 |

233

234 | 235
| 236

237 | 238
239 | 240
241

242	243
244	245
246	247

Petrus de Wolff, Petr. Fil.

254 | 255
256 | 257
258 | 259

266 | 267
268 | 269
270 | 271

272	273
274	275
276	277
278	

279 | 280
281 | 282

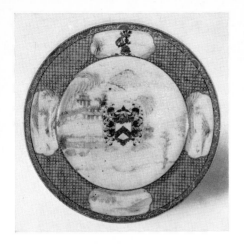

283 | 284
285 | 286
287

298 | 299
300
301

302
303 | 304
305 | 306

307
308
309 | 310

311 | 312
313 | 314
315 | 316

317 | 318
319 | 320
321 | 322

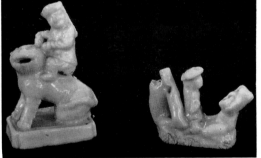

323 324 | 325
     326 | 327
     328 | 329

330 | 331
332 | 333
334 |

335 | 336
337 |
338 | 339

340 | 341
342 | 343
      | 344

349	
350	351
352	353

359 | 360
361

Notes on the monochrome plates

1. Water-colour by Gaignières, circa 1713, showing white porcelain vase mounted as a ewer with silver-gilt enamels. The vase itself 1st half fourteenth century. Ht. 28 cm. Denuded of its mounts, is now in the National Museum of Ireland, Dublin.

2. Blue-green celadon plate showing dragon in relief and engraved decoration on the rim. 13th to 14th century. D. 35 cm. *Princessehof Museum, Leeuwarden.*

3. Porcelain kilns of Ching-tê Chên. *Top,* filling and emptying beehive-type kilns; *bottom,* glaze-kilns (left) and muffle kilns. Water-colours in *Princessehof Museum, Leeuwarden.*

4. Throwing pots on the wheel. *Right,* first shaping; *left,* paring. Water colours in *Princessehof Museum, Leeuwarden.*

5. Martabani jar from Soo-Chou, brown earthenware, decorated in yellow slip with ornamental bands, birds and animals in landscape. 19th to 20th century. Ht. 73.5 cm. *Princessehof Museum, Leeuwarden.*

6. Lobed Martabani jar from Kuang-tung, glazed earthenware, decorated with overlay of twigs and leaves, and glazed in yellow and purple on green background. Late 16th or early 17th century. Ht. 33.5 cm. (Cf. similar jar in Victoria and Albert Museum, London, W. Honey, pl. 81.) *Princessehof Museum, Leeuwarden.*

7. Light-grey glazed earthenware Martabani jar, probably made in Southern China. Ht. 37 cm. *Princessehof Museum, Leeuwarden.*

8. Dish, blue-and-white, 'Swatow ware'. Central part with small dragons surrounded by *hai ma* (sea-horses); rim with eight panels, separated by tassels, showing alternately dancing dervishes and Koran sayings, 'God is health' and 'God is cure'. Late 16th, early 17th century. D. 39 cm. *Princessehof Museum, Leeuwarden.*

9. Jar, blue-and-white, 'Swatow ware', with four loops on shoulder. Decorated in two bands with *fêng-huang* and Chinese lions. Early 17th century. Ht. 35.5 cm. *Princessehof Museum, Leeuwarden.*

10. Dish, polychrome 'Swatow ware', the centre decorated with flowers and two birds; on the deep rim, panels with flowers on diaper-pattern background. Late 16th, early 17th century. D. 41 cm. *Princessehof Museum, Leeuwarden.*

11. Dish, polychrome 'Swatow ware'. Bowl painted with European ship and sea-monster, separated by small islands, the centre with compass-card and the rim with the *pa kua* (Eight Trigrams). 17th century. D. 31 cm. *Princessehof Museum, Leeuwarden.*

12. Detail of still-life by W. Kalf showing silver-mounted blue-and-white ewer. Chia Ching period. *Schloss Rohonsz, collection Thyssen Bornemisza.*

13. Ewer, blue-and-white, the silver mount stamped with a London mark and year-letter for 1585–86. Vertical panels, separated by ribs, painted with children playing. Wan Li period. Ht. 22 cm. *Victoria and Albert Museum, London.*

14. Still-life by N. Gillis (worked Haarlem 1622–32) dated 1611, showing large and small blue-and-white 'clapmuts'. *Collection W. M. J. Russel, Amsterdam.*

15. Plate, blue-and-white, with decoration of pagodas in landscape, turreted walls in

background, cranes in lotus pond on rim. 16th century. D. 27 cm. *Princessehof Museum, Leeuwarden.*

16. Scalloped-edged plate, blue-and-white, centre showing scholar in garden; on rim, wide panels with birds and fruits on branches. Wan Li period. D. 26.7 cm. *Princessehof Museum, Leeuwarden.*

17. *'Clapmuts'*, blue-and-white centre painted with river landscape with birds on rock, well-border with four wide panels of flowering and fruiting branches and symbols, alternating with narrow panels; on rim *t'ao t'ieh* masks alternating with meander pattern. Wan Li period. D. 22 cm. *Princessehof Museum, Leeuwarden.*

18. Wine-pot, blue-and-white, with spout and hoop-handle and decoration of animals, flowers and plants. Wan Li period. Ht. 15.8 cm. *Princessehof Museum, Leeuwarden.*

19. Dish, blue-and-white, centre with river landscape with geese and plants, on rim alternately wide panels of symbols and flowers and narrow panels. Wan Li period. Ht. 8.8 cm., D. 51 cm. *The Hague, Dienst voor 's Rijks Verspreide Kunstvoorwerpen.*

20. Plate, blue-and-white, on central part symbols, on rim symbols alternating with flowers. Wan Li period. D. 20.5 cm. *The Hague, Dienst voor 's Rijks Verspreide Kunstvoorwerpen.*

21. 'Persian flask', blue-and-white, painted in vertical panels with *hai ma* alternating with flowers, and narrow vertical panels with tassel-like decoration. Wan Li period. Ht. 26 cm. *Kröller-Müller Museum, Otterlo.*

22. Hexagonal bottle with tall neck, decorated in blue-and-white, the body with panels framing different floral sprays and fruits, and the shoulder and neck with different diaper pattern and symbols. Wan Li period. Ht. 25 cm. *Collection Bal, Zeeuws Museum, Middelburg.*

23. Ewer, blue-and-white, branch-shaped spout, decoration of rocks, plants and insects, on shoulder key-fret meander, on neck bird on branch. Wan Li period. Ht. 17 cm. *Princessehof Museum, Leeuwarden.*

24. *'Kraaikop'*, porringer or caudle-cup, blue-and-white, the silver mount with marks of Leeuwarden silversmith Minne Sikkes and year-letters for 1632. Wan Li period. Ht. 8.5 cm. *Fries Museum, Leeuwarden.*

25. Bowl, with blue-and-white decoration of landscape, and four biscuit reliefs of the Eight Taoist Immortals in pairs. Wan Li period. Ht. 8 cm., D. 14 cm. *Princessehof Museum, Leeuwarden.*

26. Still-life by W. Kalf. Detail showing bowl, blue-and-white, decorated in relief with the Eight Taoist Immortals in pairs. On cover (lacking in Plate 25), Chinese lion. *Private collection.*

27. Bowl, blue-and-white, decorated with swastikas in open work, and four reliefs with the Eight Taoist Immortals in pairs, a fifth relief showing Shou Lao, deity of longevity. Wan Li period, Chêng Hua mark. Ht. 5 cm., D. 9 cm. *Collection Bal, Zeeuws Museum, Middelburg.*

28. 'Character' bowl, blue-and-white, the character *shou*, longevity, being used as a background decoration for four medallions with the Eight Taoist Immortals in pairs; on inside Shou Lao on flying crane. Late Wan Li period. Ht. 9 cm., D. 21.5 cm. *Flehite Museum Amersfoort.*

29. Bowl, blue-and-white, wall divided into eight panels with conventionalized deer in vegetation. Wan Li period. Ht. 7.5 cm., D. 14.5 cm. *Princessehof Museum, Leeuwarden.* A similar cup is depicted in a still-life dated 1623, referred to by S. Hofman writing in *Bull. Rijksmuseum Amsterdam*, 1967, No. 1, pl. 2.

Notes on the monochrome plates

30. Kêndi, blue-and-white, elephant-shaped, Wan Li period. Ht. 20 cm. *Collection Bal, Zeeuws Museum, Middelburg.*

31. *'Clapmuts'*, blue-and-white, centre decorated with bird on rock and trees; rim painted with alternating wide panels of flower- and fruit-branches and symbols, and narrow panels, with tassels. Wan Li period, Ht. 6 cm., D. 16.5 cm. *Princessehof Museum, Leeuwarden.*

32. Still-life by W. Kalf. Detail showing elephant-shaped *kêndi*. Wan Li period. *Staatliche Kunstsammlungen, Weimar, Germany.*

33. Still-life by W. Kalf. Detail of *kêndi,* silver-mounted. Wan Li period. *Owner unknown.*

34. Still-life by Jan Brueghel sr. (1568–1625). Detail showing *kêndi* with spout turned to the back of painting. Wan Li period. *Thurkow collection, The Hague.*

35. Castle Zeelandia, built in 1624 on small island off the Formosa coast. Water-colour on parchment. *Zeeuws Museum, Middelburg.*

36. Covered box with *wu ts'ai* decoration on cover of high dignitary in chair of state, courtiers, and letter-bearer kneeling. Seventeenth century. Ht. 17 cm., D. 30 cm. *Rijksmuseum, Amsterdam.*

37. Bowl, white porcelain, decorated in openwork with Chinese characters. Late Wan Li period. D. 9.5 cm. *Groninger Museum.*

38. Candlestick, blue-and-white, with inverted chamber-pot for base. Decorated with figures in landscape on bowl, tulip motif and symbols on stick. Transitional period. Ht. 30 cm. *Stodel, Amsterdam.*

39. Jug, blue-and-white, decorated with palace in landscape, horizontal bands above and below and tulip motif on neck. Transitional period. Ht. 38 cm., D. 18 cm. *Rijksmuseum Meermano Westreenianum, The Hague.*

40. Jug with handle and pouring-lip, blue-and-white. Painted with garden scene, plantain and Chinaman; on neck, tulip motif. Transitional period. Ht. 22.5 cm. *Rijksmuseum voor Volkenkunde, Leiden.*

41. Still-life by W. Kalf, detail showing metal-mounted ewer. Transitional period. *Boehler, Munich, Germany.*

42. At left, jug with handle and broken spout, at right jug with handle and pouring-lip. Blue-and-white, decorated with Chinese in landscape. Transitional period. Ht. left, 17.5 cm.; right, 22 cm. *Flehite Museum, Amersfoort.*

43. Wine-ewer, blue-and-white, peach-shaped, with decoration of leaves, fruits and longevity symbol called Cadogan, Transitional period. Ht. 18 cm. *Groninger Museum.*

44. Wine-ewer, blue-and-white, with decoration of Chinese noblemen in a garden. Transitional period. Ht. 20.5 cm. *Princessehof Museum, Leeuwarden.*

45. Bowl, blue-and-white, decorated with panels alternately wide (Dutch houses and Chinese men) and narrow (variations on tulip motif). Transitional period. Ht. 15.6 cm., D. 36.4 cm. *De Sypesteyn Museum, Loosdrecht.*

46. Inside of bowl of no. 45, painted in blue with a Dutch scene showing Dutch houses, canal with boat and ducks; the sides decorated with variations of the tulip motif in wide and narrow panels interspersed with three panels showing Chinese figures on two, Dutch houses on third.

47. *Schnelle,* blue-and-white, with pewter lid, and decoration of Chinese dignitary in landscape. Transitional period. Ht. 21 cm., D. 9.5 cm. *Flehite Museum, Amersfoort.*

48. Barber's bowl, blue-and-white, decorated with, centre, Chinese gathering leaves in landscape; sides of well, Chinese in landscape with Dutch houses and deer; on rim, Dutch houses, Chinese figures, duck-pond. Transitional period. D. 31 cm. *Princessehof Museum, Leeuwarden.*

49. Double-gourd flask, blue-and-white; decoration of Chinese garden with plantain and Chinese ladies. Transitional period. Ht. 33.5 cm., D. 19.5 cm. *Rijksmuseum, Amsterdam.*

50. Vase, blue-and-white. On body four medallions with landscape and figures, above them flowering tendrils, between them winged heads copied from European models; tulip motif on neck. Transitional period. Ht. 37.5 cm. *Princessehof Museum, Leeuwarden.*

51. Ewer, blue-and-white, with metal lid and handle. On body, lotus-plant and flower in pond; on neck, tulip motif. Transitional period. Ht. 23 cm., D. 13 cm. *Princessehof Museum, Leeuwarden.*

52. '*Rolwagen*', blue-and-white, decoration of lady with two attendants, one carrying umbrella of state, the other a halberd or standard, in garden, scene from play or novel. Transitional period or early K'ang Hsi. Ht. 47.5 cm., D. 14.5 cm. *Rijksmuseum Meermanono Westreenianum, The Hague.*

53. Detail from still-life by J. van Streek (1624–84) showing globular vase with long neck; on body, Chinese figures in landscape; on neck, tulip motif. Transitional period. *Owner unknown.*

54. Bowl, Mandarin porcelain. Painted with a view of foreign trading posts ('factories') at Canton showing right, building of the Dutch East India Company and, centre, of English East India Company. D. 40 cm. *Nederlandsch Historisch Scheepvaartmuseum, Amsterdam.*

55. Transport of porcelain by bearers in wooden barrel from Ching-tê Chên to Canton via Meiling pass. Chinese painting, probably end 18th century. *British Museum, London.*

56. Packing porcelain at Ching-tê Chên before transport. Chinese painting, probably 18th century. *British Museum, London.*

57. Bowl, *famille rose,* with two Europeans in porcelain shop with dealer, porcelain exhibited in background. 2nd quarter 18th century. D. 8 cm. *Princessehof Museum, Leeuwarden.*

58. Porcelain room or hall in miniature in doll's house. 1st half 18th century. *Municipal Museum, The Hague.*

59. '*Poppegoet*', miniature vases for doll's house or porcelain cabinet. 18th century. Ht. 5–8 cm. *Collection Bal, Zeeuws Museum, Middelburg.*

60. '*Rolwagen*', blue-and-white. Upper part decorated with plants in square vases on veranda; lower part, probably covered with *hua shih* slip, because of crackle and oily glaze, with galloping horsemen. 1st quarter 18th century. Ht. 19.4 cm., D. 5.5 cm. *Collection Bal, Zeeuws Museum, Middelburg.*

61. Plate, blue-and-white 'steatite' porcelain, painted with river landscape, mountains and walled palace. Ch'ien Lung period. D. 31.5 cm. *Groninger Museum.*

62. Bowl with scalloped border, blue-and-white. Eight Taoist Immortals on clouds above, *ling chih,* longevity fungus below. Ch'êng Hua mark on bottom. K'ang Hsi period. Ht. 10 cm., D. 20 cm. *Provinciaal Overijssels Museum, Zwolle.*

63. Dish, blue-and-white. Centre scene of lady with servant girl bearing fan, burning

incense outdoors on occasion of moon-festival, two moon-hares and a crane. Border with four panels and separated by narrow tasselled meander panels. K'ang Hsi period. D. 34.5 cm. *Collection Bal, Zeeuws Museum, Middelburg.*

64. Bowl, blue-and-white, landscape with running deer, K'ang Hsi period. D. 21 cm. *Princessehof Museum, Leeuwarden.*

65. Moulded dish with scalloped rim, blue-and-white. Centre with ladies on garden terrace, surrounded by gadrooned panels painted alternately with symbols and flowers; outer rim of panels with meanders alternating with flowers. K'ang Hsi period. D. 27.5 cm. *Princessehof Museum, Leeuwarden.*

66. Plate, blue-and-white. In the centre, two Chinese ladies in front of outdoor altar-table and plantains; on rim, panels with peaches on diaper-pattern background. K'ang Hsi period. D. 20.5 cm. *Provinciaal Overijssels Museum, Zwolle.*

67. Bottle-shaped vase, blue-and-white, decorated with some of the Hundred Antiquities. Undeciphered mark on bottom, K'ang Hsi period. Ht. 19.5 cm. *Collection Bal, Zeeuws Museum, Middelburg.*

68. Dish, blue-and-white. Centre with flowering plum-tree on rock, rim with similar trees. 1st half 18th century. D. 55.5 cm. *Frans Hals Museum, Haarlem.*

69. Dish, blue-and-white, with, in centre, conventionalized lotus surrounded by flower sprays, and on rim, conventionalized lotus-tendril work and *pater noster* motif. Base of dish bears a flower mark, K'ang Hsi period. From Dresden collection of Augustus the Strong, inventory no. 301. D. 38 cm. *Dienst voor 's Rijks Verspreide Kunstvoorwerpen, The Hague.*

70. A long-necked vase, blue-and-white, with elephant-trunk handles. Decoration of Chinese ladies admiring flowering plant in pot. Mark of artemisia leaf. 1st half 18th century. Ht. 25 cm. *Collection Bal, Zeeuws Museum, Middelburg.*

71. Covered pot, blue-and-white, decorated with scene of Hsi Wang Mu gathering herbs with two lady attendants, framed by tree-peonies and two flying cranes. Lotus tendril work on neck, playing boys on cover. A stopped hole near the foot on one side was intended for a faucet and indicates that vessel was used as water-pot. 1st half 18th century. Ht. 60 cm. *Frans Hals Museum, Haarlem.*

72. Bottle, blue-and-white, 'steatite' porcelain with decoration of landscape with mountains and Chinese men. c. 1725–30. Ht. 8.6 cm. *Collection of W. Inden-van Pesch Brummen.*

73. *Kêndi,* blue-and-white, with landscape of mountain and water. K'ang Hsi period. Ht. 23 cm. *Princessehof Museum, Leeuwarden.*

74. Pot with dome-shaped cover, blue-and-white. Decorated with large panel on side of Chinese scene, audience before a high dignitary, deep frieze round base, and on cover, variations of cloud motif. For mark see fig. 7. Ht. 88 cm. *Princessehof Museum, Leeuwarden.*

75. Blue-and-white covered pot with Chinese lion on lid and lion-head shaped handles, sides painted with scene showing two Chinese ladies bearing gifts to third lady on terrace, with plantain in garden. 1st half 18th century. D. 21 cm. *Centraal Museum, Utrecht.*

76. 'Rolwagen', blue-and-white, with decoration of Dragon on Band. About 1700. Ht. 27.5 cm. *Princessehof Museum, Leeuwarden.*

77. Thick-necked vase with background of powder blue and gold, and on panel, bird on tree in *famille verte.* K'ang Hsi period. Ht. 43.5 cm. *Rijksmuseum, Amsterdam.*

78. Covered jar, powder-blue background with reserve panels decorated in *famille verte* with some of the Hundred Antiquities and flowering branches. From collection of Augustus the Strong; for mark see fig. 8. 1st decade 18th century. Ht. 25.5 cm., D. 21.5 cm. *Dienst voor 's Rijks Verspreide Kunstvoorwerpen, The Hague.*

79. Covered vase, with Chinese lion on lid, *famille rose*, decorated with landscape with *fêng huang* and birds on branches; conventionalized lotus frieze round base and, on shoulder, within meander edged panel, flowers and some of the Hundred Antiquities on *ju-i* shaped panels. Ch'ieng Lung period. Ht. 132 cm. *Collection Bal, Zeeuws Museum, Middelburg.*

80. Dish, *famille verte* with gold; two fighting sparrows, and one on flowering tree. K'ang Hsi period. D. 24 cm. *Collection Bal, Zeeuws Museum, Middelburg.*

81. Plate, with decoration in underglaze blue, green, red and yellow, of leaves, diaper patterns on rim. 17th century. D. 36 cm. *Princessehof Museum, Leeuwarden.*

82. Deep dish, *famille verte*. Centre with scene of ladies in large and small pleasure boats on lotus pond, sides of well with flowering irises (?), and rim, on diaper patterned background, with oblong panels of flowering branches, alternating with chrysanthemums in circles. 1st half 18th century. D. 38 cm. *Rijksmuseum, Amsterdam.*

83. Plate, *famille rose,* centre with decoration of cock, hen and tree peony; rim with cell-diaper pattern and three oblong panels with flowers. Ch'ien Lung period. D. 22 cm. *Collection Bal, Zeeuws Museum, Middelburg.*

84. Dish, *famille rose,* peaches on their branches. Ch'ien Lung period. *Musée Guimet, Paris.*

85. Seven-bordered plate, eggshell, ruby back, *famille rose*. Centre painted in rose-red, yellow, blue, green, brown and red enamels, with scene of two ladies seated at table and a boy. Probably Yung Chêng period. D. 22 cm. *Collection Bal, Zeeuws Museum, Middelburg.*

86. Plate, *famille rose*, decoration of flower-basket surrounded by sprays, inner rim of spearhead motif in gold, and outer rim, on star-shaped white-patterned background, intricately shaped panels with flowering branches. Ch'ien Lung period. D. 23 cm. *Collection Bal, Zeeuws Museum, Middelburg.*

87. Plate, *famille rose*, with peonies and chrysanthemums, and butterfly on centre and flowering branches on rim. Probably Yung Chêng period. D. 20.7 cm. *Rijksmuseum, Amsterdam.*

88. Dish, *famille rose*, decorated with a bouquet of flowers surrounded by eight panels, lotus-petal in shape, painted in green, purple and yellow cell-diaperwork alternately. Rim painted with flowers. After 1st quarter 18th century. D. 20.7 cm. *Princessehof Museum, Leeuwarden.*

89. Dish, *famille rose*. Centre with two over-elegant ladies in garden with willow-tree, rim with flowering branches. 1740–60. D. 42.5 cm. *Provinciaal Overijssels Museum, Zwolle.*

90. Plate, *famille rose,* decoration of flowers and cricket in centre surrounded by flowers on inner rim, and, on outer rim, variations of cloud motif and diaper pattern. Ch'ien Lung period. D. 25.7 cm. *Princessehof Museum, Leeuwarden.*

91. Vase, *famille rose*, late *ku-yüeh hsüan* type, with three ladies and boy. Cyclical date 1784. Ht. 16 cm. *Rijksmuseum, Amsterdam.*

92. Covered milk-jug, *famille noire*. Decoration, on black background, of (front) horn-blower in yellow and green enamel and gold, and (back) trumpeter; round mouthrim and on lid, spearhead motif in gold. 2nd half 18th century. Ht. 13 cm. *Collection Bal, Zeeuws Museum, Middelburg.*

93. Cup and saucer decorated in *famille noire,* outside with black background, purple branches and white flowers, inside with branches, leaves and flowers in iron-red with gold. 1st half 18th century. Cup, Ht. 4 cm., D. 9.7 cm.; saucer, D. 12 cm. *Collection Bal, Zeeuws Museum, Middelburg.*

94. Ewer, *'lakmoes'* decoration with, on front, heart-shaped flaming panel of young Buddha on lotus-throne, against black background. 2nd half 18th century. Ht. 30 cm. *Collection Bal, Zeeuws Museum, Middelburg.*

95. Verbrugge family painted by G. Lapis in 1773. On right and left of chimneypiece, on brackets, can be seen two openwork lanterns in *famille rose. B. W. G. Wittewaall Collection, The Hague.*

96. 'Surprise cup', blue-and-white; when cup is filled, a tiny figure rises from the inner openwork small inverted cup. 2nd or 3rd quarter 18th century. Ht. 4 cm., D. 8 cm. *De Sypesteyn Museum, Loosdrecht.*

97. Bowl, blue-and-white, openwork outer wall decorated with honeycomb and swastika. Ht. 7.5 cm., D. 15.5 cm. *Collection Bal, Zeeuws Museum, Middelburg.*

98. Cupboard set or *garniture de cheminée* of five pieces, blue-and-white, with decoration of leaves and flowers in lozenges. K'ang Hsi period. Ht. 55 cm. *Owner unknown.*

99. Garniture of three pieces, blue-and-white, octagonal bases, on shaped panels, decoration of figures and plants. 18th century. Ht. 30.5 cm. *Flehite Museum, Amersfoort.*

100. Garniture of five pieces, *famille rose,* decoration of flowers with birds. About 1750. Ht., without cover, 29.5 cm. *Collection Bal, Zeeuws Museum, Middelburg.*

101/102. Beaker and covered vase from garniture set of five, *famille rose.* Decoration of bamboo, peony and other flowers, arms of Sichterman family (a squirrel) on side of beaker, with the same squirrel as finial on cover of vase. Round foot, shoulder of vase, and rim of beaker, flower-painted panels set in wide bands of honeycomb motif. On inside edges of rims, motif from Meissen in gold. About 1740. Beaker, Ht. 47 cm., D. 24 cm.; covered vase, Ht. 63 cm. *Groninger Museum.*

103. Covered beer-mug with pewter hinge, *famille verte,* with decoration of the 'three friends', pine, plum and bamboo, and flying crane. K'ang Hsi period. Ht. 22.3 cm. *Collection Bal, Zeeuws Museum, Middelburg.*

104. Helmet-shaped ewer, decorated with flowery tendrils in blue with red and gold; and under pouring lip, arms of Portuguese Ataïde family, blue escutcheon with bar in gold. The decoration is less accurate than on Dutch *chine de commande.* 1st quarter 18th century. Ht. 23.5 cm. *Collection Klatte-de Waal, Overveen.*

105. Puzzle-jug, copy of Delft specimen, blue-and-white, decorated on body with three medallions of Chinese ladies on terrace with, in between, panels with landscape and meander motif. Ht. 20.5 cm., D. 12 cm. *Princessehof Museum, Leeuwarden.*

106. Ewer and saucer dish, blue-and-white, with panels, separated by diaperwork, of landscapes, trees and shrubs and pagoda. K'ang Hsi period. Ewer Ht. 20.5 cm., dish, D. 48.5 cm. *Rijksmuseum, Amsterdam.*

107. Winged vase, blue-and-white, with slender neck and trumpet-shaped mouth. Decoration of plants and flowers. K'ang Hsi period, or later. Ht. 26 cm. *Princessehof Museum, Leeuwarden.*

108. Tulip-vase, Chinese decoration with western elements, notably winged cherub on base. Copy of Delft specimen. K'ang Hsi period, mark A.P.K. Ht. 42 cm. *Groninger Museum.*

109. Spittoon, blue-and-white, with decoration on bowl of Chinese lady in garden, and flower motif inside mouth, 1st half 18th century. Ht. 8.2 cm., D. 10.5 cm. *Groninger Museum.*

110. Round sander or pounce-pot, with blue-and-white decoration of flowering plants and birds. 1st half 18th century. Ht. 7.5 cm., D. 7 cm. *Princessehof Museum, Leeuwarden.*

111. Covered butter-dish, blue-and-white, with sitting dog on lid. Decoration of European landscape. 1st half 18th century. Ht. 8 cm., D. 11 cm. *Princessehof Museum, Leeuwarden.*

112. Oil-and-vinegar set in European shapes of two small boxes connected by handle and two small jugs. Enamelled in the Netherlands in Kakiemon style in blue, green, iron-red black and gold. 1st half 18th century. Jugs, Ht. 17.7 cm. *Collection Bal, Zeeuws Museum, Middelburg.*

113. Candle-holder in the shape of an arm, decorated with *ju-i* motifs in *famille rose.* 2nd half 18th century. L. 16 cm. *Princessehof Museum, Leeuwarden.*

114. Two heads of walking-sticks, one decorated with man's head in *famille rose.* 2nd quarter 18th century. At left, 12 cm; at right, 10.5 cm. *Collection Bal, Zeeuws Museum, Middelburg.*

115. Candlestick on octagonal foot, blue-and-white. 2nd half 18th century. Ht. 16.2 cm. *Princessehof Museum, Leeuwarden.*

116. Baluster-shaped sugar-caster with openwork head. Imari style decoration in blue with red and gold. 18th century. Ht. 21.7 cm. *Princessehof Museum, Leeuwarden.*

117. Candlestick, part of 'Parasol' set, decorated in blue, iron-red and gold. 2nd quarter 18th century. Ht. 20 cm. *Palazzo Venezia, Rome.* (See Plates 175, 192–6.)

118. Round sugar-caster, blue-and-white, with bayonet lock, and painted with leaves and flowers. 2nd half 18th century. Ht. 12 cm. *Flehite Museum, Amersfoort.*

119. Scallop, *famille verte,* decorated with some of the Hundred Antiquities. K'ang Hsi period. D. 18.7 cm. *Princessehof Museum, Leeuwarden.*

120. Hexagonal pounce pot and ink-pot, with flowers in underglaze blue, overglaze red, green and blue. 1st half 18th century. At left, Ht. 5 cm., D. 6.5 cm.; at right, Ht. 5.5 cm., D. 6.5 cm. *Flehite Museum, Amersfoort.*

121. Covered water-jar of wash-hand set with hole for faucet, *famille rose.* Decoration of cartouche with archer, with acanthus leaf above and satyr's head below. 2nd half 18th century. Ht. 51.5 cm. *Rijksmuseum, Amsterdam.*

122. Bottle, blue-and-white, with birds and flowers. 1st half 17th century. Ht. 26.5 cm. *Historisch Museum Palthe-Huis, Oldenzaal.*

123. Oval basin from same set as 121, *famille rose,* decorated with flowery garlands. Ht. 34 cm. Length, 65.5 cm. Breadth, 47.5 cm.

124. Oil-and-vinegar jar, double body, two opposing spouts, blue-and-white, decoration of flowering shrubs. 18th century. Ht. 20.5 cm. *Princessehof Museum, Leeuwarden.*

125/126. Flask and basin in *famille rose,* decorated with bamboo-shoots, flowers and leaves, and basket of flowers within cartouche. 1760–80. Flask, Ht. 25 cm.; basin, Ht. 11 cm.; D. 26 cm. *Boymans-van Beuningen Museum, Rotterdam.*

127. Baluster-shaped vase, blue-and-white. Decoration of oval panel of European ladies on

flowery background. K'ang Hsi period. Ht. 67 cm., D. 47 cm. *De Sypesteyn Museum, Loosdrecht.*

128. Octagonal coffee-pot, blue-and-white, painted with Dutch landscape and in clouds above, Europa and the Bull. Early 18th century. Ht. 25 cm. *Groninger Museum.*

129. Cup and saucer, blue-and-white, with decoration of sailing-ship, Odysseus on prow, siren in sea, and inscription, *Gardes vous de la Syrène* (Beware of the siren). K'ang Hsi period. Cup Ht. 5 cm., D. 9 cm.; saucer, D. 13.7 cm. *De Sypesteyn Museum, Loosdrecht.*

130. Lidded-cup and saucer, blue-and-white. Decoration of panels with leaves alternating with kneeling Chinese and King and Queen on throne. Inscription round rim: *L'empire de la vertue est établi jusqu'au bout de l'univers* (The empire of virtue is established till the end of the universe). K'ang Hsi period. Cup, Ht. 8.5 cm., D. 8.5 cm.; saucer, D. 13.5 cm. *De Sypesteyn Museum, Loosdrecht.*

131. Medal struck by Johannes Smeltzing (died 1693) on the occasion of the Costerman troubles. See Plate 132. After a print: Gerard van Loon, *Beschrijving der Nederlandsche Historie prenten.* III, 1728, p. 508.

132. Plate, blue-and-white, of demolished house of Jacob van Zuylen van Nyevelt, mark, Ch'êng Hua, K'ang Hsi period. D. 20.5 cm. *Princessehof Museum, Leeuwarden.*

133. Plate, blue-and-white, of music-makers in oval medallion and, on rim, Chinese landscape. K'ang Hsi period. D. 34 cm. *Princessehof Museum, Leeuwarden.*

134. Tile, blue-and-white, Chinese lady and boy in garden. 18th century. D. 19 cm. *Princessehof Museum, Leeuwarden.*

135. Teapot with lower part in openwork, *famille rose,* with decoration of cocks. Ch'ien Lung. Ht. 10 cm. *Collection Bal, Zeeuws Museum, Middelburg.*

136. Pear-shaped teapot, *famille rose,* with cock decoration in shaped panel on background of cell-diaperwork. Ch'ien Lung, Ht. 10 cm. *Princessehof Museum, Leeuwarden.*

137. Still-life by P. G. van Roestraten showing left, Têhua *blanc de chine* hexagonal teapot. *Owner unknown.*

138. Coffee-pot, blue-and-white, with decoration of vase and incense-burner. Yung Chêng period. Ht. 27.5 cm., D. 21.2 cm. *Princessehof Museum, Leeuwarden.*

139. Teapot, ribbed body with straight spout. Decorated in Imari style in polychrome with flowers. 1st half 18th century. Ht. 13.5 cm., D. 12 cm. *Schotse Huizen, Veere.*

140. Tall cup with two handles, blue-and-white, at top and bottom, cloud motifs with flowers, in between, symbols. K'ang Hsi period. Ht. 11 cm. *Princessehof Museum, Leeuwarden.*

141. Cup and saucer, blue-and-white, decorated with shrubs and plants, 1st half 18th century. Cup, Ht. 5.5 cm.; saucer, D. 14.2 cm. *Princessehof Museum, Leeuwarden.*

142. Cup and saucer, blue-and-white, with Chinese lady and boy. 1st half 18th century. Cup, Ht. 4.5 cm., saucer, 10.5 cm. *Provinciaal Overijssels Museum, Zwolle.*

143. Octagonal cup and saucer, blue-and-white, decorated with plants in radiating panels. 1st half 18th century. Cup, Ht. 5 cm., saucer, D. 13.5 cm. *Princessehof Museum, Leeuwarden.*

144. Cup and saucer, blue-and-white, moulded, decoration of vase with flowers on table on veranda. 18th century. Cup, Ht. 4 cm.; saucer, D. 10.5 cm. *Flehite Museum, Amersfoort.*

145. Handled cup, painted in green, blue, yellow and iron-red, with two Chinese. 2nd half 18th century. Ht. 5.3 cm., D. 6 cm. *Zeeuws Museum, Middelburg.*

146. Still-life by P. G. van Roestraten showing, from left, Yi-hsing teapot, baluster-shaped vase, bowls, teacups. *Christie's, London, 8 May, 1936, Cat. no. 70.*

147. Cup and saucer, blue-and-white, with decoration of so-called *Koekoek uit 't huisje* (Cuckoo from its nest). 1st half 18th century. Cup, Ht. 5.6 cm.; saucer, D. 7.9 cm. *Centraal Museum, Utrecht.*

148. Two-handled covered bowl, probably for sugar, decoration on body of scrolls and shells in gold, on cover, arms of van Reverhorst family in polychrome. 1730–40. Ht. 13 cm. *Collection Klatte-De Waal, Overveen.* See Plates 173 and 274.

149. Left, oblong hexagonal tray ('*schuitje*', small boat), right, hexagonal tray, *famille rose* decoration with black and gold, of Chinese lady and two boys. 2nd quarter 18th century. Left, length, 13 cm., breadth, 8.5 cm.; right D. 8.5 cm. *Collection Bal, Zeeuws Museum, Middelburg.*

150. Quadrangular jar with cover, blue-and-white, painted with scenes from legend or history, early K'ang Hsi period. H. 31.5 cm. *Rijksmuseum, Amsterdam.*

151. Covered milk-jug and tea-jar in *famille rose* with some decoration as 149. 2nd quarter 18th century. Jug, Ht. 8.5 cm.; jar, Ht. 11.5 cm. *Collection Bal, Zeeuws Museum, Middelburg.*

152. Tea-jar, blue-and-white, rectangular, with curved shoulders and pewter lid. Decorated with scene of two ships and merman holding flag in blue, red and black (Dutch colours) with inscription 'Zoutman'; above a medallion with monogram 'J.J.J.E.' (?) and below, inscription 'Doggers Bank'. Ht. 12.2 cm. Part of set decorated in Netherlands on the occasion of the battle of Doggers Bank, 1781. Some pieces with this decoration are in the Mr. S. van Gyn Museum, Dordrecht; this piece, *Boymans-van Beuningen Museum, Rotterdam.*

153. Bulging milk-jug with handle and three splay feet; on front, inscription in gold on black background, relating to *T'Wijnheere en Biertappers gilde* (Vintners' and Alehouse-keepers' Guild) 1776. Ht. 11.5 cm. *Collection Bal, Zeeuws Museum, Middelburg.*

154. Tureen with elephant legs, two handles and lotus-leaf shaped cover. On body and cover, arms in black, blue, red and gold of Frederik Adrianus Van Reede van Renswoude, 1658–1735, flanked by flowers in blue, yellow, rose-red, green and gold. Ht. 34.5 cm., length 40 cm. *Fundatie van Renswoude, Utrecht.*

155. Tureen, boar's head handles, and cover with knob consisting of bundled stalks, decoration as no. 154. Ht. 21.5 cm., length, 32 cm. *Fundatie van Renswoude, Utrecht.*

156. *Jardinière* and tureen, polychrome, part of set allegedly ordered by Königliche Preuzische Asiatische Compagnie zu Embden, to be presented to Frederick the Great (1740–86). Both pieces are painted with the 40 quarters of the arms of this prince, the mantling in white, the arms in blue, red, silver and gold. *Jardinière*, Ht. 20 cm., D. 25.5 cm. Tureen, Ht. 18 cm., length, 32 cm. *Huis Doorn, Doorn.*

157. Two fruit-stands belonging to the same set as the piece shown in illustration 154. The stems, tree-trunks climbed by two half-nude boys; the dishes in openwork painted in brown, green, blue and gold. Ht. 37.5 cm.

158. Oval fruit-dish in openwork with flower decoration; oval dish and sauce-boat on leaf-shaped stand decorated with flowers in rose-red, green and purple enamel. 3rd quarter 18th century. Fruit-dish, Ht. 28 cm., length, 25 cm.; oval dish, length, 40 cm., breadth 32 cm. *Bisdom van Vliet Museum, Haastrecht.*

Notes on the monochrome plates

159. Colander, salt-cellar, covered butter-dish on oval tray, and covered oval tureen on tray, all from the same set as no. 158, with similar decoration. Salt-cellar, length 9 cm.; butter-dish, length 12 cm. *Bisdom van Vliet Museum, Haastrecht.*

160. Covered oval tureen, with fruit-shaped knob on cover, decorated in gold with accollée arms of Prince William V (1748–1806) and Princess Wilhelmina of Prussia (1751–1820). 4th quarter 18th century. Ht. 16 cm.; length, 32.5 cm. *Noordeinde Palace, The Hague.*

161. Accollée arms (see Plate 160) on engraved portrait of Princess Wilhelmina by Vinkeles (1741–1816) after P. C. Haag (1737–1812).

162. Lobed oval dish, sauce-boat, and oval salt-cellar decorated as in Plate 160. Dish, Ht. 4.5 cm., length 15 cm.; sauce-boat, Ht. 8 cm., length, 22 cm.; salt-cellar, Ht. 4.5 cm., length, 15 cm. *Noordeinde Palace, The Hague.*

163. Covered oval tureen, blue-and-white, with fruit-shaped knob, 4th quarter 18th century. Ht. 17 cm., length 26.5 cm. *Bisdom van Vliet Museum, Haastrecht.*

164. Covered octagonal tureen, with boar's-head shaped handles, and cover with knob in the shape of a dog. Blue-and-white with decoration of leaves and flowers. 4th quarter 18th century. Ht. 20 cm., D. 23.2 cm. *Formerly Maarten Maartenshuis, Doorn.*

165. Salad-bowl, and rectangular tureen on tray, blue-and-white. Both painted with Chinese landscape, gate and pagoda. Salad-bowl, Ht. 13 cm., length 25 cm.; tureen, Ht. 23 cm., length, 38 cm. *Bisdom van Vliet Museum, Haastrecht.*

166. Covered round tureen, on tray, blue-and-white, 4th quarter 18th century. Ht. 26.5 cm. *Bisdom van Vliet Museum, Haastrecht.*

167. Covered oval tureen on dish, with mask handles, blue-and-white, with decoration of brushwood with leaves. 2nd half 18th century. Tureen, Ht. 21 cm. *Collection O. Verhagen, The Hague.*

168. Covered butter-dish on tray, blue-and-white, painted with landscape and Chinese figures. 4th quarter 18th century. *Bisdom van Vliet Museum, Haastrecht.*

169. Oblong low bowl with scalloped rim, *famille rose* decoration of flowers. 1760–70. 4.5 × 14.5 cm. *Fundatie van Renswoude, Utrecht.*

170. Oblong butter-dish on tray, blue-and-white, with Chinese landscape. 4th quarter 18th century. Dish, Ht. 13 cm., tray 19.5 × 13 cm. *Bisdom van Vliet Museum, Haastrecht.*

171. Oval salt-cellar, with arms of F. A. van Reede van Renswoude, and flowers painted in red, blue and green. 3.5 × 10 cm. *Fundatie van Renswoude, Utrecht.*

172. Rectangular salt-cellar, decorated in *famille rose* with flowerets. Ht. 3.3 cm., length 8 cm., breadth 6 cm. *Flehite Museum, Amersfoort.*

173. Oval, covered ragout-tureen, and covered custard cup. 1735–40. From the same set as the pieces shown in Plates 148 and 274. Tureen length 21.5 cm. *Collection Klatte-De Waal, Overveen.*

174. Butter-dish, oval openwork tray, knob on cover a sitting dog. Dish, Ht. 9.5 cm., tray 20 × 17 cm. *Fundatie van Renswoude, Utrecht.*

175. Oval tureen, part of 'Parasol' set, see Plates 192–196. 2nd quarter 18th century. *Palazzo Venezia, Rome.*

176. Hexagonal salt-cellar on three legs, with walls of honeycomb openwork, blue-and-white, 1st half 18th century. Ht. 5.5 cm., D. 8.5 cm. *Princessehof Museum, Leeuwarden.*

177. Oblong octagonal dish, blue-and-white, with decoration of mountain and water landscape and palace, 'Willow pattern', 'Fitzhugh rim', 4th quarter 18th century or later. 40.7 × 32.7 cm. *Princessehof Museum, Leeuwarden.*

178. Oval dish with scalloped rim, blue-and-white, 'sunflower pattern'. 18th century. 32 × 26 cm. *Groninger Museum.*

179. Plate, blue-and-white, two Chinese ladies in garden. 4th quarter 18th century. D. 20 cm. *Bisdom van Vliet Museum, Haastrecht.*

180. Oblong, octagonal fish-platter with trivet, blue-and-white, with decoration of Chinese lake with pagodas and bridge, 'Willow pattern', 4th quarter 18th century. L. 41 cm., width 34 cm. *Bisdom van Vliet Museum, Haastrecht.*

181. Deep plate with shaped foot, with decoration in green, purple, red and yellow enamel, of Chinese men and women, in panels against a background of twigs, flowers and leaves. C. 1829–30. Ht. 15 cm., D. 25 cm. *Lange Voorhout Palace, The Hague.*

182/186. Dinner service with cat, and monogram J. G. (?), painted with garlands in red and gold. Flat covered dish Ht. 13 cm., length 25.5 cm., breadth, 21.7 cm., tureen with knob, 26.5 cm. × 36 cm. × 23.5 cm., ice-pail with removable tray, Ht. 25 cm., D. 20 cm., hot-water plate, Ht. 5 cm., D. 24.5 cm., fruit-basket in openwork, 9 × 26.5 × 18 cm. *Fries Museum, Leeuwarden.*

187. Saucer, with *café au lait* glaze on back and front, decorated with flowers in green, red and blue enamel, 18th century. D. 10.7 cm. *Flehite Museum, Amersfoort.*

188. Punch-ladle, *famille rose,* with flowerets in the 'Lowestoft' pattern, 18th century. 9.5 × 7 cm. *Centraal Museum, Utrecht.*

189. Covered pot, so called Batavian ware, with flower-shaped reserve panels in *famille rose,* painted with flowers in rose-red, and green enamel. Ht. 12 cm., D. 10 cm. *Flehite Museum, Amersfoort.*

190. Two fish-shaped tureens, with scales painted in iron-red, rose-red and gold. 2nd half 18th century. Length, 21.5 cm. *Collection Bal, Zeeuws Museum, Middelburg.*

191. Duck-shaped tureen, iron-red, brown, green and blue enamel and gold. 2nd half 18th century. Ht. 15 cm., length, 19 cm. *Collection Bal, Zeeuws Museum, Middelburg.*

192. Saucer, blue-and-white, with decoration of lady, servant girl with parasol, and birds. Early 18th century. D. 12 cm. *Groninger Museum.*

193. 'Parasol' plate, after design of fig. 34, probably by Cornelis Pronk, decorated in Imari style in underglaze blue, overglaze iron-red and gold. 1735–40. D. 23 cm. *Groninger Museum.*

194. Coffee-pot, blue-and-white, with 'Parasol' ladies. 2nd half 18th century. Ht. 22.5 cm. *Rijksmuseum, Amsterdam.*

195. 'Parasol' plate, rose-red, light blue and light green enamel. About 1735. D. 23 cm. *Municipal Museum, The Hague.*

196. Saucer, blue-and-white, incorrectly drawn 'Parasol' subject, 2nd half 18th century. D. 12 cm. *Flehite Museum, Amersfoort.*

197. Plate with decoration of the 'Doctors', probably after design by Pronk, painted in green, rose-red and red enamel and gold, the rim with medallions of fishes and birds. 1730–45. D. 21.8 cm. *Boymans-van Beuningen Museum, Rotterdam.*

198. Design for 'Doctors' plate, and for cup and saucer, with three instead of the four men shown in no. 197.

199. Saucer or deep plate, four 'Doctors', blue-and-white. 2nd quarter 18th century. D. 15.6 cm. *Princessehof Museum, Leeuwarden.*

200. Jug with handle at back, and decoration of 'Doctors' subject as no. 197. Ht. 15.5 cm. *Frans Hals Museum, Haarlem.*

201. Bottle with decoration of 'Doctors' subject as no. 197, painted in light and dark blue, rose-red, red and green enamel and gold. Middle 18th century. Ht. 28 cm. *S. Messel, Amsterdam.*

202. Plate, decorated with 'Bower' subject, ascribed to Pronk, painted in rose-red, yellow, blue and green enamel and gold, rim, on diaper pattern, medallions with insects and flowering branches, Ch'ien Lung period. D. 19.9 cm. *Boymans-van Beuningen Museum, Rotterdam.*

203. Dish, Imari style, painted in blue, red and gold, with gentleman, lady and dog in garden. 1st quarter 18th century. D. 22 cm. *Rijksmuseum, Amsterdam.*

204. Plate decorated in red, purple and light blue, with skating pair, after a mezzotint by Dusart (1660–1704). 3rd quarter 18th century. D. 23 cm. *Rijksmuseum, Amsterdam.*

205. Plate, painted in yellow, blue and red enamel, with two Scots, and on rim, four cartouches, two with Chinese landscapes, two with a bird on a branch. 2nd quarter 18th century. D. 23 cm. *Collection Bal, Zeeuws Museum, Middelburg.*

206. Plate, decorated with scene of youth fishing, after print by Bloemaert (1564–1651); rim painted with diaperwork and three medallions of Chinese landscapes, interspersed with chrysanthemums. 2nd quarter 18th century. D. 21.3 cm. *Private collection.*

207. Print of youth fishing, by or after Bloemaert, published by C. J. Visscher: the pattern for Plates 206 and 298. *Prentenkabinet, Rijksmuseum, Amsterdam.*

208. *Le Printemps,* print by De Larmessin after N. Lancret (1690–1743), the model for Plates 209 and 210.

209. Covered tea-jar with openwork foot and polychrome decoration of woman with watering-can on one side, and young gardener and girl on the other. 2nd quarter 18th century, or later. Ht. 12.3 cm. *Zeeuws Museum, Middelburg.*

210. Boat-shaped tray, *schuitje,* decorated with scene taken from print shown in Plate 208 in iron-red enamel, some black and gold. 2nd half 18th century. Length 13, width 8.5 cm. *Collection Bal, Zeeuws Museum, Middelburg.*

211. Cup and saucer with decoration in black, light green and rose-red enamels of seamstress in chair. Cup, Ht. 2.8 cm.; D. 6.9 cm., saucer, D. 11.5 cm. *Collection Bal, Zeeuws Museum, Middelburg.*

212. Bowl with polychrome decoration of man on ladder picking fruits, and a kneeling woman, after a print by N. Ponce (1746–1831). 4th quarter 18th century. H. 8.2 cm., D. 18 cm. *Collection Van Vliet, Catharina Gasthuis Municipal Museum, Gouda.* Same subject as no. 213 and no. 214.

213. Bowl, subject as 212, painted in green, lilac, red and blue enamel. 4th quarter 18th century. *A. Arondson, Amsterdam.*

214. Plate, subject similar to 212 and 213, of man on ladder throwing fruit to girl who catches them in her skirt, painted in rose-red, green, yellow and other enamels, twisted cable in gold on rim. 4th quarter 18th century. D. 23.6 cm. *De Sypesteyn Museum, Loosdrecht.*

215. Vase painted in green, red, brown and other enamels, on background of Chinese

flowerwork, two panels, one decorated with scene of gentleman at table and servant pouring gin, the other with young lady with hat in landscape. 3rd quarter 18th century. Ht. 21.3 cm. *Rijksmuseum, Amsterdam.*

216. Cup and saucer, fluted rim with decoration of European in red kimono, bordered with gold lying on blue bed. Middle 18th century. Cup, Ht. 3.5 cm., saucer, D. 10.5 cm. *Flehite Museum, Amersfoort.*

217. *Les Oies du frère Philippe,* by N. Lancret, inspired by poem of La Fontaine. *Collection Rudolphe Kahn, Paris.*

218. Plate decorated with scene taken from no. 217 in black, red, rose-red, yellow enamel and gold. 2nd quarter 18th century. D. 23.4 cm. *Collection Bal, Zeeuws Museum, Middelburg.*

219. *Les Coquettes* or *Le Retour du Bal,* by H. S. Thomassin, after Watteau (1684–1721). *Prentenkabinet, Rijksmuseum, Amsterdam.*

220. Saucer, painted in rose-red, red, green and yellow enamels, with European gentleman and lady. 2nd quarter 18th century. D. 13.5 cm. *Boymans-van Beuningen Museum, Rotterdam.*

221. Cup and saucer decorated with subject of 219 in reverse; *grisaille* decoration with rose-red, yellow and turquoise enamels. 2nd quarter 18th century. Cup, Ht. 6.2 cm., saucer, D. 13.5 cm. *Boymans-van Beuningen Museum, Rotterdam.*

222. Plate, *famille rose,* with decoration of Chinese interior, European woman with servant leading spotted dog on leash. 2nd quarter 18th century or later. D. about 23 cm. *Stodel, Amsterdam.*

223. Pilgrim bottle, with dragon-shaped handles decorated in yellow, rose-red, green and light blue enamels, with a pair of lovers under a tree, and trumpet-blowing angel on one side, and man with mirror and woman on other side; neck painted with Y-pattern in brown-red. 2nd quarter 18th century. Ht. 22 cm. *Boymans-van Beuningen Museum, Rotterdam.*

224. Dish, blue-and-white, with decoration of Neptune, mermen and mermaids, the rim with three sprays of flowers between narrow bands of diaperwork. Middle 18th century or later. D. 42.5 cm. *De Sypesteyn Museum, Loosdrecht.*

225. Plate with Judgement of Paris in centre and, on rim, scrolls and shells in gold. 2nd quarter 18th century. D. 23 cm. *Collection Bal, Zeeuws Museum, Middelburg.*

226. Plate decorated in *famille rose* with same subject as Plate 225; on rim, four panels of Chinese river and ships. 2nd quarter 18th century. D. 23 cm. *Stodel, Amsterdam.*

227. Saucer in green rose-red and blue enamels; 'Leda and the Swan', taken from subject of Plate 228. 2nd quarter 18th century. D. 12 cm. *Rijksmuseum, Amsterdam.*

228. 'Leda and the Swan', engraving by G. Duchange, *Prentenkabinet, Rijksmuseum, Amsterdam,* after painting by Correggio, *Staatliche Museen, Berlin.*

229. Saucer painted in green, rose-red, blue and yellow enamels, with Cephalus and Procris. 2nd quarter 18th century. D. 12.5 cm. *Historisch Museum, Rotterdam.*

230. Teapot decorated in green, red and brown enamel and gold, with Neptune and Amphitrite on one side and love-scene on the other. After 1750. Ht. 12.6 cm. *Collection Bal, Zeeuws Museum, Middelburg.*

231. Plate with decoration of half-nude man and woman sitting under a tree; rim painted with cell diaper background and four panels with Chinese river landscapes. 2nd quarter 18th century. D. 23.5 cm. *Stodel, Amsterdam.*

232. Plate, *famille rose*, showing one of the 'Four Elements', Earth, after a painting by Francesco Albani (1578–1660), four lightly clad women on triumphal car surrounded by nude *putti*; narrow rim painted with tendrils. 2nd or 3rd quarter 18th century. D. 23 cm. *Stodel, Amsterdam.*

233. Two plates, *famille rose,* left with Venus and Hermes, right with Apollo and Diane 1745–60. D. 22.8 cm. *Collection Bal, Zeeuws Museum, Middelburg.*

234. Plate, blue-and-white, Adam and Eve (?) in centre; on rim, leaves and flowers. Mark Ch'êng Hua, K'ang Hsi period. D. 16 cm. *Municipal Museum, Arnhem.*

235. Cup, blue-and-white, painted with Crucifixion, and spiralling clouds round rim. K'ang Hsi period. Ht. 4.6 cm. *Centraal Museum, Utrecht.*

236. Saucer, blue-and-white, with painting of Crucifixion, K'ang Hsi period. D. 12.4 cm. *Centraal Museum, Utrecht.*

237. Plate painted in red and green enamels and some gold, with Baptism of Christ; on rim, flowering branches held by eagle and four *putti*. 2nd or 3rd quarter 18th century. D. 21.5 cm. *De Sypesteyn Museum, Loosdrecht.*

238. Saucer painted in green, blue and red-brown enamels, with Crucifixion, early 18th century. D. 11.6 cm. *Rijksmuseum, Amsterdam.*

239. Saucer, decorated in *famille rose,* with Ascension with Apostles. 1st or 2nd quarter 18th century. D. 12.2 cm. *Princessehof Museum, Leeuwarden.*

240. Saucer painted in rose-red, yellow, blue and light green enamels, with Rebecca at the Well. 1st half 18th century. D. 12 cm. *Rijksmuseum, Amsterdam.*

241. Plate with purple-red and red enamels, and gold decoration, of the Resurrection; and, on rim, cornucopias and two principal Louis XIV motifs, one with leaves and the other with leafy branches. 2nd or 3rd quarter 18th century. D. 22.7 cm. *Municipal Museum, The Hague.*

242. Plate, painted in iron-red, blue and green enamels, and gold, with scene of Table Bay, Dutch ships, and, in background, Capetown; gilt rim taken from Meissen. 1735–50. D. 22.5 cm. *Rijksmuseum, Amsterdam.*

243. Plate, painted in polychrome, with scene showing New Town-inn of Amsterdam; flowerets round rim in rose-red. 4th quarter 18th century. D. 22 cm. *Stodel, Amsterdam.*

244. Plate with decoration of ship *Vryburg* on the Whampoa roads off Canton, 1756, painted in black (ship and rigging), green and red enamels, and gold; inner rim with spearhead motif. 3rd quarter 18th century. D. 38 cm. *Collection Bal, Zeeuws Museum, Middelburg.*

245. Plate, in *bianco-sopra-bianco,* with, in centre, Meissen-style cartouche enclosing harbour view. 2nd quarter 18th century. D. 23.5 cm. *Historisch Museum, Rotterdam.*

246. Saucer painted in red, yellow, blue, green and turquoise enamels, and gold, with arms of City of Amsterdam above a Chinese junk. D. 13.5 cm. *Princessehof Museum, Leeuwarden.*

247. Cup and saucer, painted in polychrome, showing Chinese fortress on Pearl River, Canton. 2nd or 3rd quarter 18th century. Cup, Ht. 4.2 cm., D. 7.8 cm.; saucer, D. 12.2 cm. *Rijksmuseum, Amsterdam.*

248. Plate, with decoration in purple, yellow, green and brown-red enamels, of young sailor taking leave of sweetheart and, on rim, four cartouches with Chinese landscapes alternating with four circles with purple flowers. 3rd quarter 18th century. D. 23 cm. *De Sypesteyn Museum, Loosdrecht.*

249. Plate, decorated in green, yellow and rose-red enamels, and gold, with Chinese lady and gentleman on either side of pedestal bearing a jar with coral-branch; *chinoiserie* after Meissen. 2nd quarter 18th century. D. 23 cm. *Princessehof Museum, Leeuwarden.*

250. Plate, decorated in black, with background in green, blue and red enamels; painted in the Netherlands with portrait of Stadtholder William IV, 1711–51, after mezzotint by J. Faber, in reverse; round top of rim, inscription *Willem Karel Hendrik Friso Prince van Oranien en Nassau & etc., etc. Stadhouder Admiraal en Capiteyn Generaal over de Seve(?) Provincien in de Nederlanden de 3 May 1747.* 2nd quarter 18th century. D. 21.5 cm. *Boymans-van Beuningen Museum, Rotterdam.*

251. Cup and saucer, in *famille rose,* with half-length portraits of Maria Theresa, Empress of Austria, and prince-consort Francis of Loraine. 3rd quarter 18th century. Cup, D. 7 cm., saucer, D. 11.5 cm. *Centraal Museum, Utrecht.*

252. Plate, painted in sepia, with portrait of P. de Wolff after original shown in no. 253; the rim decorated with yellow and blue sprays, and with inscription on well-border reading *Petrus de Wolff Petrrpil.* 2nd quarter 18th century. D. 23 cm. *Rijksmuseum, Amsterdam.*

253. Mezzotint by Petrus Schenk (1660–1718), a portrait of Petrus de Wolff. *Rijksmuseum, Amsterdam.*

254, 256, 258. Three plates, decorated in underglaze blue, red and green enamels, and gold, with inscription in black, inspired by set of caricatures entitled *Het Grote Tafereel der Dwaasheid* ('The great scene of folly'). 1725–35. D. 21 cm. *Collection Bal, Zeeuws Museum, Middelburg.*

255. Plate, painted in red and blue enamels, and gold, with spearhead motif round rim, 'The Bull's Cruelty'. 2nd quarter 18th century. D. 23 cm. *Zaanlandsche Oudheidkamer Zaandijk.*

257, 259. Two plates (cf. Plates 256, 258) painted in iron-red and gold with rim-decoration in gold, reminiscent of Meissen. 1725–35. D. 21.5 cm. *Collection Bal, Zeeuws Museum, Middelburg.*

260. Plate, blue-and-white, with arms of van der Stel family. 1715–20. D. 25.7 cm. *Centraal Museum, Utrecht.*

261. Plate, blue-and-white, with impaled arms of Van Bleyswyk and Anna van Hemert, married 1708. D. 27.2 cm. *Princessehof Museum, Leeuwarden.*

262. Plate, blue-and-white, with unknown coat of arms, and honeycomb motif on rim. 1750–70. D. 23 cm. *De Sypesteyn Museum, Loosdrecht.*

263. Plate, rim and well-border in blue-and-white, central part with arms of Chasteleyn family painted in blue, red and gold. D. 23 cm. *Collection Klatte-De Waal, Overveen.*

264. Dish, *famille verte,* with coat of arms of province of Groningen, surrounded by tendrils and birds. Well-border and rim, painted with diaperwork in underglaze blue, and panels with landscapes and flowers in blue, yellow, red and green enamels, and gold. 1st quarter 18th century. D. 42 cm. *Rijksmuseum, Amsterdam.*

265. Plate with coat of arms of province of Holland in architectural frame, probably painted in the Netherlands, and well-border and rim as no. 264. 1st quarter 18th century. D. 50 cm. *Formerly Collection Klatte-De Waal, Overveen.*

266. Plate decorated in Imari style in blue, red and gold with accollée arms, at left, of Sautein family. 1st quarter 18th century. D. 21.5 cm. *De Sypesteyn Museum, Loosdrecht.*

267. Teapot, lacking lid, painted with coat of arms of lions rampant above monogram

V.O.C. of Dutch East India Company; round rim the inscription *Res concordia parvae crescunt* (Small things grow through unity), 1728. Ht. 8 cm. *Rijksmuseum, Amsterdam.*

268. Plate, *famille rose,* with arms of de Neufville family, slanting gold cross on red enamel, and with crest on rim at top. 2nd quarter 18th century. D. 22.5 cm. *Rijksmuseum, Amsterdam.*

269. Plate, *famille rose,* ruby back, with decoration of flowery panels on Y-pattern background, the centre with flowering branches, and the panel at top including the arms of the City of Amsterdam. D. 22.5 cm. *Rijksmuseum, Amsterdam.*

270. Plate, central part *bianco-sopra-bianco,* with arms of Herzeele family in red and gold, and outer rim with Louis XIV style decoration in *grisaille.* D. 22.5 cm. *Historisch Museum, Rotterdam.*

271. Plate, decorated in centre with arms of the Verhuell family, and round rim with panels showing Chinese landscapes, alternating with sprays in rose-red, yellow and blue enamels, black and gold, between bands of spearhead motif in gold. 1785–90. D. 23 cm. *Rijksmuseum, Amsterdam.*

272. Plate decorated in red, green, rose-red enamels, and gold, the central part with accollée arms; the outer rim with Louis XIV style ornament broken by coats of arms, swags and acanthus-leaves, the well-border with wavy band motif. 2nd quarter 18th century. D. 32.5 cm. *Historisch Museum, Rotterdam.*

273. Oblong dish with arms of Falck family in red and gold, surmounted by crest of white falcon; well-border decorated with Louis XIV ornament, and outer rim with foliate scrolls, both in *grisaille.* 1765–70. Length 28 cm., breadth, 19 cm. *Rijksmuseum, Amsterdam.*

274. Plate, *famille rose,* with, in centre, arms of Van Reverhorst family; at right, arms of Schrevelius, Peenen, Groenendyck, De Vroede; at left, van Reverhorst, De Winter, Vereyck, De Bruyn; and rim-decoration of scrolls and shells in gold. 1735–40. D. 23 cm. *Rijksmuseum, Amsterdam.*

275. Cup and saucer, decorated in red and blue enamels, and gold, the centre with man in plumed hat, surrounded by festoon motif; the rim with similar decoration and dancing man. 1st half 18th century. Cup, Ht. 3 cm., D. 6.5 cm. *Provinciaal Museum, Drenthe, Assen.*

276. Cup shown with handle at back, decorated in *famille rose* and silver, with arms of Hendrik van Ijsselmonde tot Paaslo impaling Anna Elisabeth van Haersolte van Staverden, who were married in 1746; the rim painted with scrolls and shells. 1765–70. Ht. 8 cm., D. 4.5 cm. *Collection Bal, Zeeuws Museum, Middelburg.*

277. Cup and saucer, decorated in *famille rose,* with impaled arms of S. Bal and L. Cats, sprays of flowers and dentil border. 1779. Cup, Ht. 4.5 cm., D. 7.5 cm.; saucer, D. 12.5 cm. *Collection Bal, Zeeuws Museum, Middelburg.*

278. Plate, decorated in black and with white enamel, with helmet and mantling of arms of Discher family in red and gold, surrounded by inscription. 1749. D. 23 cm. *Rijksmuseum, Amsterdam.*

279. Plate decorated in red and green enamels, with coat of arms, eagle, swags, cannon, flags, Neptune's trident and staff of Hermes, crowned by two nude trumpet-blowing *putti* within borders of festoons. 4th quarter 18th century. D. 23 cm. *De Sypesteyn Museum, Loosdrecht.*

280. Cup and saucer, with decoration of Louis XVI vase, flanked by two half-nude women,

and ribbon with motto *Jamais abattu*, and surrounded by four bees (?) and festoons of flowers; also on cup. 4th quarter 18th century. Cup, Ht. 4 cm., D. 7.5 cm.; saucer, 10.5 cm.

281. Plate, *famille rose*, the centre with basket of flowers, surrounded by three concentric rings of chain, scrolled flowery tendrils and straight bands. End 18th century. D. 23 cm. *Boymans-van Beuningen Museum, Rotterdam.*

282. Plate, blue-and-white, decorated with the eight of spades in centre, and bands of lozenge-like decoration broken by four *ju-i* motifs round rim. 2nd half 18th century. D. 22 cm. *De Sypesteyn Museum, Loosdrecht.*

283. Plate decorated in black and gold, with Chinese landscape and, in centre, arms of Elwick or Ellick family. Yung Chêng period, about 1730. D. 35 cm. *Ashmolean Museum, Oxford.*

284. Plate painted in black, flesh colour, and a little gold, with wedding allegory and arms of Nic. Geelvinck and Johanna Jacoba Graafland. About 1730. D. 22.8 cm. *Rijksmuseum, Amsterdam.*

285. Plate, decorated in black and gold with portraits of Stadtholder (?) and lady. Yung Chêng period. D. 18 cm. *Centraal Museum, Utrecht.*

286. Cup and saucer painted in sepia, and some gold on rim, with Chinese landscape of walled palace. Yung Chêng period. Cup, Ht. 4 cm., D. 7 cm., saucer, D. 11.5 cm. *Collection Bal, Zeeuws Museum, Middelburg.*

287. Cup decorated in black and some gold, with portraits of lady and gentleman. Dated on back, 1733. Ht. 4 cm., D. 6.5 cm. *British Museum, London.*

288. Plate, painted in black and gold, with Chinese scene. Yung Chêng period. D. 23 cm. *Groninger Museum.*

289. Haringpakkerstoren at Amsterdam. Print by P. Schenk, from *Topografische Atlas.* About 1710. *Municipal Archives Department, Amsterdam.*

290. Deep plate, in black; in central cartouche, with gold rim, a Dutch scene—Haringpakkerstoren at Amsterdam; round rim, fleur-de-lis in red and gold. Ht. 4 cm., D. 21 cm. *Municipal Museum, Amsterdam.*

291. Plate decorated in black, sepia, and some gold, with fishing couple. 1750–70. D. 12 cm. *Private collection.*

292. Covered jug, decoration in black with cartouche of European landscape bordered in gold. About 1770. Ht. 14 cm. *British Museum, London.*

293. Cup decorated on outside in *encre de chine* with fishing couple, and on inside rim in black and gold. About 1760. Ht. 6 cm., D. 12 cm. *Private collection.*

294. Cup decorated in black and gold, with 'lacework' rim decoration, portrait of Gisbertus Voetius (1589–1676), and coat of arms of city of Utrecht. About 1750 (?). Ht. 4.5 cm., D. 7 cm. *British Museum, London.*

295. Cup and scallop-edged saucer, painted in black and gold, with 'Valentine' decoration. About 1760. Cup, Ht. 6.5 cm., D. 15 cm.; saucer, D. 11 cm. *Private collection.*

296. Covered sugar bowl, knob on lid a red rose, decorated in black, with arms of the town of Kampen. 1767. Ht. 13.9 cm. *Municipal Museum, Kampen.*

297. Cup and saucer painted in black, with 'Charlotte at Werther's tomb'. About 1790. Cup, Ht. 5 cm., D. 9.2 cm; saucer, D. 13.4 cm. *British Museum, London.*

298. Plate decorated in black, with fishing youth, after print by Bloemaert, published by

Notes on the monochrome plates

C. J. Visscher the Younger (see Plate 207); round rim, festoon with peacocks, 1750–60. D. 23.4 cm. *Rijksmuseum, Amsterdam.*

299. Four-lobed tray painted in black, with 'cither player', and with red and gold fleur-de-lis round rim. About 1770. D. 23 cm. *Fries Museum, Leeuwarden.*

300. Plate, in black, decoration of birth of Christ. About 1770. D. 12 cm. *Collection Bal, Zeeuws Museum, Middelburg.*

301. Two plates, left, Mercury and Neptune, black and gold within elaborate scrolled border. 1750–60. Right, Mercury, decorated in black, foliate scroll round rim. 1740–50 (?). Both, D. 11 cm. *Private collection.*

302. Handled cup, painted in black and some gold, with Minerva (?) and resting youth 1770–80. Ht. 6 cm. *Private collection.*

303. Handled cup, in black and flesh colour, 'unchastened' version of subject of no. 302, 1770–80. Ht. 6.3 cm. *Private collection.*

304. Bowl, with decoration in black, flesh colour, and some gold, of three red-haired European figures; inside rim also painted in black. About 1775. Ht. 6.5 cm., D. 14 cm. *Private collection.*

305. Plate, with decoration in black and some gold, of Nieuwe Kerk, Abdytoren and Mint at Middelburg. 1780–90. D. 12 cm. *Zeeuws Museum, Middelburg.*

306. Nieuwe Kerk, Abdytoren and Mint, print by Th. Koning, published in 1777 in December issue of *Zeelands Chronykalmanak. Prentenkabinet, Rijksmuseum, Amsterdam.*

307. Plate, with painting in sepia, of poultry yard, the rim with two gold bands separated by a red line. 1770–85. D. 27.5 cm. *Collection Bal, Zeeuws Museum, Middelburg.*

308. Engraving, 'Poultry-yard', by Francis Place after F. Barlow. *Prentenkabinet, Rijksmuseum, Amsterdam.*

309. Saucer, with *encre de chine* painting after botanical print (?), and rim in red and gold. 1740–60. Ht. 3 cm., D. 16 cm. *Private collection.*

310. Deep plate, decorated in black, outer rim with some gold, centre, with six Buddhist figures. About 1775. D. 23.5 cm. *Private collection.*

311. Ribbed plate with scalloped edge, decorated in Kakiemon style, in red, blue and gold, with the tale of Yang Hsiang, one of the 24 Paragons of Filial Piety, and the tiger. 1st quarter 18th century. D. 25 cm. *Princessehof Museum, Leeuwarden.*

312. Plate decorated in red and blue in Imari style, the centre with tree and flowers, the rim, alternately with Chinese flowers and cloud motif. 1st quarter 18th century. D. 40 cm. *Rijksmuseum, Amsterdam.*

313. Square tray, decorated in Imari colours, with Kakiemon decoration of cock and hen. (Cf. plate 70 in Soame Jenyns' *Japanese Porcelain.*) 1st quarter 18th century. D. 20.3 cm. *Groninger Museum.*

314. Barber's bowl, painted in Imari colours and style, with flowers and leaves, the rim with cloud motif, diaperwork and flowerets. 1st quarter 18th century. D. 26.7 cm. *Princessehof Museum, Leeuwarden.*

315. Dish with Imari decoration: in the centre a conventionalized chrysanthemum surrounded by Eight Precious Things; on the rim, panels of flowers and conventionalized chrysanthemums. 1st quarter 18th century. D. 36 cm. *Princessehof Museum, Leeuwarden.*

316. Plate painted in blue, red and gold, the centre decoration of flower-vase on platform with fence, the rim with alternately circular and *ju–i* shaped cartouches with flowers, separated by tendrils. Ex-collection of Augustus the Strong. 1st quarter 18th century. D. 35.5 cm. *Dienst van 's Rijks Verpreide Kunstvoorwerpen, The Hague.*

317. Dish of the same shape as *famille verte* armorial plates (colour plate G), decorated in blue, red and gold, with, in centre, mountain landscape with chariot and, on rim, flowery gadroons in relief. 2nd quarter 18th century. D. 34.5 cm. *Collection Van Vliet, Catharina Gasthuis Municipal Museum, Gouda.*

318. Dish, scalloped rim, iron-red, central part as no. 317; rim, flowers. 2nd or 3rd quarter 18th century. D. 27.5 cm. *Rijksmuseum, Amsterdam.*

319. Plate, decorated in iron-red, gold and black, with Chinese water landscape with boat, and background of mountains; round rim, tulip-shaped relief, panels painted with flowerets. 1st half 18th century. D. 27.4 cm. *Schotse Huizen, Veere.*

320. Two long-necked flasks painted in iron-red and gold with chrysanthemums. 1st half 18th century. Ht. 15.5 cm. *Collection Bal, Zeeuws Museum, Middelburg.*

321. Two Yi-hsing teapots in red stoneware: left, with excise office mark of T'ien Ch'i (1621–27); right, with excise office mark of Shun Chih (1644–61). Ht. 7 cm. and 11.5 cm. *Groninger Museum.*

322. Teapot, Yi-hsing, in red stoneware. 18th or 19th century. Ht. 10.2 cm., D. 10.5 cm. *Princessehof Museum, Leeuwarden.*

323. Statuette, Têhua, *blanc de chine*, of seated European, late 17th or early 18th century. Ht. 33 cm., breadth 13.2 cm. *Princessehof Museum, Leeuwarden.*

324. Incense holder, Têhua, *blanc de chine*, statuette of Chinese lion. Late 17th or early 18th century. Ht. 28 cm., breadth, 13.2 cm. *Princessehof Museum, Leeuwarden.*

325. Group of Europeans, Têhua, *blanc de chine*. Late 17th or early 18th century. Ht. 14 cm. *Kröller-Müller Museum, Otterlo.*

326. Statuettes, Têhua, *blanc de chine*: three Europeans and one lion, each a whistle. Early 18th century. Ht. 4.3 cm., 4.7 cm., 5.5 cm., and 4.5 cm. *Groninger Museum.*

327. Statuette, Têhua, *blanc de chine*; two seated ladies, heads and hands separately moulded. Late 17th or early 18th century. Ht. 15.7 cm., breadth, 16.2 cm. *Princessehof Museum, Leeuwarden.*

328. Cup, Têhua, *blanc de chine*, prunus sprays in relief. Late 17th or early 18th century. Ht. 7.2 cm., D. 7.6 cm. *Princessehof Museum, Leeuwarden.*

329. Statuettes, Têhua, *blanc de chine*; left, European on lion, right, European on dragon (?), and whistle. Early 18th century. Ht., left, 6.5 cm., right, 3.5 cm. *Flehite Museum, Amersfoort.*

330. Statuette of dog, in yellow enamel with green collar. 3rd quarter 18th century. Ht. 16.5 cm. *Collection Bal, Zeeuws Museum, Middelburg.*

331. Group decorated in polychrome of dancing pair, after western prototype J. J. Kändler or J. T. Eberlein. Middle 18th century. Ht. 15.5 cm. *Groninger Museum.*

332. Statuette of sitting dog, iron-red on white with green collar and gold bell. 3rd quarter 18th century. Ht. 25.5 cm. *Collection Bal, Zeeuws Museum, Middelburg.*

333. Statuette, in blue-and-white, of Taoist Immortal Lu Tung-pin. Early 17th century. Ht. 22 cm. *Collection Bal, Zeeuws Museum, Middelburg.*

334. Statuettes, decorated in polychrome, of Louis XIV and Madame de Montespan. Late 17th or early 18th century. Ht. 23 cm. *Private collection.*

335. Plate, decorated in underglaze blue and *famille rose.* Mandarin porcelain with two Chinese ladies at table. 1st half 18th century. D. 21 cm. *Princessehof Museum, Leeuwarden.*

336. Brush-pot, Mandarin porcelain, painted in rose-red, yellow, green and gold. 2nd half 18th century. H. 12 cm. *Centraal Museum, Utrecht.*

337. Covered cup and saucer, Mandarin porcelain, *famille rose,* decoration of lady with children in front of Chinese house. 2nd half 18th century. Ht., cup, 8.7 cm., saucer, D. 13.5 cm. *Princessehof Museum, Leeuwarden.*

338. Plate, Mandarin porcelain, with decoration in purple, green, light red and blue enamel, of mandarin ladies and child in front of Chinese house, and background of mountains. 2nd half 18th century. D. 23 cm. *Schotse Huizen, Veere.*

339. Vase, Mandarin porcelain, with polychrome decoration of Chinese figures on terrace, in panels surrounded by undulating tendrils in relief. 2nd half 18th century. Ht. 30 cm. *Groninger Museum.*

340. Plate enamelled on glaze in the Netherlands in iron-red and blue, with portrait of Willem Deurhoff (1650–1717), and, on rim, biblical scenes. 1st quarter 18th century. D. 28 cm. *Koninklijk Oudheidkundig Genootschap, Rijksmuseum, Amsterdam.*

341. Plate, enamelled on glaze in the Netherlands, in blue, green, rose-red and gold, with portrait of Anthonie van Leeuwenhoek (1632–1723), and Oude Kerk at Delft in background, surrounded by twisted rope ornament. 3rd quarter 18th century. D. 27 cm. *Municipal Museum Prinsenhof, Delft.*

342. Anthonie van Leeuwenhoek, mezzotint by Johannes Verkolje (1650–93), the pattern for no. 341. *Rijksmuseum voor de Geschiedenis der Natuurwetenschappen, Leiden.*

343. Plate, as no. 342, with decoration of sepulchral obelisk of Van Leeuwenhoek.

344. Plate, as no. 342, with decoration of coat of arms of Van Leeuwenhoek.

345. Plate, Chinese blue-and-white porcelain, enamelled on the glaze in the Netherlands. Decoration of formal flower in centre with, left, Prince William IV, and right, Princess Anna, both seated, surmounted by two trumpet-blowing amors holding up a crown, on rim, panels with birds. Inscription *Nooijt ver Eenigt altijd versteenigt* (Never united (or together), always turned to stone). 2nd quarter 18th century. D. 23.5 cm. *Historisch Museum, Rotterdam.*

346. Plate, technically as no. 345, with Princess Anna in same pose as on no. 345, and inscription, *Gij moet niet haaste of gij Raak aan het laatste* (You shall not make haste or you will not last). 2nd quarter 18th century. D. 23 cm. *Municipal Museum, Arnhem.*

347. Bowl, with underglaze blue rim, the body decorated with engraved Chinese flower-pattern, and enamelled in green and red on glaze in the Netherlands, with Gallic cock, orange-tree and Dutch lion on one side, and William IV and Anna on other. 2nd quarter 18th century. Ht. 6.7 cm., D. 14.7 cm. *Rijksmuseum voor Volkenkunde, Leiden.*

348. Plate with underglaze blue rim, enamelled in red, green and yellow, on glaze, in the Netherlands, with portraits of Prince William V and Princess Wilhelmina. 3rd quarter 18th century. D. 23 cm. *Historisch Museum, Rotterdam.*

349. Tea service, enamelled in the Netherlands in red, blue, green and purple, with 'cherry-picker' subject. 2nd or 3rd quarter 18th century. Teapot, Ht. 11.5 cm. *Centraal Museum, Utrecht.*

Notes on the monochrome plates

350. Bowl with underglaze blue rim, and engraved Chinese pattern, enamelled on the glaze in the Netherlands in red, yellow, etc., with tree and birds. 18th century. Ht. 7.5 cm., D. 14.8 cm. *Schotse Huizen, Veere.*

351. Bowl, technically as no. 350, the decoration of a Chinese lady sitting, with horse in yellow, deer in lilac, and small house in red. 18th century. Ht. 7 cm., D. 11 cm. *Schotse Huizen, Veere.*

352. Bowl, as no. 350, with decoration of so-called 'Sentry-boxes', in red, green and gold. Ht. 7 cm., D. 14 cm. *Schotse Huizen, Veere.*

353. Bowl, as no. 350, with decoration of flower-basket in red, green and gold. Ht. 7 cm., D. 11 cm. *Schotse Huizen, Veere.*

354. Plate, with Chinese engraved tendril decoration, enamelled on the glaze in the Netherlands with, in centre, town-crier and two inscriptions, and on rim, leaves and flowers. 1720–30. D. 22.2 cm. *Fries Museum, Leeuwarden.*

355. Plate, enamelled in the Netherlands on the glaze in red, green, blue and gold, with the ship *Zeeland,* 1700. 1st quarter 18th century. D. 21.5 cm. *Rijksmuseum, Amsterdam.*

356. Saucer, enamelled on the glaze in the Netherlands in green, red, yellow and blue, with whaling ship, *De Walvisvangst.* 1st half 18th century. D. 9.7 cm. *Rijksmuseum, Amsterdam.*

357. Ribbed plate, enamelled on the glaze in the Netherlands in red, green, yellow, blue and gold, with decoration in centre of musicians, and on rim, panels of the lovers, and the cherry-picker and deer hunting. 2nd half 18th century. D. 27.8 cm. *De Sypesteyn Museum, Loosdrecht.*

358. Plate, enamelled in the Netherlands in polychrome, with pattern 'The Bull's Cruelty'. 2nd half 18th century. D. 22 cm. *Zaanlandsche Oudheidkamer, Zaandijk.*

359. Japanese bottle, decorated over the glaze in the Netherlands, in red, green, blue and turquoise enamels, with scene of ship-canal between Haarlem and Leiden. Beneath the base, in underglaze blue the monogram V.O.C. of the Dutch East India Company. 3rd quarter 18th century. Ht. 32 cm., D. 25 cm. *De Lakenhal Museum, Leiden.*

360. Detail of print *Uytslag der Wind Negotie* (result of stock-jobbery), showing man with paper in left hand, inscribed *Hoornse wortelen* (Hoorn carrots). *Atlas Van Stolk, Rotterdam.*

361. Square Japanese bottle, with decoration in pseudo-Kakiemon style, of man with paper, taken from no. 360. 1725–35. Ht. 19.8 cm. *Collection Bal, Zeeuws Museum, Middelburg.*

Appendix · Collections in the Netherlands

Collections of Chinese export wares can be seen, for example, in the Stedelijk Museum in Alkmaar, in the Rijksmuseum, in the Willet Holthuysen Museum, in the Sophia-Augusta Foundation (Stedelijk Museum) all three in Amsterdam, in the Flehite Museum in Amersfoort, in the Simon van Gijn Museum in Dordrecht, in the Coopmanshüs Stedelijk Museum in Franeker, in the Frans Hals Museum in Haarlem, in the Groninger Museum voor Stad en Lande, in the Museum of the Bisdom van Vliet Foundation at Haastrecht, in the Fries Museum at Leeuwarden, in the Centraal Museum at Utrecht, in the Schotse Huizen at Veere, and in the Overijssels Museum at Zwolle. Only the collections in the Rijksmuseum at Amsterdam and in the Groninger Museum have been enlarged by important acquisitions bought as well as gifted and bequeathed. The last-named museum, opened in 1890, received almost at once an important legacy of Chinese porcelain (that of Jonkheer M. R. M. A. de Marées van Swinderen) and soon afterwards another (from Mr. A. Nap). The keeper, Miss Minke de Visser, has catalogued and enriched this collection for over twenty years. So this museum gives a good survey of Chinese ceramics from the Tang dynasty (618–906) up to the last century. Ottema's collection, and that of M. T. van Meulen, gifted to the city in 1915, were exhibited when the Princessehof Museum was opened in 1917. The museum was further enriched by legacies and gifts among which special mention should be made of the so-called Swatow porcelain of Ir. R. D. Verbeek and of his son A. D. R. Verbeek. Miedema, who after Ottema's death was the director of the Museum for a few years, put together three richly illustrated catalogues of the collection.

The interest in Eastern Art, stemming from the last years of the nineteenth century and the beginning of this, led to the setting up in 1918 of the Society of Friends of Asiatic Art. The interest of the general public was also awakened by the publication of bulletins and the holding of exhibitions. On the initiative of this society in 1932, a collection was installed in a few rooms of the Stedelijk Museum in Amsterdam; and this was moved in 1952 to the Drucker building in the Rijksmuseum. Apart from statuary and paintings from the Far East, the society also possesses a small collection of ceramics from prehistory to around the end of the sixteenth century. This is complemented by the collection of the Rijksmuseum, which through gifts, legacies and purchases was also enriched by the collections of J. G. A. N. de Vries, R. May, L. C. J. Drucker. In spite of a few gaps, there is here a good picture of the development of Chinese ceramics.

An attractive, though not extensive, collection is in the Rijksmuseum voor Volkenkunde (Ethnographical Museum) in Leiden. After the First World War, the Museum Tetar van Elvan was set up in Delft, and this has a collection almost entirely devoted to eighteenth-century Chinese porcelain as has also the De Sypesteyn Museum in Loosdrecht (opened 1927) given by the Jonkheer C. H. C. A. van Sypesteyn.

A collection of Delft earthenware and Chinese porcelain in the same way was gifted by W. K. F. Baron van Verschuur to the nation, on condition that it was kept on permanent loan to the Arnhem City Museum. In this connexion, mention should be made of the collection of Chinese porcelain, including *blanc de chine* and *famille verte*, brought together by Mrs. H. E. L. J. Kroller-Muller, and since 1935 established in the museum at Otterlo. After the First World War, the keeper of The Hague Museum, Mr. M. H. C. Gallois (died 1937), laid the foundations of a collection consisting especially of Han, Sung and early Ming. By the purchase of the Noë collection the Boymans-van Beuningen Museum in Rotterdam came into possession of a representative collection of *chine de commande,* and since the war the Rotterdam Historical Museum has also collected a number of typical pieces of *chine de commande.*[1]

The last twenty years have shown a growing interest in Eastern Art in the Netherlands, demonstrated by the exhibition of Art from the Far East held in 1954 in the Rijksmuseum. Here was shown the fine collection of Chinese ceramics belonging to H. M. Knight of Scheveningen. In 1968–9, exhibitions of Chinese porcelain of the seventeenth and eighteenth centuries were held in several museums in the Netherlands.

The Zeeuws Museum at Middelburg has shown since 1943 the mainly eighteenth-century Chinese export porcelain collected by the antiquarian W. H. Bal and his sister, and left to the nation.

[1] Only museums and collections which belong to the authorities, a Foundation or a Society are mentioned here. There is also the Dutch Historical Maritime Museum in Amsterdam and museums in the following places: Appingedam, Assen, Borculo, Delft, Denekamp, Deventer, Doorn, Enkhuizen, Enschede, Goes, Gouda, 's-Gravenhage (The Hague), Haarlem, Heino, Hilversum, Laren, Leiden, Maastricht, Oldenzaal, Oud-Zuilen, Roermond, Roosendaal, Sneek, Steenwijk, Utrecht, Zaandijk, Zutphen, Zwolle.

Bibliography

HISTORY, TRAVEL AND TRADE

Bartold, V. V., *La Découverte de l'Asie, histoire de l'orientalisme en Europe et en Russie*. Translated from the Russian by B. Nikitine. Paris, 1947.

Carletti, Francesco, *Ragionamenti del mio viaggio intorno al mondo, 1594–1606*. Translated by Herbert Weinstock as *My Voyage around the World*. London, 1965.

Debenham, Frank, *Discovery and Exploration*. London, 1960.

Downs, Joseph, 'The China Trade and its influences', *Bulletin of the Metropolitan Museum of Art*. New York, 1941.

Du Halde, J. B., *Description Géographique, Historique, Chronologique, Politique et Physique de l'Empire de la Chine et de la Tartarie Chinoise*. 4 vols. Paris, 1735. Translated by R. Brookes as *Description of the Empire of China and Chinese Tartary*. 2 vols. London, 1738–41.

The Embassy of Peter de Goyer and Jacob de Keyser from the Dutch East India Company to the Emperor of China, in 1655. Translated from the Dutch. London, 1745. *See also* Nieuhof.

Gelder, Dr. H. E. van, 'Gegevens omtrent den Porseleinhandel der Oost-Indische Compagnie' (Data relevant to the porcelain trade of the Dutch East India Company), *Economic History Yearbook*. The Hague, 1924.

Grandjean, Bredo L., *Dansk Ostindisk Porcelaen importen fra Kanton c. 1700–1822*. Copenhagen, 1965.

Grousset, René, *Histoire de la Chine*. Paris, 1942; new edn. 1957.

Houtman, Cornelis de, *The Description of a Voyage Made by Certaine Ships of Holland (under the command of Cornelis Houtman) into the East Indies*. Translated from the Dutch by W. Phillip. London, 1598. De Houtman's voyages are also included in Hakluyt's *Collection of the Early Voyages*, etc. *See also* Roufaer.

Hullu, Dr. J. de, 'Over den Chineeschen Handel der O.I.C.', *Taal, Land- en Volkenkunde*. The Hague, Vol. 73, 1917.

Bibliography

Hullu, Dr. J. de, 'De porseleinhandel der Oostindische Compagnie en Cornelis Pronk als haar teekenaar', *Oud Holland*, Vol. I. Amsterdam, 1915.

——'De Instelling van de Commissie voor Den Handel der Oost-Indische Compagnie op China in 1756', *Taal, Land- en Volkenkunde*, Vol. 79. The Hague, 1923.

Kircher, A. (Kircherius), *China Monumentis illustrata*. Amsterdam, 1667. Partly translated in *An Embassy from the East India Company*, etc., by Jan Nieuhof (q.v.).

Latham, R. E., *The Travels of Marco Polo*. Harmondsworth, 1959.

Latourette, K. S., *The Chinese, Their History and Culture*. New York, 3rd edn., 1946.

Le Comte, Louis Daniel, *Nouveaux Mémoires sur l'Etat présent de la Chine*. Amsterdam, 1697–1703. Translated as: *Memoirs and Observations . . . made in a late journey through the Empire of China*. London, 1698.

Linschoten, Jan Huyghen van, *Itinerario, Voyage of de Schipvaert naer Ooste ofte Portugaels Indien*. Edited by H. Kern and C. P. Burger, Linschoten Society, Vol. II, 1. The Hague, 1910.

Lubberhuizen-van Gelder, A. M., 'De Factorijen te Canton in de 18e eeuw', *Oud Holland*. Amsterdam, 1955.

Muller, W., *Onze vaderen in China*. Gids, Amsterdam, 1917.

Nieuhof, Jan, *Het Gezandtschap der Neêrlandtsche Oost-Indische Compagnie aan den grooten Tartarischen Cham den tegenwoordigen Keizer van China*. Edited by H. Nieuhof. Amsterdam, 1665. Translated by J. Ogilby as *An Embassy from the East-India Company of the United Provinces to the Grand Tartar Cham Emperour of China, delivered by their Excellcies P. de Goyer and J. de Keyser and ingeniously described by Mr. J. Nieuhof* (with an appendix of several remarks taken out of Father A. Kircher's *Antiquities of China*). London, 1669.

Picard, R., *Les Compagnies des Indes, Route de la Porcelaine*. Paris, 1966.

Pelliot, P., *Les Influences européennes sur l'Art Chinois au 17e et 18e siècle*. Paris, 1948.

Pontanus, Joannes, *Historische beschrijvinghe der seer wijt beroemde coop-stadt Amsterdam*. Amsterdam, 1614.

Schiedlausky, Günther, *Tee, Kaffee, Schokolade*. Munich, 1961.

Roufaer, G. P., and Ijzerman, J. W., *De eerste schipvaart der Nederlanders naar Oost-Indie onder Cornelis de Houtman 1595–1597*. Linschoten Society, Vol. VII. The Hague, 1915.

Schlegel, G., 'De betrekkingen tussen Nederland en China volgens Chineesche berichten', *Bijdragen tot de Taal, Land- en Volkenkunde*. The Hague, 1893.

Urwin, Iris, *The Face of Ancient China*. London, 1960.

Valentijn, François, *Oud en Nieuw Oostindie, vervattende een nauwkeurige uitvoerige Verhandelinge van Nederlands Mogentheyd in die Gewesten*, etc. 5 volumes. Dordrecht/Amsterdam, 1724–26.

Visser, Minke A. de, 'Iets over den handel in Chinees porselein en over porselein-versamelaars in Groningen', *Volksalmanak*. Groningen, 1929.

Bibliography

CHINESE ART, GENERAL

Buhot, Jean, *Arts de la Chine*. Paris, 1951.

Bushell, Stephen W., *Chinese Art*. London, Vol. I, 1904, Vol. II, 1910.

Dawson, Raymond, *The Legacy of China*. Oxford, 1964.

Feddersen, Martin, *Chinese Decorative Art*. London, 1961.

Grousset, René, *La Chine et son Art*. Paris, 1951.

Hansford, S. Howard, *A Glossary of Chinese Art and Archaeology*. London, 2nd edn., 1961.

Hildburgh, W. L., 'Chinese Painted Enamels with European Subjects', *The Burlington Magazine*. London, 1941.

Medley, Margaret, *A Handbook of Chinese Art*. London, 1964.

Speiser, Dr. Werner, *China, Spirit and Society*. Translated by George Lawrence. London, 1960.

Visser, H. F. E., Catalogue of the Museum of Asiatic Art in the Rijksmuseum, Amsterdam.

——*Kunst uit het Oosten*. Amsterdam, 1955.

Volker, T., *The Animal in Far Eastern Art, and especially in the art of the Japanese Netsuke, with reference to Chinese origins, traditions, legends and art*. Leiden, 1950.

Willetts, William, *Chinese Art*. Harmondsworth, 1958.

——*Foundations of Chinese Art*. London, 1965.

Williams, C. A. S., *Encyclopaedia of Chinese Symbolism and Art Motives*. New York, 1960.

CERAMICS, GENERAL

Cox, Warren E., *The Book of Pottery and Porcelain*. New York, 11th edn., 1963.

Hannover, Emil, *Pottery and Porcelain*. Translated by Bernard Rackham. London, 1925.

Leach, Bernard, *A Potter's Book*. London, 1949.

Savage, George, *Pottery through the Ages*. Harmondsworth, 1959.

——*Porcelain through the Ages*. Harmondsworth, 1954.

Sauerlandt, M., *Edelmetalfassungen in de Keramik*. Berlin, 1929.

Staehelin, W. A., *Das Buch vom Porzellan*. Berne, 1965.

Tait, Hugh, *Porcelain*. London, 1962.

Visser, Minke A. de, 'Drie Kakiemon schoteltjes versierd met haan en hen, resp. in Japan, China en te Meissen gemaakt' (Three Kakiemon saucers with cock and hen decoration made in Japan, China and Meissen). Groninger Museum Annual Report, 1961.

Vries, J. G. A. N. de, *Porselein, Chineesch en Europeesch Porselein*. The Hague, 1923.

Bibliography

CHINESE CERAMICS

Ashton, Leigh, *A Handbook to the W. G. Gulland Bequest of Chinese Porcelein: European Influence on Chinese Porcelain*. London, Victoria and Albert Museum, 1950.

Beurdeley, Michel, *Porcelaine de la Compagnie des Indes*. Fribourg, 1962. Translated by Diane Imber as *Porcelain of the East India Companies*. London, 1962.

Bluett, E. E., *Ming and Ch'ing Porcelains*. London, 1933.

Bondy, W., *K'ang Hsi*. Munich, 1923.

Boschma, Dr. C., 'Een Porseleinen Cop met Silveren Oren', *Fries Genootschap* 137. Leeuwarden, 1965.

Burton, William, *Porcelain, A Sketch of its Nature, Art and Manufacture*. London, 1906. (Includes a translation of part of the two letters from Père d'Entrecolles.)

Bushell, Stephen W., *Description of Chinese Pottery and Porcelain being a translation of the T'ao Shuo by Chu Yen* (with an appendix containing two letters by Father X. d'Entrecolles on the manufacture of porcelain at Ching-tê Chên). Oxford, 1910.

——*Oriental Ceramic art, illustrated by examples from the collection of W. T. Walters*. New York, 1899. (This work includes a partial translation of Père d'Entrecolles' letters.)

Chiang-hsi T'ung Chih (General History of Kiangsi) revised, enlarged and brought up to date under the supervision of Hsieh Min in 1732. This work includes the T'ang Ying list of porcelain made for the Emperor Yung Chêng.

Ching-te-Chen T'ao Lu by Lan P'u. Published in 1815. Partly, and inaccurately translated into French by Stanislaus Julien (q.v.). Now available in a translation by Geoffrey R. Sayer (q.v.).

Corbeiller, Clare Le, 'Trade Winds from China', *Bulletin of the Metropolitan Museum of Art*. New York, January, 1962.

Craig, Sir Algernon Tudor, *Armorial Porcelain of the Eighteenth Century*. London, 1925.

Craig, T. J., 'Armorial China and Glass', *The Concise Encyclopaedia of Antiques*, Vol. II. London, 1960.

Crisp, F. A., *Armorial China*. London, 1907.

Crossman, Carl L., *A Design Catalog of Chinese Export Porcelain for the American Market*. Peabody Museum, Salem, Massachusetts, 1964.

David, Lady, *Ch'ing Enamelled Wares in the Percival David Foundation of Chinese Art*. London, 1958.

Dexel, Thomas, *Die Formen Chineschischer Keramik*. Tubingen, 1955.

Donnelly, P. J., *Blanc de Chine*. London, 1969.

D'Entrecolles, Père X., Two letters dated 1712 and 1722 describing the manufacture of porcelain at Ching-tê Chên, first published in *Lettres édifiantes et curieuses, écrites des missions étrangères par quelques missionaires de la Compagnie de Jesus*, Vols. XII and XVI. Paris, 1717 and 1724. Reprinted in *Description of Chinese Pottery and*

Bibliography

Porcelain by S. W. Bushell (q.v.). Translated in part in *Oriental Ceramic Art* by Bushell (q.v.) and *Porcelain* by W. Burton (q.v.).

Du Boulay, Anthony, *Chinese Porcelain*. London, 1963.

Fichtner, F., 'Der Alte Bestand ostasiatische Keramik im Scholoss Favorite bei Rastadt', *Ostasiatische Zeitschrift*, No. 5/6, 1939/40.

Fontein, J., 'A pair of large blue and white vases of the Kang Hsi period', *Phoenix*, Vol. 4, 1949.

——'Chinese Ceramiek', *Sprekend Verleden*. Amsterdam, 1959.

Garner, Sir Harry, *Oriental Blue and White*. London, 3rd edn., 1970.

——'The use of imported and native cobalt in Chinese Blue and White', *Oriental Art*. London, 1956.

——'The origins of *Famille Rose*', *Transactions of the Oriental Ceramic Society*. London, 1967–69.

Goidsenhoven, J. P. van, *La Céramique Chinoise sous les Ts'ing. 1644–1851*. Brussels, 1936.

Goldschmidt, Daisy Lion, *Les Poteries et Porcelaines Chinoises*. Paris, 1957.

Griggs, W., *Illustrations of Armorial China*. London, 1887.

Gulland, W. G., *Chinese Porcelain*. London, 3rd edn., 1911.

Gutschmidt, J., 'Das chinesische Tafelservice met dem groszen Königlich Preuszischen Staatswappen', *Zeitschrift des Vereins für die Geschichte Berlins*, 52. Berlin, 1935.

Gyllensvärd, B., *Chinese Ceramics in the Carl Kempe collection*. Stockholm, 1965.

Hackenbroch, Y., 'Chinese Porcelain in European Silvermounts', *The Connoisseur*. London, 1955.

Hobson, R. L., *Chinese Pottery and Porcelain*. 2 volumes. London, 1915.

——*The Wares of the Ming Dynasty*. London, 1922; 2nd edn., Tokyo, 1962.

——*The Later Ceramic Wares of China*. London, 1925.

——*Handbook of the Pottery and Porcelain of the Far East*. London, British Museum, 3rd edn., 1948.

——'On some Armorial Porcelain in the Franks Collection', *The Connoisseur*, XXI. London, 1908.

Honey, W. B., *Guide to the Later Chinese Porcelain in the Victoria and Albert Museum*. London, 1927.

——*The Ceramic Art of China and Other Countries of the Far East*. London, 1955.

——'Dutch decorators of Chinese porcelain', *Antiques*. New York, 1932.

Hyde, J. A. Lloyd, *Oriental Lowestoft, Chinese Export Porcelain*. Newport, 1954.

——with Ricardo Espirito Santo Silva and Eduardo Malta (water-colours and descriptions), *Chinese Porcelain for the European Market*. Lisbon, 1956.

Jacquemart, A., and Le Blant, E., *Histoire Artistique Industriale et Commerciale de la Porcelaine*. 3 vols. Paris, 1862.

Jenyns, R. Soame, *Ming Pottery and Porcelain*. London, 1953.

Bibliography

Jenyns, R. Soame, *Later Chinese Porcelain*. London, 4th edn., 1971.

——'The Chinese Ko-Sometsuke and Shonsui Wares', *Transactions of the Oriental Ceramic Society*. London, 1962–63.

Jones, Alfred, 'Old Chinese Porcelain made from English Silver Models', *The Burlington Magazine,* Vol. XX. London, 1911–12.

Jourdain, Margaret and Jenyns, R. Soame, *Chinese Export Art in the Eighteenth Century*. London, 1950.

Julien, Stanislaus, *Histoire et Fabrication de la Porcelaine Chinoise, ouvrage traduit du chinois*. Paris, 1856. A partial translation of the *Ching-tê Chên T'ao Lu* is included in this work.

Kamp, P. A. van de, 'Een Rotterdams belastingdrama op Chinees porselein', *Antiek,* Vol. II. Locheim, 1967–8.

Kisch, Bruno, 'Europäerien auf Chinesischen Porzellan', *Artibus Asiae,* VI. Leipzig, 1936–37.

Lane, Arthur, 'Queen Mary II's Porcelain Collection at Hampton Court', *Transactions of the Oriental Ceramic Society*. London, 1949–50.

——*Chinese Porcelain of the Ch'ing Dynasty*. London, Victoria and Albert Museum, 1957.

Loeffler, E. P., 'China Trade Porcelain in the Museum's Collection', Bulletin of Rhode Island School of Design. Rhode Island, U.S.A., March 1962.

Lovell, Hin-Cheung, *Illustrated Catalogue of Ting Yao and Related White Wares in the Percival David Foundation of Chinese Art*. London, 1964.

——'Important finds of ancient Chinese ceramics since 1949', *Chinese Translations no. 1.* Oriental Ceramic Society, London, 1967.

Marquet de Vasselot, J. J. and Ballot, Marie-Juliette, *La Céramique Chinoise*. Paris, 1922.

Mattos Dos Santos, M., 'The marks', *Chinese Ceramics*. Lisbon, 1968.

Medley, Margaret, *Illustrated Catalogue of Porcelain Decorated in Underglaze Blue and Copper Red in the Percival David Foundation of Chinese Art*. London, 1963.

——*Illustrated Catalogue of Ming Polychrome Wares in the Percival David Foundation of Chinese Art*. London, 1966.

Miedema, H., 'Zes famille noire koppen en schotels in het Princessehof', *Report* of the Princessehof Museum, 1963.

———*Swatow*. Catalogue of the Princessehof Museum, Leeuwarden. Leeuwarden, 1964.

——*Martavanen*. Catalogue of the Princessehof Museum, Leeuwarden. Leeuwarden, 1964.

Miedema, H., *Kraakporselein en overgangsgoed*. Catalogue of the Princessehof Museum, Leeuwarden. Leeuwarden, 1964.

Monkhouse, W. Cosmo, *A History and Description of Chinese Porcelain*. London, 1901.

Mudge, Jean McClure, *Chinese Export Porcelain for the American Trade, 1785–1835*. Delaware, 1962.

Bibliography

Noë, L., 'Een versameling Chine de commande in het Museum Boymans', *Bulletin, Museum Boymans*. Rotterdam, 1957.

Ottema, Nanne, *Chineesche Ceramiek, Handboek geschreven naar aanleiding van de verzamelingen in het Princessehof te Leeuwarden* (Handbook of the collection in the Princessehof). Amsterdam, 2nd edn., 1946.

——*Chinese ceramiek*, revised by Jaap Romijn. Lochem, 1970.

——*De Praktijk van het porselein verzamelen* (The collecting of porcelain). Amsterdam, 1953.

Penkala, Maris, *Far Eastern Ceramics*. The Hague, 1963.

Perzynski, F., 'Towards a grouping of Chinese Porcelains', *The Burlington Magazine*. London, 1910–11.

Phillips, John Goldsmith, *China Trade Porcelain*. London, 1956.

Pope, J. A., *Chinese Porcelain in the Ardebil Collection*. Washington, 1956.

——'The Princessehof Museum in Leeuwarden', *Archives of the Chinese Art Society of America*, V. Washington, 1951.

Pott, P. H., 'Een in ons land overgeschilderde Chinese Kom met portret van Prins Willem V en Echtgenote', *Jaarverslag* of the National Museum for Ethnology. Leiden, The Hague, 1952.

Rahm, Siv., 'Chinese export porcelain and its influence on Dutch ceramic art', *Vrienden van de Nederlandse Ceramiek, Mededelingenblad* nr. 30. Amsterdam, 1963.

Roth, S., *Chinese Porcelain imported by the Swedish East India Company in the Gothenburg Historical Museum*. Gothernburg, 1965.

Sayer, G. R., *Ching-tê Chên T'ao Lu or The Potteries of China*, being a translation with notes and an introduction. London, 1951.

——*T'ao Ya, or Pottery Refinements* being a translation with notes and an introduction. London, 1959.

Scheurleer, D. F. Lunsingh, 'In China vervaardigde Actiebordjes'; and 'De paardjeskom en andere Chinese porseleinen op zeventiende-eeuwse schilderijen'. Both in *Antiek*, 3. Lochem, 1968–69.

——'Enige weinig voorkomende Chinese porseleinen' and 'De Nieuwe Stadsherberg in het IJ voor Amsterdam'. Both in *Antiek*, 2, 1967–68.

——Introduction to the catalogue of the exhibition of Chinese porcelain garniture sets at the Willet-Holthuysen Museum, Amsterdam, 1968. *Vrienden van de Nederlandse Ceramiek, Mededelingenblad* nr. 52. Amsterdam, 1968.

——'Een Chinees eetservies uit het einde van de achtiende eeuw', *Vrienden van de Nederlandse Ceramiek, Mededelingenblad* nr. 51. Amsterdam, 1968.

——'Een verzameling blauw en wit Chinees porselein te Brummen' and 'Een decor van twee papegaaien op Chinees porselein en Delfts aardewen werk'. Both in *Antiek*, 4, 1969–70.

——'Een Italiaanse fontein op een Chinese schotel'. *Antiek*, 5, 1970–71.

Bibliography

Spriggs, A. I., 'Red Cliff Bowls of the late Ming Period', *Oriental Art,* Vol. VII. Oxford, 1961.

——'Transitional Porcelain Ginger Jars', *Oriental Art,* Vol. XI. Oxford, 1965.

——'Oriental Porcelain in Western Paintings', *Transactions of the Oriental Ceramic Society* for 1964–65. London, 1967.

Spruit, Louise, 'De "zwarte kunst" van onze voorouders', *Vrienden van de Nederlandse Ceramiek, Mededelingenblad* nr. 30, 1963.

——'Een decor in encre de Chine', *Antiek,* 2. Lochem, 1967–68.

Sullivan, M., 'Chinese Export Porcelain', *Oriental Art,* Vol. 33, 1960–62.

T'ao Shuo by Chu Yen: *see* Bushell, Stephen W.

T'ao Ya: *see* Sayer, G. R.

Thorpe, W. A., 'The subjects of decoration on Chinese porcelain', *Handbook to the W. G. Gulland bequest.* London, 1950.

Virgin, Jan, *Ming Blue-and-white from Swedish Collections,* Catalogue of exhibition in the Museum of Far Eastern Antiquities. Stockholm, 1964.

Visser, Minke A. de, *Toelichtende Beschrijving van de verzameling Chineesch en Japansch Porselein, Chineesch en Europeesch rood steengoed en aardewerk, aan wezig in her Groningsch Museum* (Catalogues of the collections of Chinese and Japanese porcelain and pottery in the Groninger Museum). Groningen, 1930.

——'Eetservies van Chinees porselein met het wapen van de familie Feith', *Vrienden van de Nederlandse Ceramiek, Mededelingenblad* nr. 35, 1964.

——'Chineesch Porselein in Holland met Kakiemon decor voorzien', *Oud Holland,* Amsterdam, 1956.

Volker, T., *Porcelain and the Dutch East India Company.* Leiden, 1954.

——'Het "blauw-wit" porselein der V.O.C. in de 17de eeuw', *Vrienden van de Nederlandse Ceramiek, Mededelingenblad* nr. 6, 1956.

——*The Japanese Porcelain Trade of the Dutch East India Company after 1683.* Leiden, 1959.

——'Early Chine de commande', *Bulletin* of the Boymans-van Beuningen Museum. Rotterdam, 1958.

Wall, V. I. van de, 'Een Historisch Servies', *Nederlandsch Indië Oud en Nieuw.* Amsterdam, 1923–24.

Williamson, G. C., *The Book of Famille Rose.* London, 1927.

Wills, Geoffrey, 'Chinese Lowestoft and Export Porcelain', *The Concise Encyclopaedia of Antiques,* Vol. II. London, 2nd edn., 1960.

Winkworth, W. W., 'The Delft Enamellers', *The Burlington Magazine.* London, June 1928.

Yamada, Chisaburo, *Die Chinamode des Spätbarocks.* Berlin, 1935.

Yorke Hardy, S., *Tung, Ju, Kuan, Chün, Kuang-Tung and glazed I-Hsing Wares in the Percival David Foundation of Chinese Art.* London, 1953.

Bibliography

Zimmermann, E., *Porzellan der Ming dyn. in der Porzellan Sammlung zu Dresden*. Berlin, 1910.

——*Chinesisches Porzellan*. Leipzig, 1913; 2nd edn., 1923.

——'Nachdekorierung von Chinesischem Porcellan in Europa', *Kuntswanderer*. Leipzig, 1928–29.

OTHER CERAMICS

Blauwen, A. L. den, 'Ceramiek met Chinoiserien naar prenten naar Petrus Schenk jr.', *Bulletin* of the Rijksmuseum. Amsterdam, 1964.

Dixon, J. L., *English Porcelain of the 18th Century*. London, 1952.

Fontaine, G., *La Céramique Francaise*. Paris, 1964.

Garner, F. H., *English Delftware*. London, 1948.

Gelder, H. E. van, 'De Kunstenaars van ons Oud-Delfts Aardewerk', *Vrienden van de Nederlandse Ceramiek, Mededelingenblad* nr. 12. Amsterdam, 1958.

Gröger, H., *Johann Joachim Kändler, der Meister des Porzellans*. Hanau, 1956.

Hager, L., 'Ein Majolica Tafelgeschirr aus Faenza im Residenzmuseum', *Pantheon*. Munich, 1939.

Havard, H., *La Céramique Hollandaise*. Amsterdam, 1909.

Helbig, J., *Faïences Hollandaises, XVIIe et XVIIIe–debut XIXe siecle*, Musees Royaux d'Art et d'Histoire, Brussels, n.d.

Hobson, R. L., *A Guide to the Islamic Pottery of the Near East*, British Museum. London, 1932.

Honey, W. B., *European Ceramic Art from the end of the Middle Ages to about 1815: Illustrated Historical Survey*. London, 1949; *A Dictionary of Factories, Artists, Technical Terms et cetera*. London, 1952.

——*French Porcelain*. London, 2nd edn., 1972.

——*Dresden China*. London, 1964.

Hudig, Ferrand W., *Delfter Fayence*. Berlin, 1929.

Jansen, B., 'Een Delftse kan uit de fabriek van Rochus Jacobsz Hoppesteyn', *Mededelingen van de Dienst voor Schone Kunsten der-Gemeents*. 's Gravenhage, 1952.

Jenyns, Soame, *Japanese Porcelain*. London, 1965.

Jonge, Dr. C. H. de, *Oud Nederlandsche Majolica en Delftsch Aardewerk*. Amsterdam, 1947.

——'Ceramiek in het Museum der Stichting Bisdom van Vliet te Haastrecht', *Vrienden van de Nederlandse Ceramiek, Mededelingenblad* nr. 31. Amsterdam, 1963.

——*Delfts Aardewerk*. Rotterdam 's Gravenhage, 1965.

Korf, Dingeman, *Tegels*, Bussum, 1960. Translated as *Dutch Tiles*. London, 1963.

——*Nederlandse Majolica*. Bussum, 1962.

Landais, H., *La Porcelaine Française*. Paris, 1963.

Lane, Arthur, *Italian Porcelain*. London, 1954.

Bibliography

Lane, Arthur, *Tea-pots in Pottery and Porcelain*. London, Victoria and Albert Museum, 1955.

——*French Faience*. London, 2nd edn., 1970.

——*Early Islamic Pottery*. London, 5th impression (revised) 1965.

——*Later Islamic Pottery*. London, 2nd edn., 1971.

Pelinck, E., 'Een Japanse Fles beschilderd met de Leidse Trekvaart', *Jaarverslag* of the Museum de Lakenhal. Leiden, 1952.

Rackham, Bernard, *Italian Maiolica*. London, 1952.

Rakebrand, Hilde, *Meissener Tafelgeschirr des 18 Jahrhunderts*. Darmstadt, 1958.

Reidemeister, L., 'Die Porzellankabinette der Brandenburgisch Preussisches Schlösser', *Jahrbuch der Preussischen Kunstsammlungen*. 1933–34.

Rust, W. J., *Nederlands Porselein*. Amsterdam, 1952.

Schnorr von Carolsfeld, Ludwig Erich Köllmann, *Porzellan der Europäischen Fabriken*. Brunswick, 1956.

——Catalogue of exhibition *Wonen in de wijde Wereld*, Tropenmuseum. Amsterdam, 1962–64.

——Catalogue of exhibition *Oranje Boove*, Museum Willet Holthuysen. *Vrienden van de Nederlandse Ceramiek, Mededelingenblad* nr. 15. Amsterdam, 1959.

Seters, W. H. van, 'Leeuwenhoek Ceramiek', *Nederlandsch Tijdschrift voor Geneeskunde*. Haarlem, April, 1936.

Towner, Donald, *English Cream-coloured Earthenware*. London, 1957.

Watney, Bernard, *English Blue and White Porcelain of the Eighteenth Century*. London, 1963.

Weiss, G., *Ullstein Porzellanbuch*. Berlin, 1964.

Westers, A., 'Een Lampetkan van Delfts Aardewerk', *Bulletin* of the Boymans-van Beuningen Museum. Rotterdam, 1961.

Zimmermann, Ernst, *Meissener Porzellan*. Leipzig, 1926.

RELATED SUBJECTS

Berendsen, A., *Het Nederlandsche Interieur*. Utrecht, 1950.

Bontekoe, Cornelis, *Tractaat van het excellente kruyd thee*, 1678.

Brunner, H., *Altes Tafelsilber*. Munich, 1964.

Drossaers, S. W. A., 'Inventaris van de Meubelen van het Stadhouderlijk Kwartier met het Speelhuis en van het huis in het Noordeinde te 's Gravenhage'. *Oud Holland*. Amsterdam, 1930.

Dubbel, B., *Tin en tinnegieter in Nederland*. Zeist, 1965.

Frederiks, J. W., *Dutch Silver*. 4 vols. The Hague, 1952–61.

Gans, M. H., and Duyvené de Wit-Klinkhamer, Th. M., *Dutch Silver*. London, 1961.

Garner, Sir Harry, *Chinese and Japanese Cloisonné enamels*. London, 2nd edn., 1970.

Bibliography

Gelder, H. E. van, *Heda, Van Beyeren, Kalf*. Amsterdam, 1941.

——*Haagsche Goud en Zilversmeden,* etc. The Hague, 1941.

Grimwade, Arthur C., 'Silver', *The Concise Encyclopaedia of Antiques*, I. London, 3rd edn., 1956.

Honey, W. B., *Glass, A Handbook and a Guide to the Museum Collection*. London, Victoria and Albert Museum, 1946.

Honour, Hugh, *Chinoiserie, The Vision of Cathay*. London, 1961.

Hudig, C. J., *Zilver van de Nederlandse Edelsmid*. Amsterdam, 1951.

Jansen, Beatrice, *Catalogus van Noord en Zuid Nederlands Glas*. The Hague, Municipal Museum, 1962.

Kleyn, J. de, 'Een zeldzaam houten kaststel uit Ameland', *Nederlands Openlucht Museum Bijdragen en Mededelingen*. Amsterdam, 1961.

Luttervelt, Dr. R. van, *Schilders van het Stilleven*. Naarden, 1947.

Nott, S. Ch., *Chinese Jade through the Ages*. Tokyo, 1962.

Rissink, W. G. F. C., 'Ter Gedagtenisse van' ('In memory of'). *Bulletin van de Koninklijke Nederlandse Oudheidkundige Bond,* 1965.

Sauerlandt, Max, *Edelmetalfassungen in der Keramik*. Berlin, 1939.

Staring, A., *De Hollanders Thuis* (The Dutch at Home). The Hague, 1956.

Swillens, P. T. A., *Albrecht Dürer, Zijn dagboek van de Reis door de Nederlanden in 1520–1521*. Maastricht, n.d.

Taylor, Gerald, *Silver*. Harmondsworth, 1956.

Valentiner, W. R., *Pieter de Hoogh*. Berlin, 1929.

Verster, A. J. G., *Tin door de Eeuwen*. Amsterdam, 1954.

Wit, Th. Duyvené de, *see* Gans.

Index

245

Index

Bloelingh, A., 160
Bloemaert, Abr., 137, 160; *Plates 206, 207, 298*
blue and white porcelain, Ching dynasty, 74–7
    Ming dynasty, 45–6
blue colouration, 32, 33
Bomme, Leendert, 93
Bontekoe, Dr., 100
Borneo, 39, 42
Bosschaert, Abr., 49
Both, G. C., 22 n.
Böttger, 37
Boucher, François, 126, 139
Bourbon, Duke of, 179
bourdaloue, 93
Bow, composition of porcelain, 37
    decoration, 131, 164
    imitation Chinese and Japanese ware, 66
    porcelain figures, 174
    redecoration of Chinese porcelain, 178
    statuettes, 170
'Bower' motif, 136, 152; *Plate 202*
Braamcamp, Gerrit, 70
Briot, François, 90
Broecke, Pieter van den, 106
brown glazed porcelain, 175
Brueghel, Jan, the Elder, 48; *Plate 34*
Brühl, Heinrich, Count, 111
Bruynvisch (ship), 54
Bruyun family, *Plate 274*
Brydges, James, 1st Duke of Chandos, 116
Buddha, 169, 198, 200
Buddhism and decoration, 45, 75, 200–1
'The Bull's Cruelty', 145, 182; *Plates 255, 358*
Burghley, Lord, 51
bush motifs, 75, 77, 78, 88
bussepot, 72
butterfly motifs, 204; *Plate 87*

Caffieri, A. J., 70
Callot, Jacques, 129
Cambingh, 56
Canton, decoration of porcelain at, 64, 80, 114, 132,
    147, 148, 156–7
    trade with, 21, 28, 54, 60, 61–6, 90
Carletti, Francesco, 30, 46
'carrack' porcelain, 49, 55
cassia motif, 205

Castiglione, 74, 81 and n.
Catherina (ship), 48
Cats, L., 150; *Plate 277*
Catzenellebogen, Philip von, Duke, 43
celadon wares, 39, 42–3; *Plate 2*
    derivation of name, 42 n.
Celebes, 40
'Cephalus killing Procris', 141; *Plate 229*
Chan Hsi King, 73
Chang Ch'i-chung, 26, 27, 191
Chang Ch'ien, 203
Chang Chou, 167
Chang kuo-lao, 199
Ch'ang-nan, *see* Ching-tê Chên
Chantilly, decoration, 164
    imitation Chinese and Japanese ware, 68
    pâte tendre, 37
    statuettes, 170
    walking stick heads, 95
Charles III, King of Naples, 21
Charles V, Emperor, 46
'Charlotte at Werther's tomb', *Plate 297*
Charlottenburg palace, 69, 85
Chasteleyn family, 148; *Plate 263*
Chelsea, composition of porcelain, 37
    decoration, 164
    imitation Chinese and Japanese ware, 68
    porcelain figures, 174
    statuettes, 170
    tureens, 124
Ch'êng Hua, Emperor, 33, 45, 46, 98
Cheng-Ting Kuei, 24 n.
Chêng Tê, 45, 168
'Cherrypicker', 128, 138, 184; *Plates 349, 357*
Chia Ching, Emperor, and porcelain of the period,
    45, 46, 49, 60, 112, 198
Chiang Tzŭ-ya, 202
chicken motifs, 45
Chieh-tzŭ yüan hua chüan, 73 n., 163
Ch'ien Lung, Emperor, and porcelain of the period,
    27, 60, 71, 73, 76, 79, 80, 82, 175; *Plates 61, 79,*
    83, 84, 86, 90, 135–6, 202
Ch'ien Niu, 202
Chih Nü, 202
ch'i-lin, 203–4
Ch'ing dynasty, 71–84
Ch'ing dynasty, decoration, 71, 72–84

Index

247

Index

Index

Index

Index

Index